Nunavik

Katutjiniq

Le conseil régional de développement du Nunavik

Nunavik's Regional Development Council

Fondé / Est. 1980

NUNAVIK

Inuit-Controlled Education in Arctic Quebec

Ann Vick-Westgate

UNIVERSITY OF
CALGARY
PRESS

University of Calgary Press
2500 University Drive NW
Calgary, Alberta
Canada T2N 1N4
www.uofcpress.com

National Library of Canada Cataloguing in Publication Data

Vick-Westgate, Ann, 1948-
  Nunavik

  (Northern lights series, ISSN 1701-0004 ; 1)
  Includes bibliographical references and index.
  ISBN 1-55238-056-4

1. Inuit—Education—Quebéc (Province)—Nunavik.
2. Education—Quebéc (Province)—Nunavik. I. Title. II. Series.
E99.E7V51 2002   371'.009714'111   C2002-910488-2

Canada ▪▪▪   We acknowledge the financial support of the Government of Canada
through the Book Publishing Industry Development Program (BPIDP)
for our publishing activities.

The Canada Council for the Arts
Le Conseil des Arts du Canada

This book is printed on acid-free paper.

Page, cover design, and typesetting by Kristina Schuring.

Cover photo: Inukjuak 1950. At school. L to R: Allie Samsack, Johnny Kasudluak,
Johnny Palliser.
Margery Hinds Collection. Photo: Margery Hinds (INDMH04)

Back cover photo: Inukjuak 1953. Top: Simeonie Amarualik, Nungaq Aullaluk,
Mary Amarualik, unknown. Bottom, L to R: Lydia Tukai, Maggie (child),
Caroline Tukai Qinnauajuak, Ini Iqaluk, Lucy Saimautik, Minnie Allakariallak,
three children unknown, Louisa Iqaluk, Sarah, unknown children.
Margery Hinds Collection. Photo: Margery Hinds (INDMH09) Courtesy of Avataq Cultural Institute

The University of Calgary Press gratefully acknowledges financial support from Katutjiniq:
Nunavik's Regional Development Council.

To the people
of Nunavik
– past, present and future –
and
to Michael

NORTHERNLIGHTS SERIES

Nunavik
Inuit-Controlled Education in Arctic Quebec

Ann Vick-Westgate

Co-published by the University of Calgary Press, the Arctic Institute of North America, and Katutjiniq: Nunavik's Regional Development Council.

Foreword
by Zebedee Nungak

In 1845, Sir John Franklin and 129 sailors and officers of the British Royal Navy set out in two large ships from England to seek a way to the Orient through the Northwest Passage. No Qallunaat ever saw them again, and their disappearance in the Canadian Arctic remains an enduring mystery.

Franklin's expedition can rightly be described as an attempt to ram and bull a way through the Arctic ice by methods totally inappropriate to the enterprise. Their equipment was the best technology available at the time. But Franklin and his crew brought their environment with them with all its trappings. They dined on Victorian cutlery on food which did not prevent scurvy and were clothed in Royal Navy issue woefully inadequate for the harsh Arctic cold.

The end result was the death of all Franklin Expedition members in the Canadian tundra.

In 1909, Commander Robert E. Peary of the U.S. Navy supposedly sledged to the North Pole and back with the help of the Polar Inuit of High Arctic Greenland. In nearly two decades of polar exploration, he had acquired a respect for the methods and knowledge of the Inuit in whose environment he was operating. He adapted to, and adopted, the Inuit way in the vital matters of food, clothing, transportation, and shelter.

He became enlightened enough to fuse the best of two disparate worlds and cultures and utilize each part in reaching an objective: the North Pole. As a result, he is the acknowledged discoverer of that point of geography.

Now, what have these two events in Arctic history to do with the education system in Nunavik? Nothing at all, one might say!

But they do serve to illustrate how systematic approaches to an objective can result in FAILURE (Franklin) or in SUCCESS (Peary). They demonstrate that the design, and the ways and means of an enterprise, have to be appropriate to its particularities. That to reach the objective is to have respect for the lay of the land and the ways of the people who live there. That a rigid, inflexible foreign design cannot simply be imposed. Or is preordained to fail if it is. That adaptability is a necessity of life in pursuing a goal that will be relevant to, and respected by, the people whom it serves.

In short, the common enterprise, as I understand it to be described by this book, is to design a Peary-like success and avoid, if at all possible, a Franklin-like disaster. By any measure, that is a monumental task.

Zebedee Nungak
Post Lake
Kangirsuk, Nunavik,
1993

Photo: Stephen Hendrie/
Makivik Corporation

It is complicated even further by the systemic turmoil in which our contact with formal education has taken place. Consider that our grandparents, the first generation of Inuit to observe their grandchildren (us) being herded into unilingually English federal schools, were the last of countless previous generations to leave the nomadic lifestyle.

Even our parents' generation, for the most part, never saw the inside of a classroom. We, their children, the first Inuit generation to "benefit" from formal education, have been put through several wrenching wringers. To put it another way, we have lived through several systemic cataclysms which can be oversimplified into the federal/provincial/Kativik School Board periods. All within less than 40 years! All in a period when our lives, language and culture were under tremendous stress from all sides!

It is no wonder that we Inuit of Nunavik have not yet found The Way of a soundly successful "Peary"-model education system in the four decades of exposure to formal education. It can be said to be amazing that so many (yet so few!) of our people have succeeded in such a "Franklin" sort of educational environment!

The challenges to ever strive for the fundamental design of a world-class education system for ourselves are still ahead of us. As you will read within the following pages, scores of dedicated and competent people have done much in this search. If we have not yet reached an education system "promised land," it is not for lack of trying!

All the raw material and sound advice from all sectors of our society seems to be there: from professional educators, study experts, Board officials, parents, students who have been there, Commissioners, Inuttitut teachers who have taught with almost no materials, and all manner of others who all have something profound to say.

Unfortunately, the fallout and consequences of what I described earlier as systemic cataclysms have to thoroughly exhaust themselves before the collective direction can be fully dedicated to the building and operation of a "Peary"-type enterprise. It is nobody's fault that a well-entrenched "Franklin" ramming operation has to die so hard.

A systemic turnaround has its own clumsy, wondrous, unpretty dynamic. No individual or single group can claim to have the ability to steer through one of these without touching some dangerous ice pans or encountering thick fog without navigation aids. Nobody expected such an exercise to be easy, but this one is especially un-easy. Let us just not accept it as impossibly hard.

The difference between success and failure is well illustrated by the ships used by our Arctic explorers. Franklin's ships, the *Erebus* and *Terror*, were more suited for set-piece battles with the Spanish Armada in the high seas than for finding a way through the ice-fields. Peary's ship, the *Roosevelt*, was specifically designed for the latter part of his Arctic work, and served its purpose. One expedition failed, and another one succeeded.

In the pages of this book, you will read of the efforts of many to fearlessly audit the state of education in Nunavik. To diligently seek improvement of an already good system. To fix what is not necessarily broken so that those who come after us will have it even better than we did. The various tensions and differences of opinion resulting, are, to me, not contentious at all. The status quo, however good or excellent it may be, is no place to stay. I think all recognize this. Climbers and explorers, upon reaching the summit or their discovery goal, seldom say, "I will stay here for all time!"

I write these words in the hope that people will find inspiration in the analogy of the two events in Arctic exploration which I have used. And that we will challenge ourselves to seek The Way. A "Franklin" approach can search for a purpose, but will not find it because of its monolithic doomed-ness. In a "Peary" scenario, a pre-existing system of education has to incorporate elements foreign to itself in order to breathe the oxygen vital to the environment in which it operates. It has no choice but to do this.

The objective has to be to attain an effective, functioning, relevant, and responsive system. In large part, it must be designed by pulling together the deeply felt desires and convictions of the people whom it serves, and be thereby respected by them.

I write these words in earnest hope that my grandchildren will see them in school and be motivated to find The Way if by then we have not yet collectively reached that "Pole." Let us all strive to create a "Peary" success!

Zebedee Nungak was President of Makivik Corporation from August 1995 until September 1998. Actively involved as a leader in Inuit self-government for more than 25 years, Nungak helped negotiate the James Bay and Northern Quebec Agreement as Secretary-Treasurer of the Northern Quebec Inuit Association. In the 1980s he served as co-chairman of the Inuit Committee on National Issues and chaired the Inuit Justice Task Force in the early 1990s.

Introduction

I first became involved with education in Native American communities through a community and cultural history project with Oglala Lakota students and a teacher at Pine Ridge in South Dakota. In 1970, the focus of change was on cross-cultural programs, inserting indigenous information into Western curricula, substituting Native legends and themes for Western ones. Thirty years later, locally controlled school boards around the world are redefining schooling from the ground up and creating educational systems which are based on the values, concerns and goals which they as indigenous communities have for their children. Nowhere is this change more rapid or more profound than among the Inuit of Arctic Quebec (Nunavik).

One of my primary purposes in writing this book is to support the residents of Nunavik in defining education in their own terms by detailing what has happened in their schools in the past and raising questions for the future. It is also my hope to introduce non-Inuit to a portion of the Inuit world view by outlining the history and goals of Inuit-controlled education. Finally, this book proposes some of the contributions – rooted in traditional values – which indigenous communities can make to the redesign of schooling for all students in the 21st century.

This book documents an important and sophisticated debate among the residents of Arctic Quebec over how to improve their schools, beginning with a comprehensive evaluation of the school system's first eleven years of operation under Inuit control. Wherever possible, the story is told through Inuit voices. As such, it provides a window into the complexity of education in a rapidly changing traditional society where universal schooling was not introduced at the elementary level until after the Second World War. The book concludes with an analysis of what other communities and regions seeking to improve their schools and provide their young an education for the future can learn from the evaluation process initiated by the Nunavik Educational Task Force (NETF).

I am an outsider, neither Inuit nor Canadian. I have worked with and in Northern Native organizations since 1974. For several years I worked closely with Alaska Native leaders who led the land claims fight in the 1960s and 1970s and who were engaged in the late 1970s in implementing the terms of the Alaska Native Claims Settlement Act (ANCSA). As a Training Coordinator and, later, Education Programs Director at the Alaska Native Foundation (ANF), I helped shape and deliver the assistance that Native organization provided to Native village corporations created under ANCSA and to newly created, locally controlled school districts in rural Alaska.

Prior to joining the Native Foundation, I traveled for three years as an itinerant resource teacher, working with teams of students and teachers writing community and cultural histories in the villages of Southwestern Alaska. After leaving ANF, I coordinated the development of a district-wide plan of studies for the Northwest Arctic School District headquartered in Kotzebue. Through those jobs, I came to understand the challenges of providing comprehensive K-12 schooling in Alaska's villages. During eight years in Alaska, I also learned about the strength and wisdom of the elders and the intelligence and potential of the young.

From 1989 through 1993, I served as Principal Investigator of a National Science Foundation networks project which identified successful primary, elementary and secondary programs in circumpolar indigenous communities from Alaska to the Sami areas of Scandinavia. This broadened my Northern experience beyond Alaska and provided me perspective on similarities and differences in circumpolar schooling. It was through my work with the Roger Lang Clearinghouse for Circumpolar Education that I met Quebec Inuit leaders involved in the Kativik School Board (KSB), the Nunavik Educational Task Force and Makivik Corporation.

While completing this book I also worked, during the 1997-98 and 1998-99 school years, as a 'coach' in whole school change and in literacy development in three elementary schools and one high school in the City of Boston. Learning first hand how hard it is to change the culture of one of the United States' oldest public school systems, even with access to the resources of world-class universities and corporations, made me appreciate all the more how much the Inuit of Northern Quebec have accomplished.

My own history of involvement with the Kativik School Board and the Nunavik Educational Task Force began when the School Board endorsed the creation of the Roger Lang Clearinghouse for Circumpolar Education in 1988. Annie Popert, then Director General of the KSB, sent a letter of support when we sought National Science Foundation funding to initiate an exchange on what had worked in schooling in the Native villages of Alaska, Canada's North, Greenland and Northern Scandinavia. I met with several KSB administrators, including Annie Popert, at the April 1990 Circumpolar Literacy Conference in Yellowknife and returned from the Conference with KSB instructional materials for inclusion in the Clearinghouse's Curriculum Library.

In the fall of 1990, Bill Kemp, Technical Advisor to the newly created Nunavik Educational Task Force, called me to discuss the Lang Clearinghouse's potential involvement with the Task Force. In December 1990, I met with Technical Advisor Sheila Watt-Cloutier and Education Review Committee (ERC) Chair Minnie Grey at the Task Force offices in Lachine, Quebec. At their invitation, I joined ERC Commissioners Grey, Johnny N. Adams, Josepi Padlayat, and Jobie Epoo for a January 1991 field trip to Puvurnituq on the east coast of Hudson Bay. Minnie, Johnny, and I then continued on to Ivujivik and Kuujjuaq for more community meetings. The Task Force paid for my time and expenses and I submitted a report to them of my observations during the trip.

I stayed in contact with the NETF through the completion and release of the final report and recommendations and in 1994 suggested to the Commissioners the writing of a book telling the story of the inquiry and analyzing its impact. Through the Corporation of the Northern Village of Kuujjuaq, where Johnny N. Adams was then mayor, we submitted an application for financial assistance to the Regional Intervention Fund of the Kativik Regional Development Council (KRDC). In the application we stated our reasons for writing the book as follows:

- To have a record for the region's people, particularly those who will continue the process;
- To identify the political, economic, and social forces encouraging the growth of local control of education in

Northern Quebec during the last 25 years as well as
those forces impeding that development;

- To document the respective roles of the federal and
provincial governments, regional Inuit organizations,
and communities in shaping educational policy during
the same period; and

- To establish the critical junctures and events at
which decisions were made impacting local control of
education.

With support from KRDC and smaller contributions from
Makivik Corporation and two U.S. foundations, I began work
on the book in the fall of 1994. At that time I was given
the files of the Nunavik Educational Task Force, with the
exception of employment contracts for staff and consultants
and the few submissions from individuals who requested that
their comments to the Task Force be kept confidential. The
files contained all internal meeting notes; staff and consultant memos and planning documents; correspondence with
Kativik School Board, Makivik and other organizations and
individuals; reports prepared by KSB for Task Force review;
transcribed interviews with Inuit and Qallunaat (non-Inuit)
administrators, teachers, students, and parents; transcripts of
call-in shows conducted by the Education Review Committee
members over the FM radio stations in each community; consultant reports; written statements submitted by individuals
to the Task Force; and research on exemplary programs.

The files have remained in my possession through the completion of this book. I neither asked for, nor received, guidance
on which portions of the written record to use in the book. The
decisions on which documents to cite and which actions and
events to emphasize are entirely my own. Several Nunavik
leaders have read the draft manuscript, including Zebedee
Nungak, who wrote the Foreword. No substantive changes
were suggested, requested or made as a result of this review.

In writing the book, I first read through the written record
and selected the documents I felt were the most significant.
I have focused on documents that resulted in a change of
direction, a major advance in mission or a key moment.
I made these decisions based on my own knowledge and understanding of the history of the Kativik School Board, Makivik
Corporation, and the Nunavik Educational Task Force and on
my own familiarity with schools and school change in the North
and elsewhere. I have made every attempt to be objective and

balanced in my portrayal through a straightforward recounting of events and the intent to include the perspectives of all those involved in the evaluation of the Nunavik schools.

Throughout the book I have sought to emphasize the Inuit perspective. While I put together the book, it is their story.

I made the assumption that the written record contained in the files of the Task Force accurately reflected the perspectives of the key players – the Educational Review Committee, the NETF staff and consultants, the Kativik School Board staff and Commissioners, the Makivik Executive and staff, community leaders, elders, parents, teachers, and students. While the Task Force and the School Board disagreed over some of the inquiry's conclusions and recommendations, I judged that KSB submissions to the NETF were likely their best and fullest representations of their accomplishments and concerns. And, while non-Inuit staff members drafted portions of documents, Inuit leadership of the NETF, KSB or Makivik approved use of these documents to represent their positions. Wherever possible, names of the authors or speakers are cited.

The transcripts of community meetings and radio call-in programs reflect Inuit perspectives almost exclusively. Because almost all of the meetings and radio call-ins were conducted in Inuttitut, I have had to rely on English-language transcripts prepared by translators for use by the Task Force. In so doing, I acknowledge that translation is more of an art than a science, but trust in the accuracy of the work. Rather than paraphrase their content, I have chosen to include long passages from documents and transcripts and to place entire documents in the Appendices.

I have limited and clearly separated my own analysis of events from Inuit perspectives. I have further focused my comments on educational change, the area where I have the greatest experience and perspective. Much of that analysis can be found in the book's final chapter. I have not attempted to address the influence of Inuit para-political organizations such as Makivik, Inuit Tapirisat of Canada (ITC), or the Inuit Circumpolar Conference (ICC) on the shaping of Nunavik.

In an effort to portray and analyze the exchanges, decisions and events as they happened, I have concentrated on the written record of the time and have not included analysis, written or oral, offered years after the events. I expanded the written record beyond the NETF files to include newsletters, annual reports, and other publications of the Kativik School Board and Makivik Corporation. One of the most significant documents is the KSB *Report on the Community Consultation Process initiated at an expanded Education Council Meeting held in Umiujaq in April 1994,* which documents the School Board's efforts to more substantively engage the communities in educational change. I also made extensive use of the KSB publications *Reports of the Activities of the Kativik School Board 1978-1985* and *1986-1992; Report on Symposium '85; Review of the Report of the Nunavik Educational Task Force;* and *Anngutivik* newsletters March 1985 through Autumn 1990. I also utilized Makivik Corporation publications, including *Annual Reports* and the newsletter *Makivik News.*

The Avataq Cultural Institute has been very supportive in granting me access to its collection of oral histories, photographs and other resources, including copies of federal and provincial records relating to education in Arctic Quebec. Makivik Corporation has also given me permission to use some of the photographs and maps to which it holds the rights. I also utilized the curriculum collection and other resources of the Roger Lang Clearinghouse for Circumpolar Education, particularly in writing about education in the circumpolar context.

The book does contain some other updating beyond 1994, specifically related to the Kativik School Board's community consultation process, to educational changes elsewhere in the circumpolar world and to the progress toward self-government in Nunavik.

This book does not claim to be a comprehensive history of Arctic Quebec or of Canadian or Quebec history in relation to the North and its indigenous peoples. To provide some context, I begin the book with a brief history of Northern Quebec, including the relationships over time between the Inuit and the governments of Canada and Quebec and the negotiation of the 1975 James Bay and Northern Quebec Agreement (JBNQA). The education provisions of this land claims agreement gave the Inuit control of the region's federal and provincial schools. I have also included a brief discussion of education and schooling in the North prior to 1975 and of the Province of Quebec's educational system in general.

I have endeavored to provide accurate information, however the sources I cite do not by any means encompass all of the relevant literature. And while I have made brief mention of the history of Inuit occupation in the region before contact with Europeans and of the post-contact impact of whaling, the fur trade, and disease, an in-depth exploration and analysis of that history is not the purpose of this book.

Nor is this work a review of, and commentary on, all aspects of the history and operations of the Kativik School Board (KSB). The book's focus is on the Nunavik Educational Task Force and the roles the School Board, Makivik Corporation, and the communities played in relationship to that inquiry. And while the book provides an Inuit perspective on education, past and present, and on schooling, it does not address Inuit beliefs, values and practices in other areas.

I firmly believe that indigenous peoples can make significant contributions to the reform of elementary and secondary education – both within and outside their communities and regions. They are not wedded to the idea of 'school,' do not necessarily accept the established purposes and forms of formal schooling, and are skeptical about the existing systems. Many of them are able to step back from the purpose of 'school' to the purpose of 'education.'

Schools are relatively new to many indigenous communities, but community responsibility for the education of the young is not. Native peoples know, and can voice, the values underpinning their cultures. And they believe that all members of the community have responsibility for the children in that community.

The Nunavik Educational Task Force initiated a process that resulted in positive change in the schools of Northern Quebec. In doing so, they, and ultimately the Kativik School Board itself, questioned the methods of the existing system of schooling in Arctic Quebec and acknowledged the failures of that system. They recognized that the mere fact that a school system is Inuit-controlled does not mean it is effective or different from the previous system(s).

To conduct its evaluation, the Task Force consulted the communities as well as seeking perspectives from educational consultants. In seeking answers from the Inuit themselves, it sparked an alliance between the very young and the very old calling for change. This convergence of possibilities led to the Kativik School Board opening its doors more widely, acknowledging its problems and beginning to consult effectively with the communities in order to reshape education in Nunavik. There is much work still to be done, but the Inuit of Arctic Quebec have crafted a solid foundation.

Ann Vick-Westgate

The Inuit Circumpolar Region

Legend:
- Canadian Inuit
- Greenland Inuit
- Alaska Inuit
- Russian Inuit
- Other Arctic People

Makivik Corporation, Cartographic Service, 2002.
www.makivik.org
www.makivik.org/nunavikatlas

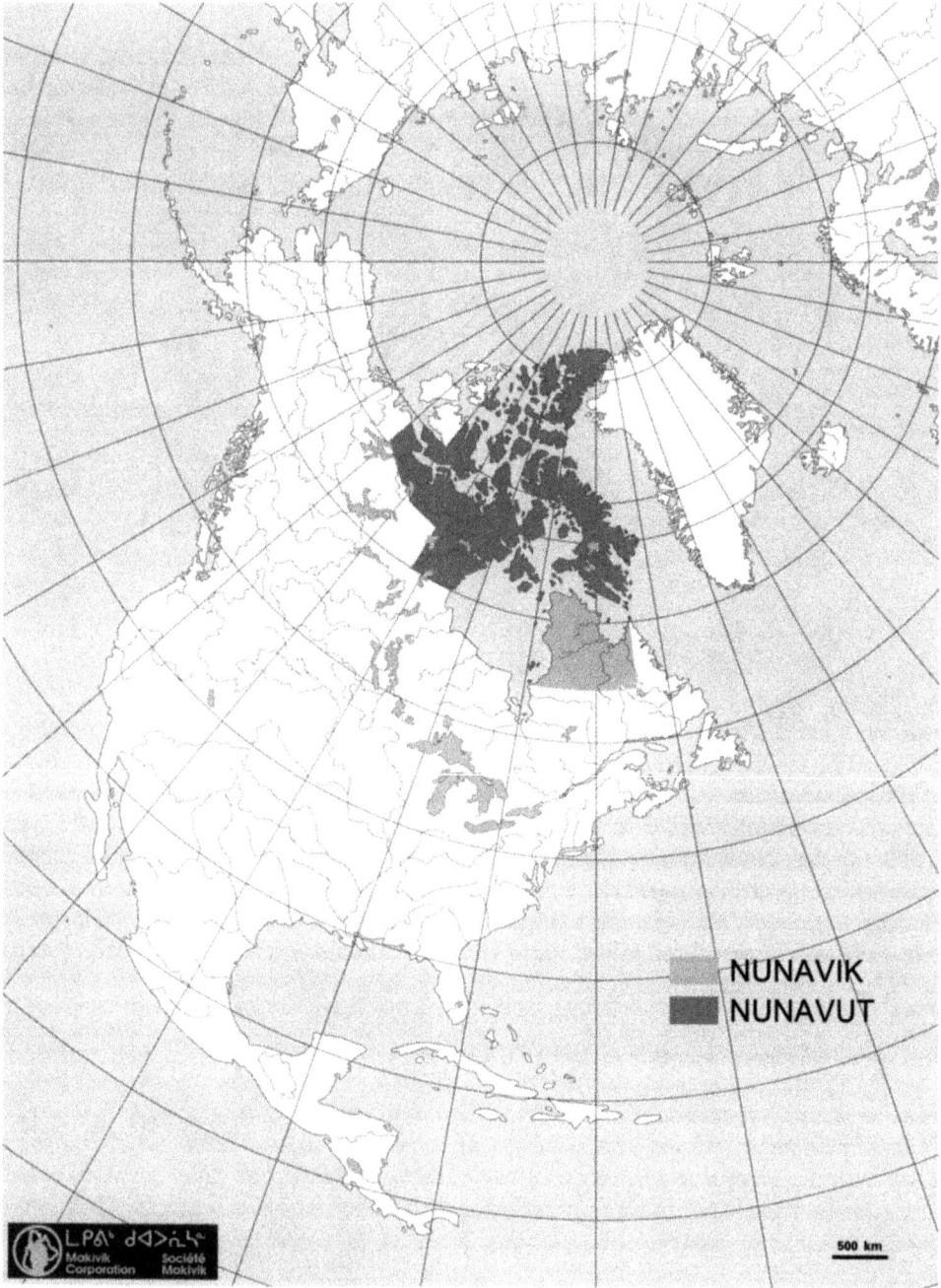

The Inuit-controlled regions of Canada's
eastern and central Arctic.

Makivik Corporation, Cartographic Service, 2002.
www.makivik.org
www.makivik.org/nunavikatlas

1

Educational Change in an Arctic World

Indigenous communities are assuming control of their schools just as Western educators are questioning the goals and methods of schooling in their own societies. Must traditional societies in the Third and Fourth Worlds that were introduced to formal education since the current Western model was developed in the late 19th century mimic that approach? Can they redefine and reinvent education? What perspectives on educational change can indigenous peoples offer Western schools?

This book documents the debate among the Inuit of Quebec over the purposes, strengths and weaknesses of the public schools in their 14 Northern communities. The Kativik School Board was the first Inuit-controlled school district established in Canada. Its Commissioners and many of its top administrators and teachers are Inuit. In 1989, after 40 years of Western-style education, 11 of them under Inuit leadership, residents of Arctic Quebec began to call for an external evaluation of the school system. Much of the pressure for change came from Inuit leaders outside the schools who assumed responsibility for questioning existing educational policies and practices, no longer content to leave education to the professional educators, Inuit or Qallunaat (non-Inuit).

Engaged in the discussion of education over the next four years would be elders who were educated traditionally, Inuit in mid-life who had a few years of education in mission and government elementary schools, as well as the first generation of Inuit to graduate from high school by going South or to residential schools (many of them 30-45 years old and in leadership positions), and the young who were currently in or recently out of the Kativik schools. Qallunaat would also be participants, as residents of Nunavik, as parents of Inuit children, as teachers and administrators and as 'expert' consultants.

The Nunavik educational story is a dynamic one which includes traditionalists (Inuit and Qallunaat), revolutionaries (Inuit and Qallunaat), advocates (Inuit and Qallunaat) for a combination of traditional Inuit perspectives with Western curricula, Qallunaat who think the Southern model of education is destructive of Inuit traditions, and Inuit who believe they and the students are best served by adopting Western educational approaches – against a background of James Bay hydroelectric development, Quebec separatism and negotiations on regional self-government.

This book begins with a summary of the history of education in Nunavik, including the methods and purpose of education in traditional Inuit society. The history of Nunavik education since 1975 has been a building back toward Inuit control.

The James Bay and Northern Quebec Agreement (JBNQA), signed by the Inuit, Cree, federal and provincial governments on November 11, 1975, was the first major land claims settlement in Canada. Unlike the 1971 Alaska Native Land Claims Settlement Act (ANCSA), the agreement with the indigenous peoples of Northern Quebec addressed education, health and social services, administration of justice, and other economic and social development issues, in addition to land ownership, mineral rights, and financial settlements.

The Kativik School Board was created as part of this Agreement. The first decade produced many innovations and accomplishments. The tasks were enormous, including the building of new schools in all of the communities and the design and initiation of a teacher education program for Inuit charged with instructing the primary grades in their own language. Inuttitut curriculum materials had to be developed for all grade levels.

In November 1985, the Kativik School Board convened a major forum in Kuujjuaq with representatives from every Nunavik community to "discuss where the education system was heading, seek direction on key issues, begin formulating a comprehensive education policy and set new priorities" (from the report on Symposium '85 issued by the School Board). In March 1989, at the Annual General Meeting (AGM) of Makivik Corporation, the Inuit institution charged with receiving and administering JBNQA compensation funds to generate revenues for economic and social development, a resolution was passed to establish an independent Task Force to evaluate the existing education system in Nunavik and to make recommendations for the future. No other school systems in the Arctic,

and few in the South, have undergone as comprehensive an assessment of their strengths and weaknesses.

The first few months of activities centered on efforts to define the scope of the Task Force's inquiry. The Kativik School Board envisioned the Nunavik Educational Task Force evaluation as a review and fine-tuning of the existing system. Between the fall of 1990 and the issuing of its report two years later, the Task Force chose to define an entirely new system involving all of the regional organizations, not just the School Board.

The balance of the book centers on the Task Force inquiry,

Inukjuak 1946
Anna attending the
qulliq (seal oil lamp).
Annie Mathewsie
behind her.

National Archives of
Canada. Photo: Bud Glunz
(APA145025). Courtesy of
Avataq Cultural Institute.

3

the community and School Board response, and the process established to review and implement Task Force and School Board recommendations in consultation with the residents of Nunavik.

The book ends with a discussion of what indigenous education might offer to the broader educational change debate. Which aspects of indigenous education might be drawn upon to strengthen the Western approach to schooling?

Educational Change
A Context for Considering the Nunavik Experience

The question of who owns the schools is a central one in educational change. Prior to the far-reaching political and social changes of the 1950s and 1960s, the question was not much asked by any sector of Western society. Schooling was the business of those who were trained to provide it. Parents and other members of the community did not dare to tell teachers and administrators how to do their business. After the 1960s, increasing numbers of people felt they not only had the right, but the responsibility, to involve themselves in local schools.

Seymour Sarason, Professor Emeritus in the Department of Psychology and the Institute of Social and Policy Studies at Yale University, writes:

> But it was only in the post-World War II era that
> the question of "Who owns the schools?" began to be
> raised ... And they were being asked for two related
> reasons: dissatisfaction with educational outcomes,
> and challenges (especially in the sixties) to every
> major social institution in society. Undergirding all of
> these questions was a moral-political one: who should
> participate in educational decision making? And
> the general answer was: any individual or group
> who directly or indirectly would be affected by
> a decision should stand in some relationship to
> the decision-making process. That answer began to
> inform decision making in various social arenas,
> such as the environment, highway construction, and
> housing complexes. It would have been surprising if
> that answer had not spurred different groups to try
> to alter the traditional style of educational decision
> making in our schools. (Sarason 1990, 53)

Conflict is to be expected in educational change. The creation, operation, and oversight of schools is an inherently political process. The business of schools is socialization of the young to society's roles and rules, and the political process is the least violent way to decide whose rules will be followed. Schools are by their nature political because they deal with values and are always resource-short (Wiles 1993). In *The New Meaning of Educational Change*, authors Michael Fullan, Dean of the Ontario Institute for Studies in Education at the University of Toronto, and Suzanne Stiegelbauer caution those involved in school change to "assume that conflict and disagreement are not only inevitable but fundamental to successful change. Since any group of people possess multiple realities, any collective change attempt will necessarily involve conflict ... Smooth implementation is often a sign that not much is really changing." (Fullan and Stiegelbauer 1991, 106)

Even if the constituency of a school district, or of an individual school, can agree on philosophy and goals, achievement of those goals is not guaranteed. Change in schools is not an exact science. In their 1994 book, *Redesigning Education*, Kenneth G. Wilson and Bennett Daviss discuss the absence of proven approaches in education: "... unlike virtually all other professions, U.S. education lacks a technical culture, a common body of proven knowledge and technique that lets all members of a profession adapt and perform to the same standards of excellence, and to redefine those standards as technology progresses" (Wilson and Daviss 1994, 79). Wilson and Daviss liken the job of a teacher to that of an artist rather than a doctor or scientist. Teachers most often work in isolation with their students without specific guidelines or regular interactions on technique and theory with their peers or supervisors: "... if we're to reform our schools, teachers must be given the tools to dismantle outworn paradigms of schooling and construct new ones in their place. But unless the teaching profession restructures itself as a collaborative, unified endeavor – a technical culture linked at all its points, from research labs and university-based teacher-preparation programs to networks of working teachers themselves – our struggle to reshape our schooling system faces a potentially devastating obstacle." (Wilson and Daviss 1994, 104).

The failure and irrelevancy of schooling is not just a topic of discussion among Inuit; it is an almost universal concern. The goal of providing schooling beyond basic literacy for all children, particularly the opportunity for many of them to continue on to college, is a relatively recent development. It wasn't until the early 1950s that a majority of children in the United States graduated from high school instead of dropping out. "A century ago [1890], less than 7 percent of the school-age population attended high school. Today, some 94 percent of our youth enroll in high school, and nearly three-quarters of them graduate ... A century ago, only 4 percent of 18-20 year olds were in college. By 1968, this country had over 50 percent of our youth enrolled in post-secondary education. By comparison, only 45 percent of Swedish children complete the 12th grade and only 15 percent of German youth are enrolled in the *Oberprimer* [Grade 13]." (Wiles 1993, 2).

Quebec did not require public school boards to provide schooling up to and including Grade 11 for all children until the 1960s. In their history of Quebec education, McGill University professors Norman Henchey and Donald Burgess point out that prior to the changes of the last three decades "with inadequate facilities, a poorly qualified teaching force, strictly enforced examination hurdles and too many 'dead end' programs, numerous children simply dropped out of school altogether" (Henchey and Burgess 1987, 67).

Whether teacher, administrator or community member, an individual's concept of what education "is" grows out of his or her own schooling experience. It is very difficult to conceive of a new design for elementary and secondary education. Critiquing what is wrong is easy; offering positive alternatives is difficult. "The culture of the school isn't contained by the buildings' walls. It becomes a part of all of us who've spent time in traditional schools. During our formative years as students, most of us absorb the attitudes and assumptions of traditional education along with our spelling lists and multiplication tables ... Those assumptions can keep us from realizing that there can be valid alternatives to even the most basic norms of conventional education. Reformers are no less human. Their efforts typically grow out of assumptions that hamper or even are antithetical to their objectives. As a result, reform suffers from inate cultural liabilities of its own" (Wilson and Daviss 1994, 127-28).

In an essay on "The Imperative for Systemic Change," Charles Reigeluth compares the current situation in the education system to the situation faced by the transportation system during the Industrial Revolution: "... as we evolved into the industrial age, the transportation needs of society began to change. It became necessary to transport large quantities of raw materials and finished goods to and from factories. Rather than trying to improve the prevailing system, an alternative paradigm was developed – the railroad. Like our current educational system, it offered a quantum improvement in meeting the needs of the industrial age, but everyone had to travel at the same rate to the same destination" (Reigeluth 1994, 5). We currently have an educational system that offers greater access and opportunities to young people than any preceding system, but it no longer meets the needs of most of the students nor provides them with the skills required in rapidly changing societies.

Another educator has drawn parallels between the needs of the educational system and advances in aviation. In a 1988 article, "Why Schools Can't Improve: The Upper Limit Hypothesis," in the *Journal of Instructional Improvement*, R.K. Branson "cites the history of aviation development to make his point, observing that by the late 1940s, the propeller-driven aircraft was performing at the peak of its effectiveness in terms of speed, payload and fuel efficiency. This condition could not be improved until a fundamental change was made in the design of the airplane, with the introduction of jet engines. With this innovation, there was a major breakthrough in efficiency and effectiveness. Branson argues that instructional delivery must experience similar dramatic change in order to significantly improve student achievement and instructional efficiency". (Morgan in Reigeluth and Garfinkle 1994, 44).

The current design for education in Canada and the United States is one that was developed by Europeans and their immigrant descendants. Like much of written history, it reflects the perspectives and values of those in power. What provided clarity and unity of purpose in an educational system designed for a homogeneous society may not be the only, or the most effective, system of schooling for multicultural or culturally distinct societies. While they may not necessarily invent a better way to fly or to educate, Inuit both inside and outside their school systems should have the opportunity to redefine and reform education to meet their needs.

Just as educational change by its nature is political and causes conflict, it is threatening to those responsible for the current system. Wiles points out that "there is resistance to change and such resistance is both natural and understandable from the standpoint of the target of change" (Wiles 1993, 34). Individual egos and institutional histories can slow down change. Those who have put blood, sweat, and tears into the

creation of an educational system will resent criticism and recommendations for change from those who were not present at
the creation and show little appreciation for the labor and good
intentions involved. The problem, as George Bernard Shaw
observed, is that "reformers have the idea that change can be
achieved by brute sanity" (Fullan and Stiegelbauer 1991, 96).

Real change is difficult to achieve. Most of the change in
schools is aimed at improving the quality of what already
exists. Fullan and Stiegelbauer point out that change often
takes place without significantly impacting the fundamental
power structure or operating rules of school districts: "... innovation can be adopted for symbolic political or personal reasons:
to appease community pressure, to appear innovative, to gain
more resources. All of these forms represent *symbolic* rather
than *real* change. The incentive system of public schools with
abstract and unclear goals, lack of performance scrutiny, and
a noncompetitive market makes it more profitable politically
and bureaucratically to 'innovate' without risking the costs of
real change" (Fullan and Stiegelbauer 1991, 28).

The key to educational reform lies in changing the underlying culture of the system. Every system, including educational
institutions, develops its own way of doing things, patterns of
response which become traditional, established methods for
dealing with conflict. This culture encourages continuity, providing a secure environment to its members. Sarason points
out that "educational reformers have trouble understanding
that change by legislative fiat or policy pronouncements from
on high is only the first and the easiest step in the change
process, a step that sets in motion the dynamic of problem creation through problem solution ... they confuse a change in
policy with a change in practice. And they also assume that
change is achieved through learning and applying new or
good ideas. They seem unable to understand what is involved
in unlearning what custom, tradition, and even research
have told educational personnel is right, natural, and proper"
(Sarason 1990, 101).

If educational change is understood as cultural change,
reformers and others will expect real change to take time.
Fullan and Stiegelbauer estimate that the time frame from initiation to institutionalization of moderately complex changes
is from three to five years. Major restructuring efforts can
take five to ten years.

Reformers must understand not only what they, as change
agents, intend, but also the perceptions of others. What

Salluit 1951
Inuit awaiting
medical
examination
aboard a boat.

National Archives of
Canada. Photo:
W. Doucette, N.F.B.
(APA126559). Courtesy of
Avataq Cultural Institute.

matters is "how people actually experience change as distinct from what might have been intended" (Fullan and Stiegelbauer 1991, 4). Reformers who do not take the time to engage, educate, and listen to the perspectives of those affected by the change may find their reforms to be shallow or short-lived, vanishing when the instigators are no longer involved.

Educational Change in Indigenous Communities

The introduction of Westernized formal education contributed greatly to cultural change and language loss in indigenous communities. Worldwide, Native peoples have historically been excluded from policy making, administration, and teaching in the school systems in their communities. Teachers come from the outside, and Western training is valued over cultural and linguistic 'on-the-ground' knowledge. Few children go on to higher education or employment other than traditional village occupations. There is little connection between having a formal education and 'making it' in the village or the outside world.

A lack of clarity about the purposes of schooling, a distrust of the formal system, parents' own negative experiences in school and their desire that children remain in the community have all contributed to the situation. But equally significant factors are lowered expectations for student performance, high teacher turnover rates, and inferior instructional materials, libraries and other resources. Egos – institutional and individual, Native and non-Native – limited funds, and issues of power and control add to the conflict.

In 1972, the National Indian Brotherhood produced a landmark policy study on Indian education in Canada, *Indian Control of Indian Education*. Underlying the study were the two fundamental principles of parental responsibility and local jurisdiction. While the federal government stated its acceptance of the basic goals expressed in the study, no legal basis existed in the Indian Act or other legislation for the transfer of control of educational programs to Indian bands or communities. During the 1970s and 1980s, increasing numbers of Indian bands assumed responsibility for administering elementary and secondary schools. The Saskatchewan Indian Federated College, an Indian-controlled university-level college with accreditation linked to the University of Regina, was established in 1976.

In 1988, the Assembly of First Nations released a nationwide review of First Nations' education. That study found that while the Canadian government had endorsed the concept of Indian control of Indian education, it had "consistently defined 'Indian control' to mean merely First Nations' participation in and administration of previously developed formal education programs." The authors of *Tradition and Education: Towards A Vision of Our Future* identified as some of the requirements for genuine control of education by an indigenous community: adequate financial and human resources; training of education authority members; community, and particularly parental, involvement at all phases of the transfer and delivery of education; the presentation of educational options to the community; the development of an education philosophy, long-term plans and evaluation procedures at the beginning of the process to guide its implementation; policies and procedures consistent with the stated philosophy; hiring of qualified staff; sufficient administration and teacher preparation; language-based and culture-based curriculum development and programming; and access to, and utilization of, technology.

While band-controlled schooling and the development of culturally relevant instruction has increased steadily, the

1990 *Fourth Report of the Canadian House of Commons Standing Committee on Aboriginal Affairs – You Took My Talk: Aboriginal Literacy and Empowerment* concluded that a lot more has to change before indigenous people gain genuine control of education in their communities. "Physical isolation and the lack of high schools on reserves are common problems in Canada. The lack of aboriginal teachers and of culturally relevant materials also represent major obstacles to the progress of aboriginal students ... Overall, the most important issues witnesses have identified are the need for greater control by aboriginal people of their own education, and the need for aboriginal language instruction" (Canada 1990, 22).

In the United States, the 1928 report by Lewis Meriam, *The Problem of Indian Administration,* had urged the Indian Bureau to adopt the "modern point of view" and educate Indian children in their communities where they could be near their families. In the late 1960s, the activities and resulting report (*Indian Education: A National Tragedy – A National Challenge*) of a special Senate subcommittee headed by Robert and then Edward Kennedy resulted in increased funding for Native American education, expanded bilingual programs, and establishment of tribally-controlled community colleges, local Native boards of education, and a National Indian Advisory Board to review the state of Native education.

In 1966, the Navajo Rough Rock Demonstration School became the first Native-controlled school in the United States. The Indian Self-Determination and Education Act, passed by Congress in 1975, expanded the number of locally controlled schools, allowing tribal councils to contract schools from the government and giving them increased control over staff hiring and curriculum. The 1990 Native American Languages Act promoted the expanded use of Native languages and authorized their utilization in instruction in schools funded by the U.S. Secretary of the Interior. In 1991, the Indian Nations At Risk Task Force, charged by the U.S. Secretary of Education with evaluating the state of education among Native Americans, endorsed the policies of community control and involvement, culturally relevant instructional programs and materials, use and development of Native languages, trained and qualified staffing, and stable but flexible settings as effective criteria for Native-controlled schooling.

While indigenous people in Canada and the United States are exercising increasing control over their children's education, steep declines in funding from federal and provincial/state governments are severely hampering the development and expansion of effective programs.

In the last 25 years, indigenous people throughout the Arctic and Subarctic have also been reassuming control of their lands and local governments as well as management of the institutions providing them with education and health care.

The circumpolar North has been called "the only round nation in the world." Arctic and subarctic in climate, the area has been home to Inuit (Eskimos and Aleuts), Dene (Athabascans), Tlingit/Haida/Tsimshian, and Saami (Lapps), as well as other Native peoples, for thousands of years. These people are now citizens of the United States (Alaska), the territories and provinces of Canada, Denmark (Greenland), Norway, Sweden, Finland, and Russia. National boundaries cut across territories traditionally occupied by indigenous groups who have shared languages and cultures.

While a number of Native people have moved to Northern cities like Anchorage and Yellowknife which have sprung up in the last 75 years, many still live in villages where they are the majority population. These communities range in size from 50-100 to several thousand inhabitants. Outside Scandinavia, most are unconnected to road systems, relying on small planes for transportation and supplies. Television, long distance phone, fax and e-mail communications are now part of life in most villages. Throughout the circumpolar world, communities are working to preserve aspects of traditional life while importing positive elements of Southern society.

The indigenous peoples of the North are faced with opportunities and problems that transcend national boundaries. Changing lifestyles, cultural differences from dominant "Southern" populations, and the challenge of preserving traditional ways while developing local economies and employment opportunities are factors which link the villages of Alaska, Canada, Greenland, the Russian Far East, and Northern Scandinavia more closely to one another than to urban areas within their individual nation-states. Shared, as well, are Arctic ecosystems – the total physical environment of which human settlements are one part. Acknowledging the bonds among them, the Native people of the circumpolar world have since the early 1970s been regularly meeting through the Inuit Circumpolar Conference (ICC) to discuss common concerns.

Chief among these concerns is education. Across the North, individuals and institutions are seeking ways to enhance decision making and control of educational programs by local communities. Formal schooling has traditionally been the purveyor of cultural change. As elementary and secondary education increasingly comes under local control, respect for traditional ways and recognition of human and other resources within communities are increasing. There is still, however, a tendency in any community – whether a Southern metropolis or a village north of the Arctic Circle – to leave schooling to the trained professionals or to expect formal education to be the way it has always been, rather than to develop new ways of teaching and learning. The village school was, and still too often is, a Westernized formal institution that has excluded the knowledge and values of the community it serves and done a poor job of preparing young people for future roles.

Educational policy and instructional programs in the Arctic have traditionally been developed in the South and shipped North. Historically these materials have gone into Northern classrooms with little adaptation. Since the 1970s, with the advent of locally elected school boards and a growing recognition by all educators that effective schooling begins with the child's world and radiates outward, programs and materials have been reshaped to reflect the culture and environment of Arctic communities. Working with community members, curriculum developers, particularly in the Northwest Territories and Nunavut, have created entire programs and processes using Northern contexts rather than adapting a Southern design.

Increased local control, which includes recognition of the need for Native teachers and administrators to take the lead in reshaping Northern education, is one of the strongest factors evident in Arctic education today. In Greenland, on January 1, 1980, primary school education, evening school classes, the Teacher Training College, the Social Pedagogue School, the Educational Association, the Church, the Greenland Broadcasting Corporation, and the Southern Greenland Publishing Company were all transferred to the control of the Home Rule Government. The post of Director of Education became the Department of Education and Culture and later the Department of Education, Culture and Employment. On June 1 of the same year, Greenland's Teacher Training College (Ilinniarfissuaq) graduated more Native-born Greenlanders than in any previous year since the founding of the college in 1841. Greenland's University (Ilisimatusarfik) was established in 1984 and now offers degree courses in Eskimology, theology and administration, focusing on providing the Home Rule Government with civil servants.

In Scandinavia, the Nordic Sami Institute was founded in 1974 as a research, educational and service institute for the Sami populations of Norway, Finland and Sweden. In the following year, the Sami Educational Council was established to advise the Norwegian Ministry of Education on questions relating to training and education for Sami. The Council now initiates the development of framework curricula and subject syllabuses; develops textbooks and teaching materials; examines and approves textbooks; and advises on counseling services, education, and in-service training for teachers and boarding school staffs in the Sami areas.

In 1989, the Sami College (Sami Allaskuvla), previously a department in the regional college at Alta in northernmost Norway, became an independent College of Education, located, like the Nordic Sami Institute and the Sami Educational Council, in Guovdageaidnu (Kautokeino). Staff and students are creating an institution with a "Sami environment" in language, culture and content, offering a variety of post-secondary courses and programs, including teacher training. All students and staff must be fluent in Sami, as a majority of classes are conducted in that language and no permanent appointment is made to the faculty until language fluency is proven.

Sami education is particularly vibrant in the kindergarten (preschool) sector. Teachers design the kindergarten program annually and then discuss it with parents. Under Norwegian law, kindergarten instructional programs cannot be made or implemented without parents' consent.

Another force in education change, in the Arctic as elsewhere since the 1960s, is the recognition of parental and community input and involvement as an essential element in effective schools. In a 1985 study of 162 of Alaska's small rural high schools, University of Alaska researchers Judith S. Kleinfeld, G. Williamson McDiarmid, and David Hagstrom found school-community relations and relations among local professionals, community members, and central office administrators to be two of five major factors in differences between good schools and poor schools. In effective schools, professional educators consult regularly with community members, and a partnership is formed to set and achieve educational goals.

There is also dissatisfaction with the instructional programs and performance expectations in village schools and a belief that coursework is not as demanding or comprehensive as

that offered elsewhere. Across the North, parents and commu- Inukjuak 1950
nity leaders are calling for significantly higher expectations Lucy Saimmautik
for student performance, including tougher coursework and
regular assessment of skills development.

Margery Hinds Collection
Photo: Margery Hinds
(INDMH02). Courtesy of
Avataq Cultural Institute.

Another concern is that graduates be able to function "in
both worlds" – confident in their cultural identity and proud
of their people while possessing the academic skills they
will need in order to have choices for future studies and
careers. The objectives for schooling adopted in the 1980s by
Canada's Baffin Divisional Board of Education (now part of
the Department of Education of the Territory of Nunavut in
Canada's Eastern Arctic) included "developing human relations skills; developing a strong Inuit identity along with a
sense of pride and confidence in oneself; preparing students
to function well in their own communities; developing knowledge of and skills in aspects of Inuit culture such as survival
on the land; developing competency in Inuttitut; preparing
students to function in the English language; developing basic
skills in reading, writing and mathematics in both Inuttitut
and English; developing in students a strong personal value
system; preparing students for college or university level
training; and developing physical fitness."

A related concern is that students are not receiving a firm grounding in either the Native or a second language. Many educators recognize that students who have strong skills in their first language will more easily acquire English language skills as well as the content of upper level courses taught in English. In a report prepared under contract with the Government of the Yukon for presentation at the Circumpolar Education Conference at Umea, Sweden in June 1990, Jim Cummins of the Ontario Institute for Studies in Education reviewed a number of programs supporting aboriginal language development among school children and concluded that "the research data are very clear that reinforcement of the aboriginal language in all of these types of programs will have no adverse effects on development of English or French academic skills. Many of the international examples of bilingual programs, in fact, suggest that academic skills in the major school language are enhanced when the child continues to develop his/her aboriginal language."

Another recent influence on Arctic elementary and secondary education is the acknowledgement of indigenous scientific world views, including systems of land and resource management. This acknowledgement is coupled with a recognition that the experiential approach which Southern educators are increasingly adopting in science education is a traditional Native teaching and learning style.

The Dene Cultural Institute (DCI) in the Northwest Territories has focused on traditional environmental knowledge as an area of major research since 1987. DCI initiatives include a pilot project documenting this knowledge in the communities of Fort Good Hope and Colville Lake. DCI staff reports that data from the project which may provide new information to scientists include "the use of winter food caches by marten, the difference in winter temperature between valley and upland and the response of marten to it; the presence of a small variety or subspecies of barren-ground caribou that has not been 'recognized' in the scientific literature, and the possible presence and use of mineral licks by barren-ground caribou." DCI has also worked with the NWT Department of Education and the Northern Heritage Society to integrate traditional knowledge into social studies and science curricula.

Instructional processes and materials that investigate and teach traditional Native sciences and technologies are needed. The relationship between Western and indigenous science must be more fully explored and defined. In this area, important work is being done through the Alaska Rural Systemic Initiative (AKRSI), a project of the Alaska Federation of Natives and the University of Alaska Fairbanks. Initiated in the mid-1990s with funding from the National Science Foundation, AKRSI initiatives include the development of an indigenous science knowledge base, emphasizing a cultural atlas; culturally aligned curriculum, emphasizing cultural standards; and Native ways of knowing and teaching, emphasizing parental involvement.

Some of the most innovative projects and materials are being developed at the elementary level. Most school systems have begun at the primary level and worked their way up both in restructuring instructional programs and in developing materials. The holistic, interdisciplinary approach to teaching and learning, with an emphasis on co-operative learning, is one which is common both to Native traditions and to elementary school programs. It is at the secondary level that the educational system begins to compartmentalize knowledge.

The Baffin Divisional Board of Education's *Piniaqtavut* ("Where We Are Going") Program, a grade K-9 program of studies including a methodology and content for developing relevant, culture-based schooling for Inuit children, was one of the first holistic programs created for system-wide use in the Arctic. A HyperCard stack developed to introduce new teachers to the program described how "the interaction of the Inuit world view with cultural identity and social customs, the cycle of the seasons, history (past, present and future) and geography (local, regional, NWT, Canada, world) form the philosophical base for *Piniaqtavut*. This philosophical base underlies a developmental learning framework of how children learn which spirals upward and outward to provide appropriate learning experiences for a child's age and cultural background ... The *Piniaqtavut* Program suggests thematic units for each grade that are consistent with the underlying philosophical base and developmental learning framework."

One of the greatest challenges facing communities, educators and researchers in the Arctic is that of developing genuinely Inuit, Dene and other approaches to education, not just sprinkling cultural materials into approaches designed for Southern systems. Native and other Northern educators, most of them trained in southern systems, will have to think outside the boundaries of those systems.

Even more basic is the need for redefinition of the purposes

Ivujivik ca. 1951

Archives Deschâtelets
Collection.
Photo: Father Chauvel,
o.m.i. (ADES35). Courtesy
of Avataq Cultural Institute.

of schooling. Southern goals espoused by non-Native teachers are not necessarily the goals of Arctic residents. Parents and educators, both Native and non-Native, must agree on goals. Movement is needed on both sides. Some parents do not recognize the value of formal education. Some teachers and administrators see preparation for college as the only desirable goal. The goals of schooling must be agreed upon and then reflected in ongoing school district operations.

New materials and programs are needed. Over the years many good materials have been developed and subsequently lost. Institutional memory is lacking. Exemplary materials are few – particularly in math and science and for upper level coursework in all subjects. The processes and commitment for the creation of culture-based programs and materials are in place in some school systems, but inadequate funds and staffing are limiting this development.

Deficiencies in science and math education identified elsewhere in the United States and Canada (for example, inadequate teacher preparation, fewer students choosing upper level courses, too much reliance on textbooks and not

Housing in Nunavik, circa 1990
Inukjuak, Quebec

Photo: Stephen Hendrie/
Makivik Corporation

enough on experiential approaches, students seeing little 'real-life' use for science) are mirrored in the Arctic, and schools must find creative approaches to correct these deficiencies. Research done by scientists and other professionals in Arctic communities can be translated into materials for school and community use, including elementary and secondary education.

Funding continues to be a problem. Severe budget cuts at the state or provincial, district or divisional board and individual school level are retarding the development of new approaches to elementary and secondary education. The decline in public sector funding is compounded by limited private foundation support in the Arctic. Private sector support is restricted by the perception that revenues and income from oil and other resources have generated sufficient funds for education and other needs.

These are some of the issues that formed the context within which the Nunavik Educational Task Force, jointly funded by the Kativik School Board and Makivik Corporation, began its assessment of the schools in Northern Quebec.

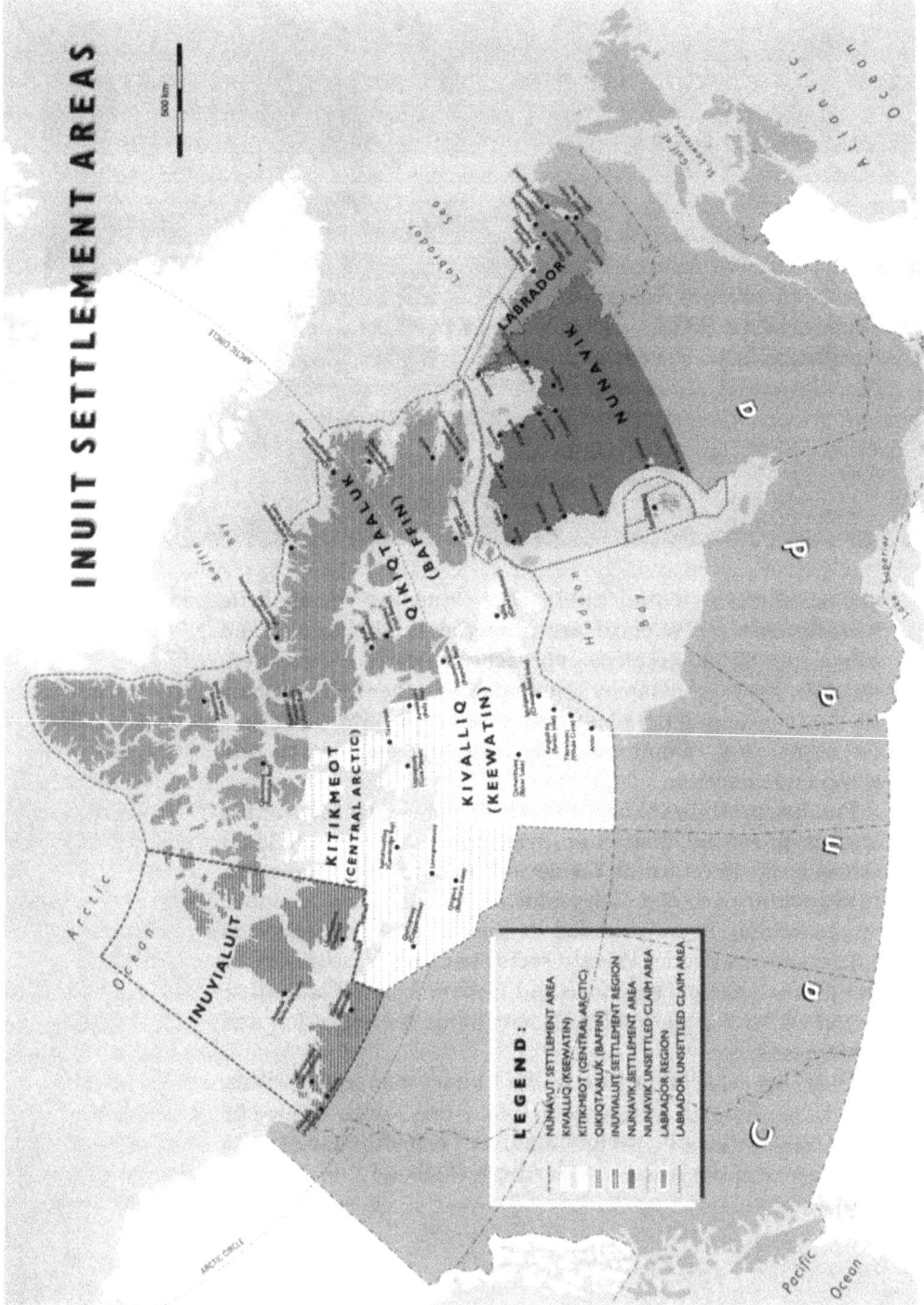

INUIT SETTLEMENT AREAS

500 km

LEGEND:

NUNAVUT SETTLEMENT AREA
KIVALLIQ (KEEWATIN)
KITIKMEOT (CENTRAL ARCTIC)
QIKIQTAALUK (BAFFIN)
INUVIALUIT SETTLEMENT REGION
NUNAVIK SETTLEMENT AREA
NUNAVIK UNSETTLED CLAIM AREA
LABRADOR REGION
LABRADOR UNSETTLED CLAIM AREA

Makivik Corporation, Cartographic Service, 2002.
www.makivik.org
www.makivik.org/nunavikatlas

20

2

A History of Nunavik

The Arctic is defined best by the nature of the terrain, not by the latitude. Not all Arctic terrain lies north of the Arctic Circle, latitude 66°30'N, above which there is at least one day a year when the sun does not set and one night when it does not rise in a 24-hour period. Most of Nunavik, with a northernmost point just over 62°N, is Arctic in environment, with plants and animals much like those on the North Slope of Alaska.

The Nunavik region was formerly called Ungava. In his article "Inuit of Quebec" in the Arctic volume (5) of the Smithsonian's *Handbook of North American Indians*, Bernard Saladin d'Anglure traces the evolution of the region's geographic name: "Ungava ... was much used during the nineteenth century because it became official on maps for the bay, was adopted to label the region served by the Hudson's Bay Company post at Fort-Chimo, and finally was extended to cover the federal district created in 1895 in the northeast Labrador peninsula. Although at first it was only a relative geographical term used by the Moravians in Labrador for the unknown regions in the northwest, and then labeled the territory of a precise local band, Ungava gradually acquired, especially in English, a very extended regional meaning that was not supplanted even after the adoption in French of the term Nouveau-Québec for the same territory, which was incorporated into the province of Quebec in 1912" (1984, 476).

A referendum to formally select an Inuit name for the entire region was held in October and November 1986. The name was accepted through a resolution of Avataq, the region's cultural institute, and Makivik in 1987; it was made official by the Commission de Toponymie Quebec in April 1988. The meaning is, literally, "a land where to live."

Quebec, Canada's largest province, is slightly bigger than

Alaska. In 1763, the northernmost boundary of Quebec extended no further than 50 to 250 kilometers (30 to 150 miles) north of the Saint Lawrence. Quebec's boundaries, including its territorial waters, were redrawn in 1895, 1897, 1912, 1918, and finally 1927, when lands were reallocated between Canada (Quebec) and Great Britain (Labrador). Nunavik is 501,800 square kilometers (193,000 square miles) – 32% of the province of Quebec and 5% of Canada's land mass.

Placing Nunavik's size in national or international perspective:

sq. kilometers	
21,386	Massachusetts
86,027	Maine
244,102	United Kingdom
356,829	Germany
372,313	Japan
381,087	Montana
386,617	Norway
404,517	Newfoundland & Labrador
411,015	California
450,089	Sweden
482,515	Yukon Territory
501,800	NUNAVIK
504,741	Spain
513,113	Thailand
547,026	France
603,700	Ukraine
650,087	Manitoba
651,900	Saskatchewan
692,405	Texas
756,626	Chile
1,068,582	Ontario
1,527,474	Alaska
1,540,680	Quebec
2,175,600	Greenland
9,528,318	U.S.A.
9,922,330	Canada

Nunavik is bounded by Hudson Bay to the west, Hudson Strait to the north, the Torngat Mountains to the east, and 55°N to the south. Straight east from Kuujjuaq, located at the base of Ungava Bay and the largest community in Nunavik, is Cape John O'Groats at the northern tip of Scotland, 3200 kilometers (2000 miles) to the east, then Talinn in Estonia,

Kangirsukallak 1904
Inuit women and
children aboard the
ship. (Erik Cove
expedition of
1904-05 P.Q.)

National Archives
of Canada
Photo: J.D. Moodie
(APAC 001815). Courtesy
of Avataq Cultural Institute.

the northern portion of the Kamchatka Peninsula in eastern Russia, and eventually Kodiak Island in Alaska, 3840 kilometers (2400 miles) west of Kuujjuaq. Straight south is Cape Horn, on the same latitude as Kuujjuaq, 57° in the southern hemisphere. On the way south are Eastport in Maine, Bermuda, San Juan, Caracas and La Paz. Iqaluit (Frobisher Bay) is 480 kilometers (300 miles) north of Kuujjuaq on Baffin Island, Thule 1600 kilometers (1000 miles) northeast, and Sept Iles 800 kilometers (500 miles) south. Kuujjuaq is 1584 kilometers (990 miles) north of Montreal, just over two hours' flying time in a 737 jet. Ivujivik, the northernmost community in Nunavik, is 253 kilometers (158 miles) further north.

Nunavik lies on the Canadian Shield, ancient rock that occupies half of Canada's landmass and is centered around Hudson Bay. With the retreat of glacial ice after the last Ice Age, the shield is still gradually rising, while portions of North America's East Coast, including Cape Cod, are gradually sinking. The tree line crosses Nunavik just north of the village of Umiujaq on Hudson Bay and of the Ungava Bay communities of Tasiujaq, Kuujjuaq and Kangiqsualujjuaq.

Geographical landmarks in Nunavik include the Torngat Mountains, which divide Quebec from Labrador and have many peaks over 1000 meters (3300 feet), topped by 1768-meter

Qilalugarsiuvik 1865
Successful whale
hunt at Little Whale
River.

National Archives
of Canada
Photo: G.S. McTavish
(APAC 008160). Courtesy
of Avataq Cultural Institute.

(5834-foot) Mount Iberville (Caubvik Mountain), with the only active glacier on the mainland of Eastern Canada. Also distinctive is the Pingualuit crater, 400 meters (1312 feet) across, and 3.4 kilometers (2.18 miles) in diameter, with a lake 267 meters (876 feet) deep in the center, created by meteor impact about 1.4 million years ago. The water in the crater lake is among the purest and most transparent in the world. The crater is located 88 kilometers (53 miles) west of the community of Kangiqsujuaq. More than 300,000 small lakes and ponds dot Nunavik, and several fjords indent the coastline at Hudson Strait.

The Inuit of Nunavik are closely related to other Inuit in Canada's Northwest Territories and Nunavut, to the Inupiat of Alaska and to the Greenlanders. The Inuttitut spoken by the Quebec Inuit is part of a continuum of closely related dialects spoken from the Bering Sea coast north of the Yukon River mouth and across Arctic Canada to Greenland.

Inuit and their predecessors have lived in Arctic Quebec for more than 3500 years, beginning with successive migrations of the pre-Dorset people from the west between 2500 and 1000 B.C. Pre-Dorset sites have been identified at Ivujivik and Kuujjuarapik. About 900 B.C. the people of the Dorset culture arrived. Numerous Dorset sites are found along the Nunavik coast, testimony to 2000 years of occupation. Thule people, direct ancestors of today's Inuit, arrived from Alaska and the northwest via southern Baffin Island before the 14th century A.D. These people introduced the technologies of whaling, the bow and arrow, the igloo, the kayak, and the dog sled to the region.

The territory historically occupied and exploited by the Quebec Inuit comprises "an immense region in the northern part of the Quebec-Labrador peninsula, including almost all the coasts, most of the adjacent islands, and a large part of the interior. This occupation was effectively limited by Indian use of the entire wooded part of the peninsula, particularly in Ungava Bay" (Saladin D'Anglure 1984, 477).

At the time of their initial contact with British, Danish and French explorers searching for the Northwest Passage to China in the late 16th century, Quebec Inuit lived in bands, about 50 of them, each composed of two to five families. The highest population density was in the north of the Ungava Peninsula, where food, particularly sea mammals, was abundant. Only occasional forays were made to the treed regions in southern Nunavik because of potential conflicts with Indians.

In 1773, Moravian missionary Jens Haven recorded ten local Inuit bands in Arctic Quebec/Labrador/South Baffin (Saladin D'Anglure 1984, 476). These bands, identified for Haven by two Inuit from Ungava Bay, closely parallel the names of today's Nunavik communities. In the following list, the first word is as recorded by Haven; the second, Haven's term in modern orthography; the third, a modern village; and the fourth, other names by which that community has been known:

- Killinek/killiniq/Killiniq (abandoned village)/Port Burwell;
- Kangiva/kangirsualujjuaq/Kangiqsualujjuaq/George River, Port-Nouveau Québec;
- Tessiugak/tasiujaq/Tasiujaq/Leaf Bay, Baie-aux-Feuilles;
- Aukpaluk/aupaluk/Aupaluk/near Hopes Advance Bay;
- Ungava/ungava/at the mouth of and somewhat north of the Riviére Arnaud, near the modern village of Kangirsuk/Payne Bay, Bellin;
- Tuak/tuvaq/Quaqtaq/near Diana Bay, Koartac;
- Aiviktol/aivirtuuq/hunting zone used by today's residents of Kangirsujuaq/Wakeham, Maricourt;
- Novangok/nuvunnguq/Cape Wolstenholme near the modern community of Ivujivik;
- Iqlurarsome/illuajuk/Inuit of the southern part of Baffin Island, so named by the illualummiut, "occupants of big igloos," on the south shore of Hudson Strait;
- Ittibime/itivi/people of "the other side" – name applied by Ungava Bay Inuit to all Inuit from the east coast of Hudson Bay.

Killiniq 1903
View of the
surrounding
landscape of the
station.

National Archives of
Canada
Photo: A.P. Low
(APA053570). Courtesy of
Avataq Cultural Institute.

In 1888, L.M. Turner recorded four additional Inuit terms used by Kuujjuaq (Fort Chimo) area people to designate the principal regional groupings of Quebec Inuit (Saladin D'Anglure 1984, 476-77):

• Suhinimyut/siqinirmiut (modern orthography)/"occupants of the sunny side" from the Atlantic coast of Labrador west to Tasiujaq;
• Tahagmiut/tarramiut/"occupants of the shady side" of the west coast of Ungava Bay, southern Hudson Strait, and the northern part of the east coast of Hudson Bay – the Nunavik coast from the villages of Aupaluk (Hopes Advance Bay) to Akulivik (Cape Smith);
• Itivimiut/ itivimiut/"occupants of the other side of the country" from the east coast of Hudson Bay from Cape Smith to the entrance of James Bay;
• Kikiktaqmyut/qikirmiut/"occupants of the islands" along the east coast of Hudson Bay. The Belcher Islands (the community of Sanikiluaq) are the only islands in this area still occupied year-round by Inuit. Historically and culturally, the Inuit of Sanikiluaq are related to the people of Nunavik; however, the Northwest Territories retained title to the offshore islands when the landmass of Arctic Quebec was transferred to that province. The Islands are now administratively within Nunavut, the new territory formed on April 1, 1999 from the eastern Northwest Territories.

The Kuujjuaq Inuit also identified the Nunamiut, "occupants of the interior," as a distinct group. The last Inuit residing near large lakes in the interior of the Ungava Peninsula were integrated into coastal Inuit groups by about 1930.

Nunavik, with a January 1996 population of 8,709 in its 14 communities, had about .16 of 1% of the province of Quebec and .04 of 1% of Canada's population at that time (Statistics Canada). In 1985, Nunavik's population was 6,053, 7,693 in 1991, and 8,709 in 1996. The July 2001 population figures from the Kativik Regional Government report a population of 10, 324, a growth rate of 3.7%, one of the highest in the world. Placing Nunavik's current population in national or international perspective yields the following selective ranking according to the most recent census or projections:

	1996 Census	**2000 (proj)**
Falkland Islands		2,000
St. Helena		6,000
St. Pierre et Miquelon		7,000
Nunavik	**8,709**	**10,324**
British Virgin Islands		21,000
Nunavut	24,330	
Yukon Territories	30,776	
Liechtenstein		32,000
Cayman Islands		38,000
Northwest Territories	39,625	
Faeroe Islands		43,000
Greenland		56,000
Bermuda		65,000
Andorra		78,000
Prince Edward Island	131,800	
Iceland		281,000
Newfoundland and Labrador	545,825	
Quebec	7,138,795	
Canada		31,081,900

[Author's note: Kativik Regional Government provided 2001 figures for Nunavik; Statistics Canada is the source for Provincial Canadian Census (1996) figures; national populations are from the UN Population Division, 2000 population estimates (1998 revision).]

Most of the contemporary communities of Nunavik grew from trading posts and missions established near camps which had been used by Inuit for thousands of years.

Kuujjuaq and Kuujjuarapik (Great Whale, Poste-de-la-Baleine, Whapmagoostui in Cree) became major transportation and communication hubs with the construction of air fields and other defense facilities during and after the Second World War. Kuujjuaq, Salluit (Saglouc, Sugluk), Ivujivik, Puvirnituq (Povungnituk), Inukjuak (Port Harrison) and Kuujjuarapik became permanent settlements for Inuit in the late 1940s and early to mid-1950s. Kangirsuk and Kangiqsualujjuaq were formally established in the late 1950s; Tasiujaq, Kangiqsujuaq and Quaqtaq in the 1960s. In 1976, some Puvirnituq residents moved back to the Cape Smith area and established Akulivik. Aupaluk was a hunting camp resettled in the late 1970s by a few people from Kangirsuk. The newest of the Nunavik communities is Umiujaq, settled in the 1980s by Inuit from the large community of Kuujjuarapik.

In July 2001, the populations of JBNQA beneficiaries in the Nunavik communities were:

Akulivik	476
Aupaluk	159
Inukjuak	1,213
Ivujivik	249
Kangiqsualujjuaq	660
Kangiqsujjuaq	545
Kangirsuk	468
Kuujjuaq	1,560
Kuujjuaraapik	585
Puvirnituq	1,353
Quaqtaq	321
Salluit	1,076
Tasiujaq	228
Umiujaq	373
Chisasibi	109
TOTAL	**9,424**

[Author's note: Chisasibi is a community located in the Cree territory of Northern Quebec. The Cree School Board is responsible for the schooling of children in this community.]

While the great majority of beneficiaries of the James Bay and Northern Quebec Agreement are Inuit, the numbers do include a few non-Inuit spouses and adopted children of Quebec Inuit. There are an additional 900 Nunavik residents who are non-Inuit.

Kuujjuaq 1939
Men repairing the
Hudson's Bay
Company roof.

Daisy Watt Collection
Photo: Daisy Watt (INK
12 DAI 117). Courtesy of
Avataq Cultural Institute.

European Impact

Missionaries came to the west coast of Greenland early in the 1700s and moved on to Labrador in 1771. In Arctic Quebec, the impact of the white man was later and more gradual. Henry Hudson sailed into the body of water which would bear his name in 1610 and much of the east coast of Hudson Bay was mapped in 1629, but the vast majority of Arctic explorers and whalers of the 17th, 18th and 19th centuries travelled through the islands north of the mainland and had little contact with Inuit on the south shore of Hudson Strait. The first Hudson's Bay Company trading post north of the 55th parallel was established at Kuujjuaq in 1830, closed in 1842, and reestablished in 1866. Missionaries did not arrive until the last half of the 19th century and then only in the southern portions of James Bay and at Kuujjuaq.

Western technology preceded actual contact. Guns, needles, and metal tools, including cooking utensils, began to change the way skills were practiced, often enhancing productivity. As they had in the past and would in the future, the Inuit adopted and adapted the technology that met their needs and improved their lives. To acquire the new goods, the Inuit began trapping the Arctic fox, an animal for which they had had little use as food or clothing but one which the traders were interested in acquiring. The demands of the fur trade began to alter the cycle of the year as people added trapping to subsistence hunting and fishing.

The missionaries had also introduced a new skill which the Inuit found useful.

Seeking a way to spread their religious teachings, the missionaries had developed a method of writing the Inuit language using symbols representing syllables in the spoken language. Invented by a missionary familiar with the shorthand way of writing the English language, syllabics enabled Inuit for the first time to communicate with one another through the written word. An Inuttitut speaker could learn the syllabic system in a matter of hours and pass it on to others. The Inuit added syllabics to the repertoire of essential skills and achieved a literacy rate of more than 90%. Ironically, the establishment of formal schooling, largely taught in English by outsiders who could not speak the Inuttitut language, would lead to a decline in the Inuttitut literacy rate in the Eastern Arctic.

While the Inuit learned syllabics through the study of religious texts, they rapidly adapted its use for everyday purposes. Writing in the September 1983 issue of *Inuktitut Magazine*, historian Kenn Harper reports the observations of a member of an expedition led by Inuit and Danish explorer and ethnologist Knud Rasmussen across the North American Arctic: "... on the Fifth Thule Expedition from 1921 to 1924, Therkel Mathiassen noted of the Iglulik Inuit: 'The Peck Syllabic Writing has spread widely among the Iglulik Eskimos, where the mothers teach it to their children and the latter teach each other; most Iglulik Eskimos can read and write this fairly simple but rather imperfect language and they often write letters to each other; pencils and pocket-books are consequently in great demand among them'" (Harper 1983, 18).

But syllabics also served the role for which it had been invented, to spread the teachings of Christianity among the Inuit. A few Qallunaat missionaries were fluent in Inuttitut, but much of the responsibility for teaching was assumed by the Inuit themselves: "In 1914 Reverend Greenshield wrote that there were at that time 12 Inuit men and six women scattered in different parts of the country, the men acting as preachers and the women teaching the children: 'They are all voluntary workers, and are doing a good work in a humble, quiet way. Our two old friends at Blacklead Island, Peter Tooloogakjuak and Luke Kidlapik, are known and respected by all for hundreds of miles round the coast. They are now in full charge of the northern district where there is no white missionary at present" (Harper 1983, 22).

Inuit had been teaching in Western-style educational institutions in Greenland and Labrador for generations. Reading and writing in Inuttitut, using the Roman script instead of syllabics, Greenland Inuit had written books and had translated works from other cultures into their own language since long before the introduction of syllabics to Canada. Of literacy in Labrador, Diamond Jenness observed: "Now, by the first decade of the twentieth century, [the Moravians] had advanced the Eskimos to a stage where, in Grenfell's judgement, they were the most literate people along the Labrador coast and were teaching their own children in the mission schools while the white missionaries taught the children of the settlers" (Jenness 1965, 31).

Harper further describes the Inuit system in Labrador: "All instruction in the Inuit schools was carried on in Inuttut and Inuit teachers ran the schools. The most notable of these teachers were Nathaniel Llinniatitsijuk, who taught for 50 years, and his wife Frederika, who taught for 30 years. Such was the situation until 1949 when Newfoundland joined Canada, at which time all instruction in Inuttut was discontinued. Only since the mid-1970s have attempts been made to reinstate Inuttut in the schools" (Harper 1983, 28).

The Canadian Presence

Northern Quebec was for 200 years part of Rupert's Land, under the management of the Hudson's Bay Company, a corporation incorporated in England in 1670 "to seek a northwest passage to the Pacific, to occupy the lands adjacent to Hudson Bay, and to carry on any commerce with those lands that might prove profitable." In 1867, events in Alaska and southern Canada led to a change in ownership of Rupert's Land. In that year, the United States acquired Alaska from the Russian Imperial Government, which needed funds to recover from its recent war with Britain in the Crimea and to compensate landowners for the liberation of their serfs. Also in 1867, through the British North America Act passed by the British Parliament, Upper (now Ontario) and Lower (southern Quebec) Canada, Nova Scotia and New Brunswick were joined into the Dominion of Canada. In 1870, Rupert's Land was bought from the Hudson's Bay Company by the Dominion of Canada, and Arctic Quebec became part of the North-Western Territories.

In 1880, the Arctic Archipelago, the islands north of the mainland, was transferred by Britain to the Dominion of Canada, in part in response to American interest in mineral rights on Baffin Island. Arctic exploration continued, focused on reaching the North Pole. In 1898, explorer Otto Sverdrup discovered and claimed for Norway three islands just west of Ellesmere Island which are now named after him. Increasing interest in the North by other nations forced Canada to begin establishing a presence there to protect its own interests. Also in 1898, the Canadian government created the Yukon Territory to provide for a governmental presence and to protect Canadian interests in the face of the Gold Rush.

In 1903, three police posts were established, at Herschel Island and Fort MacPherson in the Western Arctic and at Fullerton Harbor on the west coast of Hudson Bay. In 1905, large portions of Saskatchewan and Alberta were carved out of the North-Western Territories, and an administrator in Ottawa was responsible for what remained.

Residents of Arctic Quebec also began to see some signs of Canadian presence. In his 1969 book on social and economic development in Salluit, Nelson H.H. Graburn details the activities:

> In the late nineteenth century the Canadian government started to send official expeditions to explore the regions of the Hudson Bay and the North. One of the more famous authorities was Bell of the Canadian Geological Survey, who explored both the east and west coasts of the Hudson Bay – mainly for geological reasons. In addition to having an official interest in the geological resources of the area, the Canadian Parliament raised the possibility of opening a sea route to England from Fort Churchill via the Hudson Strait ... Although the distances were known to be shorter, there were questions about the feasibility of the navigation of the Hudson Straits because of the well-recognized difficulties of ice, currents, and weather. The Canadian Government Expedition of 1884-86 was mounted to solve some of these problems. A ship was chartered and sent north to make observations of the conditions. In addition, a number of observation posts/weather stations were set up on land at various points on the Hudson Strait, the most important objective being the reporting of ice and weather conditions. These observation stations were at Port Burwell (near Cape Chidley), where Mr. Burwell was in charge; Ashe Inlet (Big Island), where Mr. Ashe was left; Stupart Bay, just east of

Wakeham Bay, where Mr. Stupart was in charge and Mr. Payne stayed; Nottingham Island; and Point Laperriere, Digges Islands. These measures not only made great contributions to the Canadian economy and meteorology, but also resulted in a number of publications describing the Eskimos and resources of the areas around Wakeham Bay ... (Graburn 1969, 83).

Kangiqsujuaq 1884 Hudson Bay Expedition – observation station.

National Archives of Canada
Photo: Robert Bell (APAC 086360). Courtesy of Avataq Cultural Institute.

In a 1912 boundary extension, the Government of Canada transferred Northern Quebec from the Northwest Territories to the Province of Quebec. At that time the name of the territory was changed from Ungava to Nouveau Quebec. Quebec did not establish any governmental presence in the area at the time the land was transferred.

Neither Canada nor Quebec paid much attention to the North until the Second World War. The missionaries and the Hudson's Bay Company (HBC – 'Here Before Christ') were the first and constant sources of Western influence in the Inuit world. The RCMP had also entered the picture, but their posts were few and mostly on the islands of the Arctic Archipelago. The Eastern Arctic patrol visited these trading posts in the summers, beginning in the early 20th century.

Canada's energies were drawn to other opportunities and problems. According to anthropologist Diamond Jenness, who wrote a history and analysis of the different ways in which Canada, the United States, Denmark and Russia administered their northern territories settled by Inuit: "The [Minister of the Interior, Prime Minister and Parliament] were all preoccupied with other matters – a northern transcontinental railroad and the further opening up of Western Canada, in Europe the increasing power and aggressiveness of Imperial Germany, and then the First World War. Compared with these continent-shaking events, what was happening in the Arctic seemed unimportant; and as long as Canada's sovereignty remained unchallenged, the development of that region could await an indefinite future. As for its Eskimos, whom the authorities considered wards of the government but not Indians, and accordingly not the responsibility of any one department, they could safely be entrusted for a period to the fur-traders and the missionaries" (Jenness 1968, 22).

In 1920, oil and gas was discovered on the Mackenzie River at Norman Wells. Concerns about management of the resources and a rush of outsiders to the area led to the establishment of a special Northwest Territories and Yukon Branch in the federal Department of the Interior. Although his background was as Gold Commissioner of the Yukon, Director O.S. Finnie saw his branch as having responsibilities for more than the mineral resources. His attempts to institute social policies and to have the government begin to take some responsibility for Inuit welfare and education were short circuited by the advent of the Depression, by bureaucratic inertia and by prevailing attitudes.

"Government policy in the 1920s was influenced more by economic considerations than social concern ... Hence, since it was in the interests of the fur trade that the Inuit and Indians remain healthy, Finnie was able to convince the Northwest Territories Council to appoint several medical officers and to provide modest grants to the mission hospitals in an effort to control the increasing number of epidemics. Native education, however, was not considered essential to the fur trade, and so his plan to institute a programme of vocational training gained no support" (Grant 1988, 18). Scientific field studies in the Arctic were also ended because of lack of funding.

Raleigh Parkin, founder of the Arctic Institute of North America, observed that "northern policy in the 1930s appeared limited to asserting authority; catching malefactors; trapping foxes; and saving souls." Policy was shaped by the perception that Indians in Canada had become too dependent on the government. The Inuit traditions of self-reliance and survival under extreme conditions were emphasized. The government relied on Hudson's Bay Company employees and missionaries for much of what it knew about the Natives. Official reports

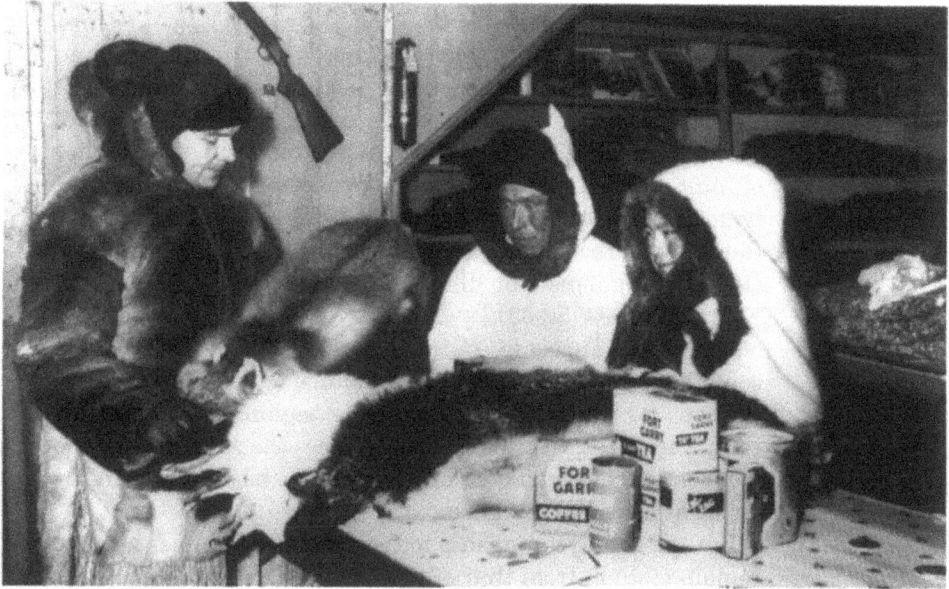

of the era are filled with observations from Qallunaat living in the North; language barriers and cultural biases meant that there was little direct input from Inuit.

The Depression also meant slumping fur prices. In Arctic Quebec, declining income from fur sales was compounded by a crash in the caribou population. People began to go hungry. Fur traders established a system of credit that advanced hunters the equipment and supplies they would need against the value of the furs they would trap during the coming season. When trapping was good and prices were high, the system worked. When times got rough, debts mounted.

Hunger in Arctic Quebec led to a court battle between Quebec and Canada over the status of Eskimos. Under the British North America Act, which established the Canadian Confederation, Indians were the responsibility of the federal government. Neither Parliament nor the courts had ever addressed the status of the Eskimos as wards of the state. Administrators in the Northwest Territories had been treating Eskimos like all other citizens. After the 1912 boundaries extension, Ottawa had continued to provide support to mission day schools in Ungava and to provide relief assistance to the Quebec Inuit. As costs mounted and the Depression reduced resources, Ottawa asked Quebec for reimbursement of the costs for relief in Ungava.

Quebec brought suit in 1935 before the Supreme Court of Canada, asserting that the Eskimos, like the Indians, were

Inukjuak 1947
Josie Nowra and
Minnie Palliser
inside HBC store
with trader
Angajuguluk.

National Archives of
Canada
Photo: Richard Harrington
(APA129927). Courtesy of
Avataq Cultural Institute.

35

Ottawa's responsibility. In response, "the Dominion placed great weight on the fact that Inuit had been treated differently from Indians, noting the lack of a treaty with Inuit, the fact that the Indian Act had not been applied to Inuit, the absence of Inuit reservations, and the Inuit's different experience with liquor regulations. The position was quintessentially liberal. Rather than recognize special status for Inuit, they were considered Canadians – no different from any other" (Tester and Kulchyski 1994, 32-33).

In 1939 the Supreme Court ruled in favor of Quebec. Canada could have appealed to the Privy Council in London, but preparations for war with Germany were beginning to preoccupy the government. Ottawa, or its designees the missions and the Hudson's Bay Company, would continue to have responsibility for Inuit heath and welfare.

But the Inuit relationship to the federal government was to remain distinct from that of the Indian. The Inuit had never signed treaties with the Qallunaat. Inuit remained isolated from sustained contact with non-Natives far longer. Inuit were scattered in small numbers across a vast and, to the Western eye, inhospitable land. And by the time Inuit policy was being developed, government policy makers had recognized some of the mistakes made by their predecessors in dealing with Indians. No one suggested reservations for the Inuit.

In his study of Eskimo administrations, Diamond Jenness compares approximate expenditures in 1939 on Eskimo education, health and welfare and on policing, graphically illustrating where each government with Arctic responsibilities placed its priorities:

	Alaska	Canada	Greenland
Inuit Population	19,000	7,000	18,000
Education, Health, Welfare	$844,000	$ 88,000	$338,822
Police	8,000	119,000	0

The world began to shrink with the coming of the war. Advances in aviation meant the North was closer to population centers and under the most direct flight path from Asia to Europe. Air bases were constructed in Canada's North, including in 1942 in Kuujjuaq (then Fort Chimo), by the U.S. Army. After the war, the Distant Early Warning (DEW) System, including the northern-most DEW Line and the mid-Canada

Line (MCL), resulted in a string of radar stations across Alaska and Canada to warn of incoming Soviet aircraft and missiles. Submarines and ice breakers began to traverse the Arctic Ocean.

As Canada looked northward for opportunities, it also began to assume greater responsibility for the health and education of the Inuit. The war had brought more Southerners to the North and opened to public view conditions of life which government reports had never reported frankly. As part of a growing social welfare system, the Department of National Health and Welfare had been created to improve health care for all Canadians. The federal government also initiated old age pensions and family allowances. A new generation of government professionals was in office, one which saw improving living conditions as part of its mandate. "In the final years of the war, there were increasing demands from the private sector for a redirection of government policies and administration in the north. They received enthusiastic support from younger reform-minded civil servants and equally strong opposition from the conservative old guard. Raleigh Parkin was one of the key figures responsible for generating outside concern and protest ... Recurrent themes in Parkin's correspondence were government neglect, Canadians' lack of knowledge about their own Arctic regions, and the under-development of northern resources. He also pointed to a new awareness 'that our north country was not a closed barrier but on the contrary, the front door to this continent'" (Grant 1988, 138).

The federal departments dealing with the North were reorganized and, with the naming in 1947 of Hugh Keenleyside as Deputy Minister of Mines and Resources, began constructing government schools across the Northwest Territories and Northern Quebec. A Permanent Committee on Eskimo Affairs began operation in May 1952 with representation from government, church, and private agencies. A separate committee on education was also established. "As participation in these initiatives was gradually extended to Inuit representatives, they were increasingly used by Inuit to dissent from and to resist many of the decisions supposedly being made for their benefit. Ultimately, they provided a base from which demands for land claims and self-government developed in the 1970s" (Tester and Kulchyski 1994, 60).

In 1953, the Department of Northern Affairs and National Resources was created.

In introducing the bill establishing the Department ...
Prime Minister Louis St. Laurent made an often-
quoted observation that Canada had administered
her northern territories "in an almost continuing
state of absence of mind" ... St. Laurent's remarks
were generous. With the exception of military
and commercial matters, primarily mining and
exploration, the Inuit had been largely ignored
by the administration, especially prior to 1945 ...
However, by the late 1940s many different factors
were conspiring to make government initiatives
imperative: the internal bickering between Catholic
and Anglican faiths; the rate at which social and
material circumstances were changing; and the
inability of private sector interests (notably the
Hudson's Bay Company) and the churches to meet
educational, health, and welfare needs. If nothing
was done, Canada would be embarrassed over the
treatment of indigenous people on an international
stage, where, under the tutelage of Lester Pearson
and his colleagues, it was trying to play a leading role
in world affairs (Tester and Kulchyski 1994, 56).

The 1950s and 1960s were to bring a profound change to Inuit
life – the movement into permanent settlements. A declining
fur trade, need for medical care, opportunities for part-time
employment, and government policies encouraged movement
into settlements. The Inuit saw the traditional life changing
and new ways of living arriving in the North. Teachers and
others promised that schooling would teach the new ways
of life and prepare students for employment in the Western
economy. Parents moved to town to give their children those
and other options. But such decisions were not made without
misgivings.

Elizabeth Simms, a teacher at the Federal day school in
Purvirnituq from 1962-1964, was given an Inuit perspective
on formal education by Kooyoo, a camp leader:

[He] came in to me about a month after I started
teaching. He was in for his semi-annual fur trade, a
two-week session ... In very carefully chosen Eskimo
which I was able to understand, Kooyoo explained to
me that he was an old man and he had to finish living
his life the way he thought was best for him by his

Kuujjuarapik 1927
A group of men and
boys on the dock
unloading supplies
for H.B.C.

National Archives of
Canada
Photo: L.T. Burwash
(APA096714). Courtesy of
Avataq Cultural Institute.

standards. He knew I represented a new era of people living in the north. He knew his children would have to cope with the changes that I was able to teach them about, but his camp was to remain intact for his lifetime for the older people. He couldn't let the children come to school on a regular basis. When he died he was sure that the younger men would make this decision, and they would all move in, but, as long as he was alive, he was going to keep the camp intact, the way he knew best. I agreed with him because I thought it was the best thing to do, and I offered to make up little packages of lessons which the fathers could pick up whenever they were in the settlement. I'd have them ready with the kids' names on them in little envelopes with books and papers and things they could work on on their own. The fathers could pick them up at trading time, take them back to the kids and let them work for two or three months and, whenever they came in again, I would correct the work and prepare new work ... He agreed and I was pleased. He also suggested that, in the summer-time when it was easy to travel, they could use the big boat and bring the kids in, if I was going to be there in the summer, which I was ... I could have them in the school classroom for as long as they were there, for maybe three or four hours a day. It wouldn't interfere with what his objectives were for the camp, and they would be continuing their education. So we agreed and we did that for two summers. Kids came in and we were together for one week or ten days ... as long as the ship was there. We later heard through friends that Kooyoo did die at a very ripe age and the camp was disbanded. The decision was made to bring the children in to school and they were able to be placed in school at a level much higher than if they hadn't had those correspondence courses (Macpherson 1991, 212-13).

3

Traditional Education and European Impact

In the traditional Inuit lifestyle, education was not separated from day-to-day living. It was not something you studied, it was something you did. The essence of education was getting ready to assume adult life roles. The pace varied with each child – there were no set ages for acquiring skills or precise paths that had to be followed. A child began to learn a skill when he or she began to pay attention, to notice how an adult did something and to try to imitate those actions.

Successful learning was demonstrated by performance. A boy showed he had learned to hunt by bringing in game, by feeding the community. A girl was judged a woman when she could preserve food for the winter's meals, when her boots kept her family's feet dry, when she trimmed the wick on the oil lamp so that it provided the amount of light and heat needed in her home.

Traditional Inuit education 'worked' because its methods and purposes were clearly understood by all members of the community and because it effectively prepared young people for the pre-established roles and responsibilities they would inherit as adults. A Kangirsuk caller to a January 26, 1991 FM radio discussion on education in that Arctic Quebec community said it best: "...when a youth is 18 under the Qallunaat law he is considered a grown man and capable of taking care of himself … Under the Inuit way of teaching, an Inuk was not an adult until he was capable of providing for the family or the community." Once they had mastered these tasks, even young Inuit, considered children still by Qallunaat, often performed adult tasks, carried adult responsibilities, and were talked with in an adult way.

The coming of the Europeans disrupted the traditional cycles. The world began to change, and people were no longer

Inukjuak 1950
Two little girls with
babies on their
back, playing
mother.

Margery Hinds Collection
Photo: Margery Hinds
(INDMH26). Courtesy of
Avataq Cultural Institute.

as sure about the skills needed to survive or the roles and responsibilities of adult men and women. New technologies and tools appeared.

Change was not new to the Inuit. Successful adaptation to changing conditions had enabled the Inuit to survive in the Arctic for millennia. Their culture in the 15th century was not the same as it had been 500 years earlier. When the Thule people, ancestors of today's Inuit, had first come to Canada's Arctic, the weather had been warmer, the ice less, and the big whales closer to shore. The weather turned colder, the migration patterns of the whales changed in response to the sea ice, new methods had to be developed to hunt on and under the ice and on land for new sources of nourishment. As they came into each new area, the people adapted their lives to the weather

Kuujjuarapik 1946
Congregation with
the Reverend
George Neilson in
front of the Anglican
church just after the
morning service.

National Archives of
Canada
Photo: Bud Glunz
(APA115409). Courtesy of
Avataq Cultural Institute.

and food resources they found there. They adapted existing tools or invented the new technology they needed to survive in each environment.

The first Qallunaat educators in the North were missionaries. Churches came to the western Northwest Territories about 1860; the earliest missionaries in Arctic Quebec north of the 55th parallel arrived in Kuujjuaq in 1872. The primary mission of the churches was to spread Christianity. The purpose of literacy was to read the sacred texts. Mission schools functioned as windows to Qallunaat society, teaching skills and attitudes that would enable students to function in a non-Inuit world.

Curriculum, a plan for instruction, was nonexistent. The missionaries taught from their individual perspectives and orientations and used methods from their own school days in various European countries. Some sought to respect Native traditions and values. Many in the early days sincerely thought they could best serve the Inuit by helping them adopt non-Native ways.

Schooling was sporadic. Prior to the 1950s, most people lived in camps and came into posts only to trade furs or when the hospital ship visited. Some Inuit had acquired English and math skills through work with the Hudson's Bay Company. A few found employment for short periods of time on the army bases or with other governmental activities.

In the late 19th century, the government had begun to provide some financial support to mission schools educating Native children. The support amounted to a few hundred dollars per day school per year and the provision of some supplies. Boarding schools received slightly more. In *Dreams & Visions: Education in the Northwest Territories From Early Days to 1984*, author Norm Macpherson describes the system: "According to tradition at least, any type of school could receive the grant from the Territorial Government and also from the Department of Indian Affairs. The teachers were certified, according to the original Ordinance, by the resident or visiting Minister; the minimum attendance was four students per quarter and the teachers required no qualifications; there were no restrictions on the text books used, or the curriculum followed; and nothing was stipulated about the length of the school day. All in all, it was a very loose arrangement for an education system, but it was indeed the one that prevailed in the NWT until after the end of World War II" (Macpherson 1991, 52). [Author's note: *Dreams and Visions*, written by a respected civil servant with decades of experience in the North with views that were considered advanced in his time, is a compilation of oral histories collected by Macpherson. In his introduction, he describes the book as containing "the dreams of the past, and the visions of the future as succeeding generations of teachers and administrators strive toward that unattainable goal – a system of education that meets the needs and serves the interests of every individual in the Northwest Territories." Because it includes, in their own words, the stories of the Qallunaats who taught in the first schools in Arctic Quebec, I have made extensive use of those interviews in this chapter.]

In an article on teacher training in the circumpolar world, McGill Professor Jack Cram talked about the impact of formal schooling on Native families: "In interviewing McGill Inuit graduates, I heard over and over again personal stories of forcible separation of children from parents by school authorities and of the apprehension, indeed, many times, the terror, involved in boarding school life in northern Canada in the 1950's and '60's. In one instance, ' ... the priests arrived with two canoes at our camp on Gerry Lake and took all us children. They told our parents the government made them do it, and we were going to school. My mother didn't know what a school was but they said it was good. We went to school in Chesterfield Inlet for two years and never saw our parents. When I went home, my mother was very surprised. She thought I was dead'" (Cram 1987, 114).

In 1944, as part of a series of studies intended to publicize conditions in Canada's North, the Canadian Social Science Research Council sponsored Andrew Moore to survey the state of education in the Mackenzie District. The Moore Report "called for a complete overhaul of the existing school system and the appointment of a director of education for both white and native schools. Additional recommendations included sweeping changes in the curriculum to meet the specific needs of the native population, upgrading of teachers' qualifications, and construction of new and improved facilities. Furthermore, Moore strongly advocated an end to the mission school system" (Grant 1988, 142).

The Northwest Territories administration undertook its own studies, for the first time focusing on conditions in the Eastern Arctic. In a 1946 report to R.A. Gibson, Deputy Commissioner of the Northwest Territories, Superintendent of the Eastern Arctic J.G. Wright wrote:

> The problem of education in the Eastern Arctic is very complex. The thinly scattered population, the transportation difficulties over great distances, the nomadic habits of the natives, the necessity for Eskimo children to learn the native way of life, the frequent changes in the personnel of the white population and, to some extent, the language and religious question, all have a bearing on the subject ... There are only two residential schools for Eskimos in the Eastern Arctic, both operated by missions at Fort George (now Chisasibi). The Roman Catholic mission has an average attendance of 8 Eskimo and the Church of England has 6. We pay these schools an annual grant of $200 per pupil ... Some of missionaries,

of course, insist on religious schools. Those laymen
who recommend education for the Eskimo want
government schools. Some do not think the Eskimo
should be given much education or he will become
dissatisfied with his lot. There is little but the fur
trade to support him in the north and he would have
a hard time competing with whites outside. Practically
all agree that any education given should be provided
in the north and that it would be a grave mistake
to transport native children any distance from their
homes for education since they rapidly become unfitted
for the native way of life. This has been amply
demonstrated in the case of children brought outside
for hospitalization (Macpherson 1991, 88-90).

The 1948 report of H. R. Lamberton and the 1949 observations of S. J. Bailey and Dr. Carter B. Storr on the existing
mission education system were presented at a 1949 session
of the Northwest Territories Council, the interdepartmental
body which governed the Arctic:

Ordinarily, regular classes are not held, the procedure
being, as explained by various missionary teachers, to
talk to a child when he appears, and if the child has
nothing more interesting on his mind at the moment
he may be induced to work for a few minutes with
his school books. This haphazard procedure produces
very meager results as can be expected, the most
tangible being the preparation of notebooks in which
certain phrases or sentences are painstakingly copied,
either in Eskimo, English or French. There is little,
if anything, meaningful to the children in what they
do. Furthermore, it must be pointed out that in
many instances more attention is given to religious
teaching than to secular education. In a few localities
an attempt is made to conduct regular classes, but
again the lack of competent qualified teachers is most
evident. True, the individual missionaries may be
sincere and may be devoting a considerable amount
of time and energy to this work; they may each be
satisfied with their results, but in the opinion of all
the Government observers the missions have not and
are not now supplying adequate educational facilities
to the Eskimo people (Macpherson 1991, 53).

Inukjuak 1940s
Classroom in the
Nursing Station.

Margery Hinds Collection
Photo: Margery Hinds
(INDMH03). Courtesy of
Avataq Cultural Institute.

Ninety years of mission-based education was ending. By 1955, all church schools in the Northwest Territories would be under the supervision of the federal government, and by 1956 all teachers were federal employees. However, churches continued to strongly influence education by insisting on co-religionist teacher staffing in their schools and hostels.

In the late 1940s the first government schools came to the North. Federal involvement in education in the Arctic Quebec had begun through the nursing stations. The first nursing station was at Inukjuak (Port Harrison) on the Hudson Bay side of the Ungava Peninsula. "In Inukjuak in the 1940s, the nurse Andy [Iona M.B. Andrew] had done some part-time teaching in combination with a nutrition program she ran that was known as the 'breakfast club'. Children would visit the nursing station in the mornings for milk, porridge, a vitaminized biscuit, a vitamin pill and cod liver oil. The nurse

47

assistant, Frederica Knight, who had spent much of her life in the region and spoke Inuttitut fluently, would teach the children some basic reading, writing and math. People remember her well. 'Paningaaaq [Frederica Knight] was the first one to teach us ABC's and 123's and feed us milk and porridge before Margery came'" (Madsen 1995, 31).

Margery Hinds was the welfare teacher assigned to Inukjuak in 1950. With her came Elijah Menarick, the first Inuk teacher in the federal schools in the North. Menarick had worked as a translator for the RCMP, and he acted in that capacity for Margery Hinds and the nurse. He was also responsible for teaching the beginning students their first lessons.

Margery Hinds describes the educational tasks facing the first teachers:

> All except the youngest could read and write the
> Eskimo syllabic script, but none knew more than a
> word or two of English. One of my first jobs was to
> make a dictionary, as none existed; the one compiled by
> Father Thibert, O.M.I. was not published until 1954 ...
> Also, there were many children in camps who wanted
> to learn so I had to hektograph [make copies of] lessons
> for them and also try to teach the camp children
> who accompanied their fathers when they came to
> Port Harrison to trade ... In May almost all the Port
> Harrison children went with their parents to their
> sealing camp on Harrison Island. I went too and
> conducted school in a tent for about three weeks ...
> It seemed to me that the basic principles of teaching
> – i.e., proceed from the known to the unknown –
> had been completely ignored by those who planned
> the education of the Eskimos in the Eastern Arctic.
> These people had very little contact with white people
> and therefore they could not speak English. They had
> little idea of the way of life of white people in white
> communities ... To teach reading, for instance, not
> only was the language foreign to them, the subject
> matter was also foreign. I tried to make pre-primer
> readers based on the day-to-day life of children at Port
> Harrison, and illustrated by Isa Smiler, using the same
> method as the Dick and Jane pre-primers. I considered
> the method excellent, with its repetition of common,
> simple words. This was not accepted by the education
> department in Ottawa" (Macpherson 1991, 74-75).

Iqaluit 1950-60s
Elijah Menarick and
Leah Idlout at the
CBC Radio Station.

Peter Murdoch Collection
Photo: Peter Murdoch
(INDPMUR0151). Courtesy
of Avataq Cultural Institute.

Welfare teachers had to do much more than teach lessons. In some settlements with no other federal employees in permanent residence, teachers had responsibility for administering public assistance payments, dispensing medical supplies and services, running the electrical generating plant, and even enforcing the Dog Ordinance (Macpherson 1991, 107). Teachers were on duty for up to 12-plus hours a day and 49 weeks of the year.

Inuit found jobs in the federal schools as teacher's aides and janitors. Because of the language and cultural differences between the Qallunaat teachers and their students, the Inuit staff taught the teachers a lot, sometimes subtly shaping the way the system operated.

Mick Mallon, who taught at Puvirnituq from 1959 to 1963, illustrates the point:

> The janitors were vital to the way the school was run.
> First was Lukasi Tukaluk, then Aisa Sivuarappik, and
> finally Samisa. As time went on, and we got used
> to each other, I learned to rely on them more and
> more. For one thing, they were usually the only people
> who could begin to understand my Inuktitut. Parents
> would come to see me. If the janitor wasn't around,

49

the conversation would begin with a great flurry
of memorized civilities on my part. Encouraged by
this, the parent would launch into the heart of the
matter. At that point, my linguistic skills would usually
collapse, a fog of miscomprehension would descend on
us all, the parent refusing to believe that anyone who
had been so witty and sparkling a moment ago on
the topic of the weather, the whiteness of snow, the
noisiness of dogs and the arrival of air-planes could
now be so dense about the simple matter of a boy
taking his grandmother fishing. ("Grandmother? ...
Grandmother?..." I would say, "She's dead? ... Oh, she's
not dead ... She's sick maybe? ... Fish, fish? ... You
want me to buy some fish from your grandmother?") By
this time Aisa or Samisa would have appeared, would
grasp the crux of the matter, and would transform
it into the slow simple sentence patterns that were
my claim to bilinguality. It was more than that, of
course. I learned to take their advice on absenteeism,
on the scheduling of hunting holidays, on a myriad of
connections between the alien school on the hill and
the world of the village (Macpherson 1991, 143-144).

[Author's note: Since that time Mallon has gone on to teach Inuttitut
to second language students at the college level.]

Sometimes the Inuit impact was not linguistic but structural.
Peter Balt recounts how the school schedule was changed at
Ivujivik in the mid-1960s: "One very nasty Saturday morning,
Peta came over to the house to tell me it was time for school.
Not being wide awake and not realizing it was Saturday
I went to school, worked with the kids until the fog got
out of my brain, and thought, 'This is Saturday. what am I
doing teaching school on Saturday?' I was ready to dismiss
the kids when Isaacie (the school janitor, mechanic and all-
around maintenance man) came in and told me, 'Well, today
is Saturday, but it's a poor day, but maybe Tuesday will be
nice and then there would be no school; everybody could go
hunting because there would be no point in having school.'
So that's how I operated it and it wasn't put in the records.
It seemed to me a pretty reasonable system all around"
(Macpherson 1991, 208).

In 1952, the Sub-Committee on Eskimo Education had been

Nunatsiaq 1936.

National Archives
of Canada
Photo: A.G. McKinnon
(APA101941). Courtesy of
Avataq Cultural Institute.

formed. Composed of administrators from Northern Affairs and National Resources, representatives from the Anglican and Roman Catholic missions, officials from the Indian Affairs Branch, and invited observers, the Sub-Committee was to play a critical role in setting educational policy at its biannual meetings in Ottawa, which continued until March 1960. From the minutes of the first meeting:

> What do we want to accomplish in educating the Eskimo? It was agreed that the Eskimo should not be permitted to remain illiterate even though their economy may be largely restricted to hunting, fishing and trapping. They should be furnished with the kind of education which will enable them to live a fuller life in their own environment and at the same time be able to take advantage of opportunities that may arise from the encroachment of outside civilization. The present objective should be to teach them reading and writing in elementary English and simple arithmetic. There should be both child and adult instruction in health and hygiene, coupled with some geography of the world and simple social and natural science. The course should include a fair proportion of time devoted to manual instruction, such as craftsmanship, sewing and handicrafts. The more promising students should be encouraged to continue their studies and fit themselves by more formal education to become

leaders in the community and to occupy positions
filled, of necessity, by white persons ... Instruction
should be in English. The use of Inuktitut should
not be discouraged, but the use of Roman characters
in writing it should be encouraged. The Book of
Wisdom [published in Inuttitut in 1947 by the federal
Department of Mines and Resources] should be
expanded for home study (Macpherson 1991, 116).

In some communities in Arctic Quebec, the federal government supported hostels so that parents could continue their
lifestyle of traveling from place to place to harvest wild foods
and run traplines while their children learned. But parents
did not like being separated from their children. The separation, combined with declining fur prices and caribou harvests,
the need for medical care, and the availability of government
assistance and occasional wage labor, encouraged people to
move into the settlements.

In a statement on the Inuit Education Concept prepared
in the late 1970s, the staff of the Inuit Cultural Institute in
Arviat depicted the dilemmas faced by both Inuit and government administrators:

Initially settlements were started by the Government
as a response to what they considered a desperate
situation, and the assumption was made that
settlements would be permanent.

The 1959 opening address to the Council of
the Northwest Territories speaks of economic,
educational, housing, health, and pension benefits for
Inuit, the issues at hand being the instability of the
fur market and the development of the wage sector
of the economy for the security of Inuit. Settlements
would act as on-going social and economic units
with at least half of the population continuing to
follow a modified land-based economy and selective
assimilation into wage labour would occur. Simply, the
Government with all good intentions felt Inuit should
participate in, and be entitled to, the same lifestyle
and services as other Canadians.

Many Government studies indicated that to put
this plan into action certain values of Inuit
would have to change. Such change could best be
accomplished through learning, the obvious device

for enculturation being formal education for Inuit children and adults. In a way education would teach Inuit to become like Qablunaat: to handle finances, to work for a living; to develop a sense of community; to understand the judicial system, town planning etc. Many of the values associated with this lifestyle are now being seriously considered by Inuit as they become more and more conscious of what it is to be a "modern Inuk"....

When Inuit moved to the settlements the Government made many promises which appeared encouraging to Inuit. The settlements offered health facilities, housing, and a certain amount of security in relation to making a living. Some people moved to be closer to their children who were in school. Many saw this new lifestyle as perhaps promising a "better life" for their children. Inuit trusted and tried to live in this setting. At that time they believed Qablunaat to be the same as Inuit with the same family ties and values. Inuit could not foresee the whole process and did not understand that, to achieve the same lifestyle, many of the values they held dear would have to be changed.

We were told education was the key. With an education we could become settlement managers, store managers, and area development officers. We were also told we could become professionals like the teachers, doctors, nurses and lawyers we saw. This "education" would bring a good job, high wages and housing...

Inuit parents accepted this because their children would grow up to get good jobs. Inuit would be 'successful' as Qablunaat defined the word...

Formal schooling increased rapidly. Gordon Robertson, Deputy Minister of the Department of Northern Affairs and National Resources and Commissioner of the Northwest Territories, estimated in 1953 that only about 5% of school-age Inuit children in the Northwest Territories and Arctic Quebec were receiving any "reasonably consistent education." About 30% of Indian and Métis children had access to regular educational services. By 1962, federal schools had opened in every settlement in Arctic Quebec.

Community	Year federal schooling started
Kuujjuarapik	1957
Inukjuak	1950
Puvirnituq	1958
Ivujivik	1960
Salluit	1957
Kangirsujuaq	1960
Quartaq	1960
Kangirsuk	1960
Kuujjuaq	1949
Kangirsualujjuaq	1962

In Arctic Quebec in September 1962 the following enrollments were recorded (Macpherson 1991, 207):

	Number of teachers	Number of pupils	Grades taught
Kuujjuarapik	8	156	1-4
Inukjuak	2	45	1-6
Purvirnituq	5	117	1-6
Ivujivik	1	23	1-5
Salluit	2	60	1-6
Kangiqsujuaq	2	35	1-5
Quartaq	1	18	1-4
Kangirsuk	2	41	1-2
Kuujjuaq	6	139	1-8
Kangiqsualujjuaq	1	32	1
TOTAL	30	666	

The instructional program was based on the curriculum used by the Protestant School Board of Quebec. Courses of study from other provinces were used in the Northwest Territories. The Mackenzie District used that of Alberta, the Keewatin Manitoba's, and the Baffin District adopted the Ontario curriculum.

Access to secondary education was still very limited. A small number of students went to southern Canada for secondary schooling.

In a 1959 pamphlet, the NANR Educational Division detailed the accomplishments of the preceding ten years in the Northwest Territories and Arctic Quebec:

Inukjuak 1953-54.
Bill Applewhite Collection
Photo: Bill Applewhite
(INDAPP046). Courtesy of
Avataq Cultural Institute.

In 1949, eight different authorities operated schools
in the north. Only three classrooms were operated by
the Department. Some schools operated for only four
hours a day, four days a week, and 35% of the teachers
in such schools did not hold teaching certificates.
Classroom visitations were infrequent. Film services
and adult education classes were provided in only
three communities. There was no vocational training
program nor were there any teachers employed
to teach hospital patients. There was little or no
provision for any program of in-service training and
there were no plans for using a curriculum, other than
that of the Province of Alberta. Community libraries
were almost unknown. There were only 117 Eskimo
children attending school on a full-time basis ...
[In the ten-year period between 1949 and 1959]
the number of Eskimos in schools has increased
over 1000% and the number of federal schools has
increased from three schools with one classroom each,
to a total of 51 schools with 182 classrooms. The
total enrollment in all schools has increased from
1,121 pupils in 1949, to 3,928 in September, 1958.
In 1949, there were 103 pupils enrolled in the junior
and senior high school grades. By September 1, 1958,
this enrollment had increased to 576 pupils. A gradual

consolidation of the various types of schools began in
1954 and in 1955 schools formerly operated by Indian
Affairs Branch were transferred to the Department of
Northern Affairs. In 1956, all mission school teachers
became federal employees, as part of a program of
consolidation of mission schools with federal schools.
By 1960, there will be only two authorities operating
schools in the Northwest Territories ... These will be
federally-operated and municipally-operated schools.
All schools now offer a full five hours of instruction
daily for five days a week (Macpherson 1991, 156).

In 1964, the federal government opened a vocational high
school in Churchill which was to provide secondary education
to many Inuit who currently hold leadership positions in Arctic
Quebec. Educator Ralph Ritcey was an Education Officer with
the federal government from 1961-84 with major responsibility for the Churchill Vocational Centre:

The first week of August 1964, Mr. Devitt received
a phone call from R.A.J. Phillips, the Director, who
asked "How soon can you occupy Fort Churchill as
a vocational school for Eskimos?" Mr. Devitt replied:
"Thirty days." At that time we had no teachers, no
students, no equipment ... in thirty days we hired
fifteen teachers, fifteen child-care workers, entered
into an agreement with the C.N.I.B. to feed the people,
and also recruited and arranged transportation for
150 students ... The first year in the school we had
150 pupils, the second year ... we ran about 256 ...
I do think on the whole that it was a very successful
experiment and a great many young people who today
are leaders in the Inuit community in the Eastern
Arctic are graduates of the C.V.C. and very proud of it.
People have asked why the school was closed in 1974
when it seemed to be such a successful experiment.
The thinking was this: the buildings were worn out,
they had been built by the Armed Forces in 1950
for a 20-year life. The heating and plumbing would
be finished by 1975. The buildings were going to be
disbanded by 1970, and the Arctic Quebec students
would be a different responsibility than NWT students
(Macpherson 1991, 187-88).

Quebec and Education

Federal schools operated in Arctic Quebec until the mid-1970s. In the 1960s, Quebec provincial schools were also established in most communities. During the 1970-71 school year in Northern Quebec there were 2,148 students enrolled in 24 federal and provincial elementary schools. 2,098 of the students were Natives, both Inuit and Indian (Man in the North Project: Education Task Force 1973, 115). From 1964 through 1974, Quebec also operated a residential trade school for older students in Kuujjuarapik.

The vast majority of the teachers in both systems were from the South. A study on teacher preparation done during that time by the Arctic Institute of North America found that "teachers trained in southern Canada know very little about the northern reality present or past, and consequently are badly equipped to help Eskimo or Indian children of the North continue their learning process on the basis of their natural curiosity, the preoccupations of their milieu, and the environment they have seen around them since they were born" (Man in the North Project: Education Task Force 1973, 14). The study concluded that only 23% of the teachers stayed in the North for longer than three years. And since the Education Task Force members believed that "the southern teacher spends his first two years in the North coming to terms with his environment and the new professional problems he faces ... over 50% of elementary-level teachers leave when they just begin to be productive, and when a real integration with their northern community becomes a possibility" (Man in the North Project: Education Task Force 1973, 119).

The Quebec provincial schools initiated instruction for the first time in French and Inuttitut. Kindergarten classes were also begun, something which the federal schools did not offer. Of 145 teachers (not including teachers' assistants) employed in Arctic Quebec's 24 elementary schools in 1970-71, 27 were Natives – most of them Inuit teaching at kindergarten, Grade 1 and Grade 2 in Quebec provincial schools. (Man in the North Project: Education Task Force 1973, 115-116)

The Quebec presence in its North also reflected changes taking place in Quebec society as a whole. While control of education was established as a provincial power under Section 93 of the British North America Act, Quebec officials had left education to the churches. Under the French regime, Quebec education had been closely patterned after that of the mother country and largely under the direction of the Catholic Church. That pattern stayed in place after the conquest. In their 1987 history, *Between Past and Future: Quebec Education in Transition*, McGill professors Norman Henchey and Donald Burgess cite the increasing importance of religious institutions in Quebec after 1760: "One resource to which [French Canadians] turned was the Catholic Church, virtually the only organized institution that the British permitted to remain in the colony. During the years following the conquest, the Church gradually assumed a predominant role in providing social and educational services to the French-speaking population ... A number of attempts were made to form a centralized school system, common to all ... The Catholic clergy feared that a common school, dominantly controlled by English-speaking and Protestant authorities, would inevitably lead to the assimilation and 'Protestantization' of the French Catholic population" (Henchey and Burgess 1987, 22-23).

Thus a dual system, Catholic and Protestant, educated the children of Quebec. Courses of study were developed by each system, teachers were of the same religion as their pupils, the Catholic schools taught in French and the Protestant in English. A Council of Public Instruction composed of Catholic and Protestant confessional committees oversaw the schools. Unlike all the other Canadian provinces, Quebec had no Ministry of Education.

The majority of the Inuit in Arctic Quebec were Anglicans, and those who spoke a second language spoke English. The history of mission schools and the subsequent adoption of the Protestant School Board of Quebec curriculum by the federal system meant that the operating principals of the Northern schools were quite similar to those in southern Quebec.

In the 1960s, profound changes occurred in the government and institutions of Quebec. An increasing population, a demand for expanded and improved social services, migration from rural villages to urban areas, and a sense that Quebec needed to modernize in the post-war world encouraged an exploration of new paths. Combined with this was a swelling nationalism among the French majority. Business and financial power was still largely in the hands of English Quebeckers. French-speaking residents of Quebec began to expect more opportunities and to use their majority status as a political wedge to achieve them. In 1960, a new Liberal government had come to power replacing the Union Nationale, which had been in power since 1944. In 1962, the Liberals were reelected, and a major part of their platform was the nationalization of the hydroelectric industry as one means of generating income to fuel the modernization of Quebec.

Though its Département des Recherches Hydrauliques and later with the formation of Hydro-Québec, the government had begun to look northward for more resources. Concurrent with this was the desire to establish a provincial presence in Arctic Quebec. Quebec began to assert to the Canadian government its jurisdiction over Inuit affairs. The first provincial schools were opened in 1963 in Kangirsujuaq and Kuujjuaq, and by 1970 provincial schools were in every Inuit community.

Expansion of educational opportunities for Quebec Inuit coincided with legislative and policy changes in the south:

> At the beginning of the 1960s, the government had set up a Royal Commission of Inquiry ... Most of the education reforms during this period stemmed directly from the report of this Commission [the Parent Report]. In 1964, a Ministry of Education was established to replace the Council of Public Instruction and its Catholic and Protestant committees as the official authority for all education policy in the province ... Regional school boards were created throughout the province to provide universal and comprehensive secondary education; the classical colleges were replaced by a new network of post-secondary colleges known as Colleges d'enseignement général et professionnel (CEGEPs); teacher training was reorganized and upgraded; and the number of university places was increased. The degree programs in both English and French universities were revised and given a common structure and the Ministry issued a series of regulations changing the organization and content of elementary and secondary education. In sum, these reforms completely changed the face of education in Quebec and resulted in a spectacular increase in the proportion of the provincial budget devoted to education services (Henchey and Burgess 1987, 27).

Quebec's presence in its North offered to the Inuit some alternatives to the existing federal system. Initially there was skepticism among the Inuit concerning Quebec's intentions.

Quebec did not have a history of caring about Inuit welfare. Some Inuit talked of moving to the Belcher Islands or north to Baffin in order to stay in the Northwest Territories (Tester and Kulchyski 1994, 39).

In July 1964, René Lévesque, then a minister in the Liberal government of Jean Lesage which had been reelected in 1962, met in Kuujjuaq with Inuit representatives from each community in Arctic Quebec. Paulussie Napartuk, president of the Eskimo Council of Kuujjuarapik, made a tape of the meeting with Lévesque, an English transcript of which was located by Avataq Cultural Institute researchers in the federal archives in Ottawa (RG 85, VOL. 1958. FILE A-1006-8, PART 4). The excerpts below capture the intent of the provincial government as well as the concerns of the Inuit:

Lévesque: "Some day soon, all administration in northern Quebec is going to be Quebec. The only reason why we wait is because we want [the Inuit] to understand, we don't want to force them, in other words ... the only thing we want is for Quebec administration to take over and for the people to have the same rights and privileges as other Quebec citizens ... And I would like to give [the Inuit] just one advice – instead of fighting against it they should try and understand it and work together so that we can work together. This is because it is something that will come soon and we will have to be friends and not enemies – because the government that is the government that will never, never, never disappear is the Quebec government."

Inuit Questioner: "If Quebec takes over, we don't want any promises broken."

Lévesque: "The only promise that we have made is that no services given by the federal government will be taken away – they will be better if anything ... I am going to tell them something they probably didn't know – the Quebec government already pays pensions, widow's pensions, etc. This money comes from the Quebec people. I don't know if they have been told – DNA [the federal government] may give the cheques but it's Quebec's money ... If they are worried about promises and things like that they just have to know that the Quebec government has always, in its field of administration, game laws or pensions, done its duty and will keep on doing its duty, that's what I mean ... They say they know that but a lot of liars have been telling lies about the Quebec government."

Kuujjuarapik 1948
Group of Inuit
facing Constable
Van Blarcom.

National Archives of
Canada
Photo: S.J. Baily
(APA027644). Courtesy of
Avataq Cultural Institute.

Inuit Questioner: "How long has the Quebec government been administering in this territory?"

Lévesque: "Since 1912, 50 years."

Inuit Questioner: "Why didn't Quebec come up here before DNA came?"

Lévesque: "The reason is this – until the war there were no airplanes. Was anyone taking care of them before airplanes came? In other words, before the war when there were no airplanes, there was no DNA and no Quebec, and no government at all because we couldn't come up. Second there was a war. The war was mostly National Defence ... When there is a war the Quebec government is not involved. It is always Ottawa – so that's why Ottawa came here first. The only reason the federal government came up first was the war, and they came to Chimo [Kuujjuaq] because there was a base, otherwise there would be no one here. Now there is no war and the only government that is really interested, really interested, is the Quebec government."

Inuit Questioner: "Shortly after the war – how come Quebec government didn't come in then when DNA came in?"

Lévesque: "Because Quebec was not ready. That is very simple. Because at the time the Quebec government had too many problems down south and was not ready to come up. Now it is ready and it will come up. A government is exactly like a man – a man has trouble with his wife and trouble with

61

his dogs, he is going to take care of one before he takes care of the other. He can't do both at the same time."

Inuit Questioner: "We have nothing against Quebec but we are satisfied with the administration here now and we don't want Quebec to take over."

Lévesque: "If the people have a reason for resisting the change, what is their main reason?"

Inuit Questioner: "We have no reason. We only think the changeover has been too fast. We don't want to change from what we now know to the other one too fast."

Lévesque: "What do the people think the big change is going to be? Are they afraid of a change? What kind of change?"

Inuit Questioner: "We really have no reason. But we are afraid that if Quebec takes over there will be new rules and regulations coming in and we have to get used to these things. We have had to get used to them before and we don't want this to happen again."

Lévesque: "We are making only one promise basically. I said that before. There will be no change in services or in anything the people get except if it is to make it better..."

The pace of change was picking up. Through settlement councils and co-operatives, the impact of which is explored in the following chapter, the Inuit began to assume some of the decision-making powers which Qallunaat institutions had previously denied them. The Inuit movement to take back control of their own lives and communities had begun.

4

The James Bay and Northern Quebec Agreement

After the Second World War and the movement of Inuit into settlements, Northern administrators established community councils. Initially, the councils had little real power and functioned more as intermediaries, carriers of complaints and questions, than as partners in the governing of communities. With the establishment of provincial schools in Arctic Quebec, parent committees were created, something federal schools had never initiated. In reality, the parent committees made few decisions, had little impact on the day-to-day operations of the schools and none on the instructional program or overall policy. Inuit were invited to participate, but the Qallunaat set the limits of that involvement.

Mark R. Gordon, a leader in the negotiations which led to the James Bay Agreement and the recognition of aboriginal rights in the 1982 Canadian Constitution, described the post-war system at a 1984 forum on Self-Determination and Indigenous Peoples in Copenhagen:

> We had an education system being provided for
> us by two different governments, by the provincial
> government and by the federal government. We had
> absolutely no control of this education system – no
> say in what it could do. The federal government
> had not even allowed us to form a committee to
> advise on how education should be given to our
> children. The provincial government, being a bit more
> democratic, allowed us to form a committee. They
> gave us authority over certain matters in school:
> 1) to hire the janitor, and 2) to hire the man who
> went to pick up the smallest children in kindergarten
> to take them to school. That was the limit of our
> authority over our education ... The federal and

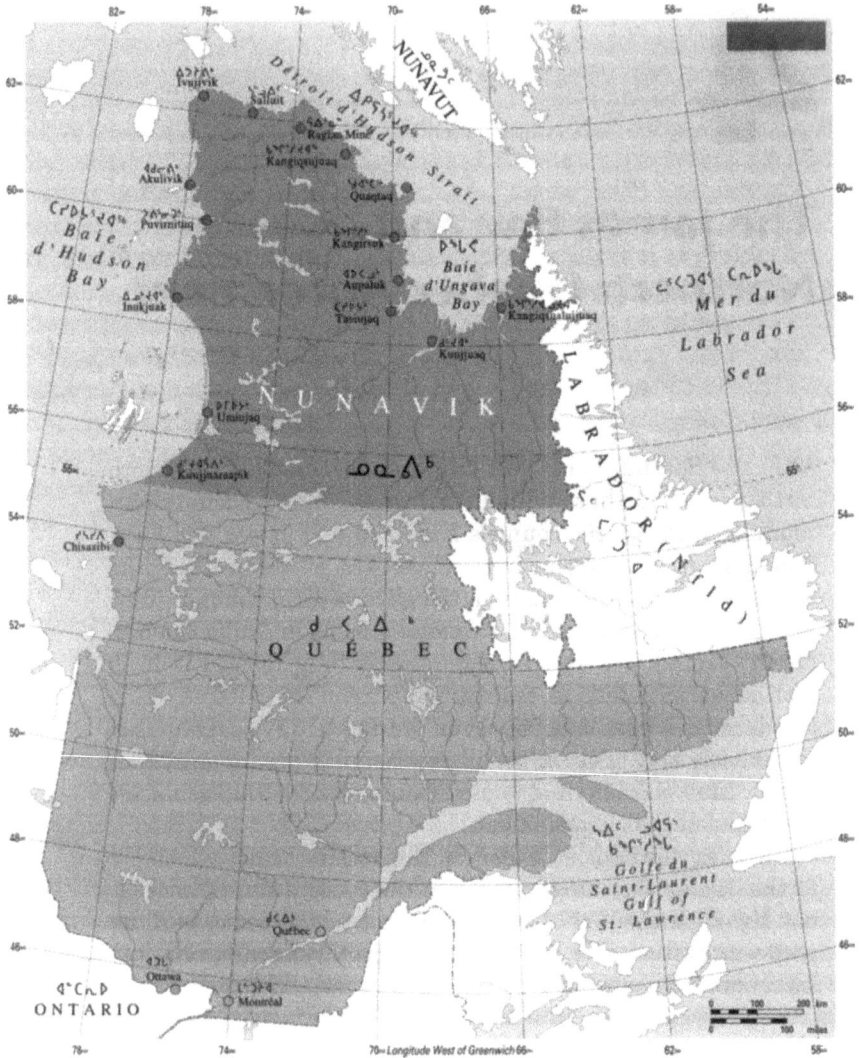

Province of Quebec
showing the Inuit-
controlled region
of Nunavik.

Makivik Corporation,
Cartographic Service,
2002.
www.makivik.org
www.makivik.org/
nunavikatlas

provincial governments have never done anything
really malicious to us; they thought they were
acting for our own good. Even recognizing that
they were trying to do some good, they made some
pretty bad mistakes. We had no authority over our
communities. There were government agents in my
community [Kuujjuaq] who could control the entire
administration of the village. They could decide who
got jobs, who got the welfare and who could go away
to school – everything. All our villages were run by a
government agent (Gordon 1987, 123).

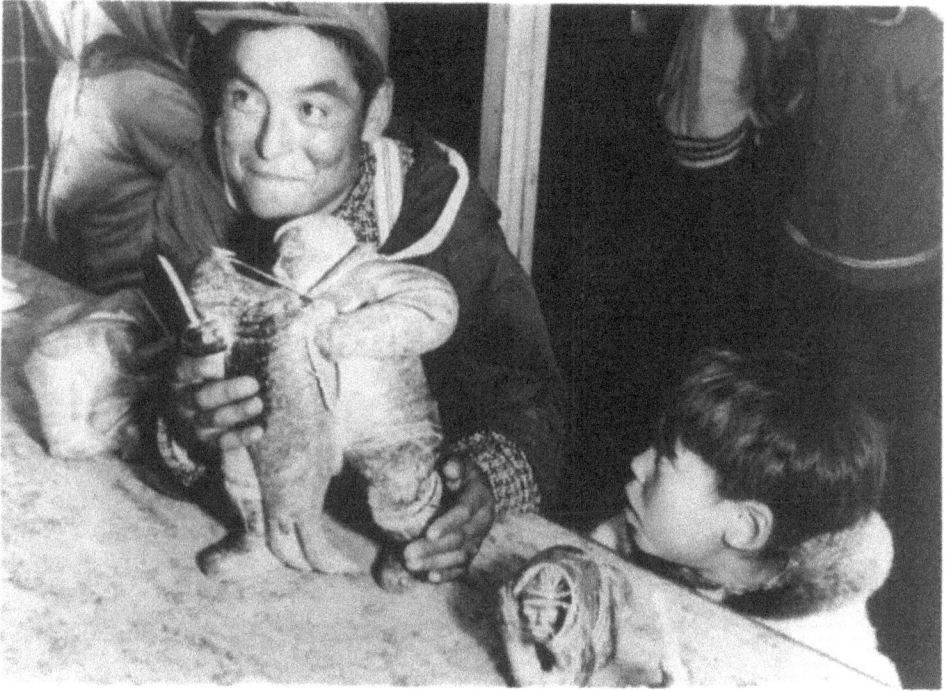

Diamond Jenness, a generation older and a Qallunaat, also saw the contradictions in the system:

Puvirnituq 1950-60s
Levi Piirti with an
unknown boy.

Peter Murdoch Collection
Photo: Peter Murdoch
(INDPMUR0242). Courtesy
of Avataq Cultural Institute.

> We have set up a complex government in their
> territory, but offered them no real place in it; and,
> what is worse, we have not inspired any hope that
> there will be real places for them, which is one reason,
> perhaps, why the local councils we have fostered
> in several places failed to take root. We, or the
> missions, have banished their old dance-houses as
> strongholds of heathenism, not realizing that they
> were community centres [providing] each band or
> group of families its stability; and we vainly try to
> substitute for them churches and schools that we
> build after our own designs and lock with keys that
> we keep in our own hands (Jenness 1964, 161).

It was through the co-operative movement that the Inuit first began to assert control economically and politically in the new settlements. The federal government had begun encouraging the formation of co-operatives in the 1950s as a way to foster the economic development of the communities and to introduce Inuit to the cash economy, Western banking

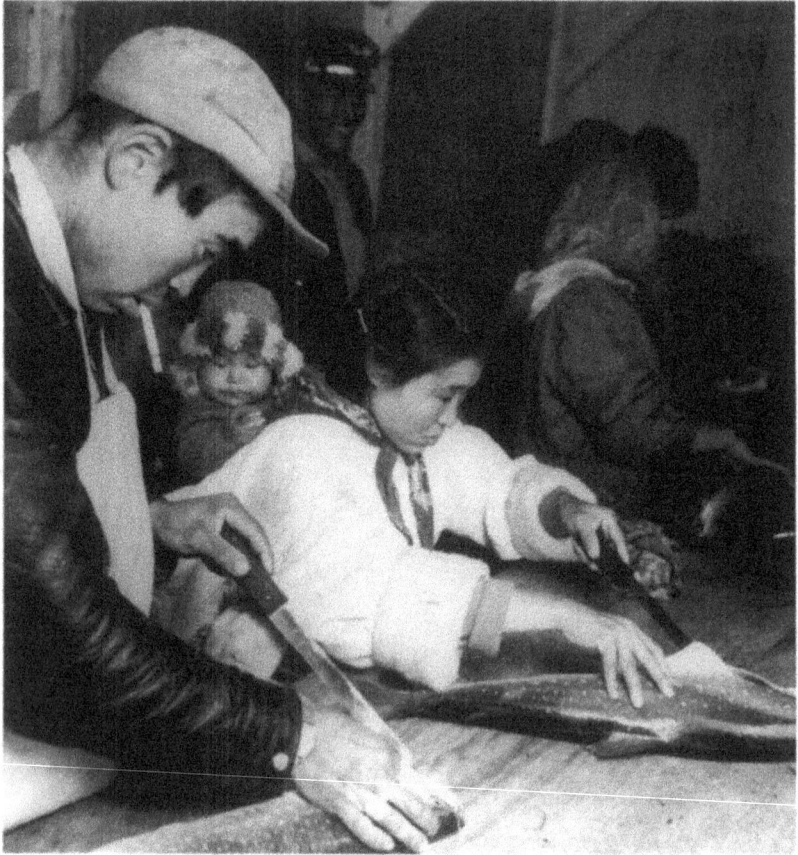

Kangiqsualujjuaq
1960
Cleaning Arctic
char.

National Archives
of Canada
Photo: Rosemary Gilliat.
Courtesy of Avataq
Cultural Institute.

and credit systems (Iglauer 2000, 15). Through co-operatives, communities sold fish and other products to the outside. Inuit began carving, making prints and sewing handicrafts for Southern markets. As they expanded, the co-operatives opened general stores, giving village residents an alternative to the HBC stores at competitive prices. They also became fuel distributors and operated small hotels and fishing lodges for visitors. While the idea of starting the co-operatives and the initial funding had come from outside, the co-operatives became truly Inuit-controlled institutions, owned and run by village residents for their own purposes.

In an interview in a special edition of the *Makivik News* marking the 20th anniversary of the signing of the James Bay and Northern Quebec Agreement, Makivik President Zebedee Nungak discussed the role of the co-operatives in awakening Inuit politically:

Kangiqlliniq
1950-60s
L to R: Taamusi
Qumaq with three
men in training.

Peter Murdoch Collection
Photo: Peter Murdoch
(INDPMUR0242). Courtesy
of Avataq Cultural Institute.

And there was a decade, basically a ten-year period, from about the mid sixties to the mid seventies when the communities in the Nunavik coast were the subject of competition between two levels of government ... We had no say in how the government administers its programs and its services to our people. We could only aspire to being employed one day at either level of government, never in a senior capacity...

Around the beginning of the 1970s, the Indians of Quebec were organizing politically, Inuit Tapirisat of Canada was being launched on a national level, and people in the Western Arctic, under their own organization called Committee for Original People's Entitlement (COPE), were engaged in efforts to get the government to recognize certain rights, and to get the people, those of us who live in Arctic regions, more say in how the governments govern the North and its people ....

And with the seed of those thoughts, and with some bold young leadership, especially on the part of Charlie Watt, who was a government employee at the time, as I was, we got the communities and the region into a

very lively debate about whether an organization like
our own is the best way to go. Now there was a certain
resistance to this idea because none of this had ever
happened before. And the only other forum in which
Inuit in this region could engage in any sort of political
discussion was through the Co-op meetings.

The Co-ops had organized in the late 1950s and
1960s and they started organizing in a regional way in
the late 1960s, and they were great places where Inuit
could express their aspirations, their profound wishes
for their communities and their region. Of course, it
was the wrong forum in that the Co-op Movement,
and what it had on its plate, could not satisfy the
yearning for political activity in a complete way.

But there was a very definite seed that was planted
in the first Co-op meetings where people started
talking about doing things for themselves, running
the show, expressing self-determination in ways that
government either federal or provincial could never
have imagined. People were becoming aware of their
identity, and their rights as a collective.

Political and societal changes outside Canada in the 1960s
and 1970s were also to have an impact on the Quebec Inuit.
Former colonies in Asia, Africa and the Caribbean had become
independent nations and were making their presence and concerns felt in the United Nations and at other international
forums. The Civil Rights Movement was forcing change in the
United States. In 1964, the Norwegian Sami Council was created as a national advisory body representing the concerns of
the indigenous people of Scandinavia before national and local
governments. The Council's powers continued to expand and
were assumed by the Norwegian Sami Parliament in 1989. A
Sami Parliament was established in Finland in 1973.

In both Canada and the United States, federal funds were
being made available to aboriginal and other minority groups
to create regional and national organizations to spur economic and social improvements in their communities. Through
the Johnson administration's Office for Economic Opportunity
(OEO), community action programs were initiated throughout
rural Alaska, and Native leaders were able to come together
regularly from across the state for the first time to discuss
shared concerns. Out of that sharing came a common agenda
for change. In 1966, the first statewide Alaska Native political

organization, the Alaska Federation of Natives (AFN), was founded. In 1971, Inuit leaders from across Canada established Inuit Tapirisat (ITC) as the coordinating organization for six regional Inuit organizations seeking land claims settlements. Among those regional organizations was the Northern Quebec Inuit Association (NQIA). The Inuit were now representing themselves in negotiations with the federal and provincial governments. The establishment of the Inuit Circumpolar Conference in 1977 provided an Arctic-wide forum for Inuit to share concerns and strategies across national boundaries.

One of the first issues around which the Inuit of Northern Quebec successfully organized, and through that organization redirected government plans, was telecommunications. Responding to Inuit concerns and pressure, the Canadian Broadcasting Corporation agreed in 1973 not to initiate television broadcasts in English and French in Arctic Quebec until Inuttitut language programming could be developed. Broadcasts began eight years later when they could include programs in Inuttitut.

One of the major developments stimulating Native political organization was the expanding exploration of the North by companies and governments seeking energy resources for growing markets. On the North Slope of Alaska and in the Mackenzie Valley of the Northwest Territories, the search was for oil and gas reserves. In Arctic Quebec, the Sami territory of Norway, and at Rampart on the Yukon River in Alaska, it was water and the potential to generate electricity. The agendas of national governments and energy companies were to collide head-on with the determination of indigenous peoples that they had the right to participate in decisions affecting lands they traditionally occupied.

Under the 1958 Alaska Statehood Act, the United States government agreed to transfer 103 million acres of federal land in the former territory to the new state for its development. In its land selections, the State of Alaska promised to respect Native claims to land which Eskimos, Indians, and Aleuts had historically used and occupied. Congress was to settle the claims issue with the Alaska Natives. But as the state began making its selections, no action had been taken by Congress on the lands surrounding Alaska's 178 predominantly Native villages. In 1966, the Alaska Federation of Natives persuaded U.S. Secretary of the Interior Stewart Udall to stop transfer of all federal lands in the state until the issue of Native land claims was settled by Congress. This also halted sale of drilling rights and leases of federal lands to oil and gas companies. Stopped by the freeze was a permit from the U.S. Department of the Interior to a consortium of companies eager to begin construction of a pipeline from Prudhoe Bay, where a major oil and gas field had been discovered in 1968, to Valdez.

The Alaska Native Claims Settlement Act (ANCSA) was signed into law by President Nixon on December 18, 1971. Under the Agreement, Alaska Natives became the recognized owners of more land – 40 million acres – than was then held in trust for all other American Indians. Natives also received $962.5 million in financial compensation for lands they gave up. The cash settlement, to be paid out over 11 years from Congressional appropriations and mineral revenues from state and federal lands, was almost four times the amount all other tribes had won from the Indian Claims Commission since its creation in the 1940s (Arnold 1976, 147-48). Lands and cash were to be distributed to village and regional corporations with Alaska Natives as shareholders.

In Quebec, three Crown corporations, the James Bay Development Corporation, the James Bay Energy Corporation, and Hydro-Québec, had begun development of a major hydro-electric scheme in the province's North. In July 1971, the Cree of the James Bay region had sent a petition to the Minister of Indian Affairs requesting federal assistance in stopping the intrusion of the Government of Quebec into Cree territory. As in Alaska, no treaty had ever been signed by any government with the Cree and Inuit of Northern Quebec.

In the 20th anniversary issue of *Makivik News*, Zebedee Nungak tells how protesting the development of the James Bay project drew the Quebec Inuit onto the national stage and into major constitutional issues of aboriginal claims and indigenous rights:

> Charlie Watt and I crashed a meeting of the Indians of Quebec Association that was being held in Fort George, which was the community before Chisasibi came into being in May 1972 ... from that meeting was planted the seed of the requirement that Inuit be involved in any activity, whether they be negotiations for claims, whether they be in going to court to try to stop the project, or any other activity.
>
> So, from that moment on, we came to an understanding that, "Yes, we are in there", we will work with the Crees, or any other group. That

developed into working with the Crees who became very quickly more autonomous than the other Indian groups, and set up their own organization.

And, from that we determined to take the government to court, to try to stop the James Bay project. And that activity was very intense. We were immediately engaged in activities that were totally foreign to us: holding press conferences, giving speeches, going to meetings, trying to convince a skeptical government agency [Hydro-Québec], the proponents of the project, that what they are doing is wrong because they haven't satisfied an obligation to make sure that the rights of the Crees and the rights of the Inuit are in some way dealt with and recognized. During this period we became very aware of the fact that we could use "the system" to our advantage, the legal system, or at least try to activate something that will get the attention of the government.

... in the end, we were successful in getting an injunction, the Malouf decision that stopped the project for one week. Mind you, it didn't stop the project in the end, but the legal activity reached a crossroads with the Malouf decision where they say the court told the government, "Yeah, these people do have a case. You should negotiate a settlement with them." And thereby the negotiations started forthwith, and we were at them steady for two years...

The James Bay and Northern Quebec Agreement (JBNQA), signed by the Inuit, Cree, the federal and provincial governments, and the Crown corporations involved in the development projects on November 11, 1975, was the first major land claims settlement in Canada. Unlike the 1971 Alaska Native Land Claims Settlement Act (ANCSA), the agreement with the indigenous peoples of Arctic Quebec addressed education, health and social services, administration of justice and other economic and social development issues in addition to land ownership and financial settlements.

Quebec's motivations for agreeing to the settlement were clearly stated by National Assembly member John Ciaccia, the special representative of Premier Robert Bourassa in the negotiations, when he presented the Agreement to the Standing Parliamentary Committee on Natural Resources and Lands and Forests for consideration on November 5, 1975:

Signing the James
Bay and Northern
Quebec Agreement
November 11, 1975
Quebec City

Photo: Makivik
Corporation Archives

Until now, the native peoples have lived, legally
speaking, in a kind of limbo. The limits of federal
responsibility were never quite clear, nor was it
quite clear that Québec had any effective jurisdiction.
The land these people inhabited was in Québec,
after 1912, and yet Québec's title was not properly
defined. This Agreement will remove any grounds for
further doubt or mis-understanding. Jurisdiction will
be established in a precise and definitive manner.
Until now, Québec's presence in the North has
not been complete. Today we are completing and
reaffirming this presence...

The Category I lands, therefore, are not reserves
in the classical sense, as I hope I have made clear.
This Agreement will, in fact, take precedence over the
federal Indian Act. It is our aim that a new concept will
exist, to be implemented by Québec law. This concept
is that of a community which the Crees or the Inuit,
as the case may be, will inhabit as their own, and
which will be built around their traditional activities,
but which will be accessible to the rest of society...

In undertaking the negotiations with the native
peoples, we have followed two guiding principles,
two principles of equal importance. The first is that
Québec needs to use the resources of its territory, all

its territory, for the benefit of all its people ... The
second principle is that we must recognize the needs
of the native peoples, the Crees and the Inuit, who
have a different culture and a different way of life
from those of other peoples of Québec...

   If the State does not succeed in establishing
principles aimed at assuring the survival of these
minorities, it could well happen that we might not even
be able to guarantee our own ... (Quebec 1976, XXI).

Not all of the Quebec Inuit agreed with the settlement.
Representatives of Puvirnituq and Ivujivik, as well as a part
of Salluit, were opposed to that or any other settlement which
included a provision for surrender and extinguishment of
aboriginal rights. They did not sign the Agreement. Puvirnituq
and Ivujivik refused for a number of years to recognize the
authority of the Kativik School Board, Makivik Corporation
and other organizations because they were established through
the James Bay and Northern Quebec Agreement.

   The leadership who had negotiated on behalf of the Quebec
Inuit acknowledged that the Agreement had limitations. Mark
R. Gordon:

   Eventually we accepted the James Bay Agreement.
The Agreement was very important to my people
because it allowed them to take control of their
communities, especially the basic services. It allowed
us to take control of our education and of our health
services. Many of these services and benefits are what
most Canadians take for granted as being their right
to have. But the native people of Northern Quebec
had to give up their land rights. They had to give up
aboriginal rights to be able to gain the basic services
which southerners enjoy without having to give up
anything.

   We knew that it was not a perfect solution by any
means and we were called "sell-outs" by many people;
but they didn't understand one thing – if we had not
signed the James Bay Agreement the court judgment
that came out one week after would have undone the
legal precedents that had been created before by the
Nishga Case...

   And as we slowly push and try to gain some of these
things that we believe are rightfully ours, it reminds

Puvirnituq 1950-60s
Isa Sivuaraapik

Peter Murdoch Collection
Photo: Peter Murdoch
(INDPMUR0277). Courtesy
of Avataq Cultural Institute.

me of a story I heard about six people hunting only one generation ago. These six people were starving and trying to find food for their family. They saw a snow-owl who had just eaten a lemming. Snow-owls are very picky about their food, so they won't eat the insides of the animal but only the meat. These six hunters had to divide what the snow-owl would not eat. Our trying to get legal concepts and legal rights recognized by the government is often like the snow-owl – we often have to eat what he won't eat, and we have to make do with that. But hopefully that will give us enough energy to go on with the hunt (Gordon 1987, 129-30).

Education Provisions of the Agreement

Under the Section 17 of the James Bay and Northern Quebec Agreement and subsequent enabling legislation, the Inuit assumed responsibility for elementary, secondary, and adult education in the region north of the 55th parallel. The Province of Quebec assumed responsibility for oversight of the Kativik School Board, including approval of annual budgets. Operating and capital costs were to come from the Quebec (75%) and the Canadian governments (25%). (In the case of the Cree School Board, Canada was to provide 75% and Quebec 25% of the approved budgets.) Existing federal and provincial educational facilities, including teacher housing, would be transferred to the new School Board. The Agreement provided for a minimum transition period of two years.

The indigenous school boards began operations at a time of profound change in Quebec education as a whole. In Canada, education is a provincial power – there is not even an Education Minister in the federal Cabinet. Prior to the 1960s, however, local authorities, heavily influenced by the churches, controlled education in Quebec. Local school boards and their teachers were sectarian, the majority Catholic. It was not until 1961 that the Quebec government required school boards in the province to provide schooling through grade 11 for all students at no cost.

In 1964, a Quebec Ministry of Education was created, and power began to shift away from local and religious control and toward the establishment of provincial standards. In 1979, the Ministry was to initiate a series of curriculum regulations (régimes pédagogiques), strictly prescribing the content of schools' instructional programs and limiting individual school boards' powers to regulate the curriculum.

Linguistic nationalism was also on the rise, and in 1976 the Parti Québécois assumed power, introducing and passing legislation which mandated French language use in education and business. Instruction in English was to be the exception rather than the rule. The CEGEP system of colleges was established, opening the opportunity for post-secondary education to a much larger segment of the Quebec population. Revision of teacher training and implementation of non-sectarian programs further reduced the influence of religious institutions. Education spending at the provincial level vastly increased.

At a time when Quebec was establishing provincial control over education and, for the first time, instituting strict controls over languages of instruction and content of curriculum, it was granting the Inuit extraordinary powers to design and administer education in their communities. Powers and duties of the Kativik School Board (KSB) under the Education Act of the Province of Quebec and the James Bay and Northern Quebec Agreement, with amendments since 1978, included establishment of Inuttitut as the teaching language, with the Board's commissioners determining the rate of introduction of French and English "after consultation with the parents' committee and having regard to the requirements of subsequent education." The KSB Council was authorized to establish programs, teach subjects and employ teaching materials in three languages based on Inuit culture and language. The Board was to adopt one or more school calendars "making use of existing rules but taking into consideration the special needs of its clientele."

While KSB teachers were to be subject to the basic salary, marginal benefits, and work loads negotiated at the provincial level for teachers in all schools, the Board could establish special training courses allowing Inuit to become qualified teachers and non-Inuit teachers "to become familiar with the special needs of its clientele." The Council was given further authority to set criteria for Native teachers of Inuit culture and language, and those teachers were exempted from provincial regulations concerning teacher qualifications. Any student was also exempted from compulsory school attendance who was needed to "maintain or help to maintain his family." The School Board could request that any regulation enacted under the Quebec Education Act be declared "inapplicable in whole or in part."

The major control to be exercised by the Ministry of Education lay in the approval of annual budgets. The James Bay and Northern Quebec Agreement committed Quebec and Canada to "providing adequate funding for currently available services and programs." Quebec was to provide 75% and Canada 25% of actual operation and capital costs of the Kativik School Board in budgets approved annually by a joint committee named by Quebec and Canada. The arrangement with the Cree, reflecting the responsibilities historically assumed by the federal government toward Indians, obligated Quebec to cover 25%. The percentage contributions were to be reviewed every five years "taking into account the ratio of Native students to non-Native students" receiving services. What constituted adequate funding became a predictable source of disagreement between the School Board and the Ministry of Education. (The full text of the Inuit education provisions of the James Bay and Northern Quebec Act can be found in Appendix A.)

The Kativik School Board became the first Inuit-controlled school board in Canada and one of the first indigenous school districts in the world.

Internationally, the out-of-court settlement in 1975 of a class action suit brought against the Alaska Department of Education by parents in rural communities mandated the State of Alaska to provide a secondary education program in any village which requested it. Twenty-six new Rural Education Attendance Areas (REAAs) were established in 1976, with regional school boards elected to replace the State Operated School (SOS) system and its appointed board. Revenues from the now flowing trans-Alaska oil pipeline fueled a massive construction program of new schools. In the Lower 48, the federal Bureau of Indian Affairs had begun to contract with tribes to operate schools on reservations. Greenland achieved Home Rule in 1979, including responsibility for the educational system.

Implementation of the James Bay and Northern Quebec Agreement

In 1964, Diamond Jenness, in his study on Eskimo administration, had discussed the role education in traditional language and culture played in sustaining nationalistic fervor in Wales, Poland and Cyprus. But he dismissed the relevance

Puvirnituq 1950-60s
L to R: Adamie?
Sivuaraapik, two
unknown, Charlie
Sivuaraapik, Saamisa
Ivillaq, Akinisie?,
Rebecca Ivillaq
holding her baby.

Peter Murdoch Collection
Photo: Peter Murdoch
(INDPMUR0308). Courtesy
of Avataq Cultural Institute.

of this experience to the Inuit, saying, "It would be a mistake to compare these European regions with our Arctic, because our Eskimos lack all cohesion outside their family groups, and cannot comprehend the structure of a nation or understand the fires of nationalism" (Jenness 1964, 127-28). Jenness, like others, underestimated the rapidly growing political sophistication of the Inuit. They were to initiate, and consummate, major land claims agreements within 15 years of the publication of Jenness' book. The Inuit were becoming part of the political framework of Canada.

The signing of the James Bay and Northern Quebec Agreement on November 11, 1975 was only the first small step toward making the agreed-upon changes in the lives of the Inuit of Arctic Quebec. For the JBNQA to be enacted, the Canadian Parliament and the National Assembly of the Province of Quebec had to pass legislation reflecting the negotiated agreements. The James Bay and Northern Quebec Native Claims Settlement was passed after lengthy debate by the House of Commons in May 1977 and proclaimed in October of that year. The process of enacting the necessary legislation in Quebec took even longer.

New institutions, including the Kativik Regional Government, the Kativik School Board, Makivik Corporation, as well as municipal governments and landholding corporations in each of the Inuit settlements, had to be created and staffed once their enabling legislation was passed. Major changes were also mandated in the administration of justice and in the delivery of health care. Bureaucracies at the federal and provincial levels modified their operations to reflect the new relationships with the Inuit and Cree.

By a special act of the National Assembly on June 23, 1978, Makivik Corporation assumed the responsibilities of the Northern Quebec Inuit Association and began receiving and administering compensation funds to generate revenues for economic and social development. The official transfer to Kativik School Board of the students, teachers, and property of both the federal and provincial school systems took place in July 1978.

As the components of the Agreement became operational, the strengths and weaknesses of the settlement became more obvious. Some criticized Inuit leaders for coming to terms with the governments and development corporations instead of continuing the attempt to block construction of the hydro projects. Other aboriginal groups voiced concerns that the Inuit acceptance of provincial authority might have an adverse impact on their own land claims negotiations, threatening the long-standing trust relationship between the federal government and Canada's Native peoples. The James Bay and Northern Quebec Agreement was described as the last of the old-time treaties and hailed as the first modern land claims settlement in Canada (Dickason 1992, 404).

The Inuit leadership had never maintained it was the best possible settlement. It reflected what was attainable at the time. Most importantly, they saw it as a work in progress, to be amended, redefined, and improved over time. Zebedee Nungak:

> I knew that it does not satisfy anybody's ideas of how Inuit in this territory should govern themselves. But it was also negotiated at a time when the political leadership in Quebec and in Canada was not very enlightened about how aboriginal rights ought to be recognized and what place they ought to be given in the political structure of the country.
>
> So, in a way, it was a major accomplishment just to have reached an Agreement, incomplete as it was, and deficient and defective as it was. It gave us certain basic tools, certain basic institutions that would do nothing but advance our desire to be more self-governing...

So, these things were what caused the leadership to say, "Yes, we understand the objections of people who have very strong feelings about the extinguishment clause. Yes, we understand we are not getting absolutely everything we wanted originally when we started the negotiations." But all of us regarded it as a step in the right direction that will launch Inuit in the villages and in the region [toward] an ability that we never had before, to run our own institutions, to try to improve living conditions, and to have more control, have the control we never had when the federal and provincial governments were running their services...

It caused a fundamental shift in the power relationship between us as Inuit, former governees, and them as governments, who did whatever they damn well pleased, without any regard to how people in the territory saw themselves fitting in to the structure (Makivik News 20th anniversary Issue).

In March 1981, Inuit and Cree leaders testified before the House of Commons Standing Committee on Indian Affairs and Northern Development that Canada and Quebec had failed to implement major provisions of the James Bay and Northern Quebec Agreement. Minister of Indian Affairs and Northern Development John Munro and Minister of Justice Jean Chretien called for a review of Canada's performance in implementing the Agreement. The results of the review were made public in February 1982.

The review found that "the contentiousness of the issues and the opposing positions of the parties were such that some of the most important provisions of the Agreement were only finalized during almost non-stop negotiating sessions during the last two weeks preceding the signing of the Final Agreement on November 11, 1975 ... The pressure under which the Agreement was negotiated, the inherent complexity of its provisions, and the fact that negotiating is by its nature a process of compromise, resulted in a document with many provisions which are vague, ambiguous and open to widely varying interpretations." This lack of specificity had led to problems, the federal reviewers concluded, "because parties to the Agreement, both native and governmental, have inter-preted the Agreement to give them what they had been bargaining for rather then what was actually put into the Agreement."

In considering specific grievances raised by the Inuit, the review found that shrinking federal budgets since 1975 had "played a major role in delaying or limiting the achievement of goals." The Inuit maintained that they needed additional funding just to bring the existing housing and educational facilities to a level comparable to that of other Inuit communities in the Northwest Territories. Under the JBNQA, Inuit villages were to become Quebec municipalities while the Cree communities maintained their band council forms of government with a continuing special relationship to the federal government. The Inuit contended that their acceptance of municipal status was contingent on a level of programs and services which Canada should have provided while the communities

Inukjuak 1950
Top, from left:
Johnny Palliser,
Eliasie Kiinakittuq,
Joe Palliser, Johnny
Williams, Alicie
Mina, Lydia Phillips,
Ikumak Aqiattusuk,
Mina Ajagutainnaq.
Bottom, from left:
Carolyn Naalatti,
Lizzie Naalatti
Uitaluktuk.

Margery Hinds Collection
Photo: Margery Hinds
(INDMH07). Courtesy of
Avataq Cultural Institute.

81

were under federal control and should have required Quebec to continue upon transfer of responsibilities to the province.

In tours of Inuit communities during the implementation review, federal officials had been "particularly impressed by the validity of the Inuit concern regarding the condition of their school facilities. Many of the school facilities are seriously inadequate. Many of the buildings are seriously overcrowded, lack proper sanitation and fire protection facilities and are in general disrepair. Many of the buildings used as schools were not intended as such and have not been properly adapted for school use. Some do not even provide adequate basic shelter let alone a proper learning environment ... In recent years significant increases in enrollment and retention have tended to compound the problem." The officials concluded that "regarding the existing conditions of Inuit and Cree housing and infrastructure there is little doubt that, despite the Federal expenditure, conditions are, in general, still below acceptable standards."

In addition to reduced government expenditures, economic development efforts by the Inuit themselves had been slowed by severe cash flow problems caused by the phased paying out of compensation funds and having to divert funds from development projects to legal and other costs associated with continuing implementation negotiations.

The lack of a specific funding arrangement committing Canada and Quebec to specific levels of expenditures beyond the compensation funds was a critical failing in the JBNQA. The federal reviewers concluded that this vague wording meant that "the determination of when and how commitments are fulfilled and the level of funding are, in the context of the agreement, usually matters of public policy and not law. The fair test of Canada's performance can, therefore, not be solely as to whether the legal obligations have been met ... Many important provisions of the Agreement are not specific enough to commit Canada to specific levels of service or funding, or to commit the government to achieve goals by a defined date..."

The reviewers did concur with the Inuit leadership on both the long-range intent and the potential of the Agreement: "The Agreement was designed to allow for the evolution of Inuit and Cree self-government and to allow for the adaptation of specific rights, benefits, and institutions to changing conditions and circumstances. The Agreement was not intended to be a fixed and static legal document but rather a flexible agreement which would allow problems to be worked out through ongoing interaction..."

In February 1984, the Canadian government established a Secretariat within the Department of Indian Affairs and Northern Development to ensure the proper implementation of the Agreement. In the fall of that year, Makivik executives met with newly-elected Prime Minister Brian Mulroney over their concerns that progress on all Northern Quebec Inuit issues were "at a standstill." Negotiations with the federal government on implementation of the James Bay and Northern Quebec Agreement began again in earnest in March 1988.

An Agreement-in-Principle was reached in late 1989 between the Quebec Inuit and the Government of Canada which included the payment to Makivik of an additional $20 million to implement portions of the JBNQA for which funding had not initially been provided, among them construction of northern transportation facilities and support for landholding corporations, local wildlife committees, and wildlife studies. An additional $500,000 was included to cover some of Makivik's costs in negotiating the new agreement. The Agreement also provided for regular meetings of the Canadian and Quebec representatives with Inuit leadership to "discuss progress and new issues."

As implementation negotiations continued, with a Final Agreement announced in May 1993, progress had begun on self-government for the region. Premier René Lévesque had indicated in November 1983 that his government would be prepared to negotiate self-government for the region when the Inuit presented a unified plan for assuming that responsibility. The Northern Quebec Task Force on Self-Government (Ujjituijiit) was established a few months later. In April 1989, village residents elected a working group to develop a constitution for Nunavik, the name they had selected in 1987 for their region of Northern Quebec. The Nunavik Constitutional Committee (NCC) and the Government of Quebec signed a Memorandum of Agreement on Self-Government in July 1991. Three years later, in July 1994, the parties signed a Negotiation Framework Agreement specifying objectives and the process to be followed in reaching agreement.

Political developments were also occurring outside Nunavik. In 1976, Inuit Tapirisat of Canada proposed the establishment of a new territory in the Eastern Arctic of the Northwest Territories. In the same year, the federal government published the Inuit Land Use and Occupancy Report, documenting that the Inuit of the Northwest Territories were continuing to use all the land their ancestors had used for hunting, fishing and trapping. In the Northwest Territories the number of Inuit and Dene elected to the territorial legislature was steadily increasing. By 1979, the majority of representatives to the Northwest Territories Legislative Assembly were Native. In Greenland, Home Rule was enacted, with the Greenlandic government assuming responsibility for education and culture, public health, housing, management of natural and renewable resources, transportation, public works, and environmental protection. Denmark retained responsibility for national defense and foreign relations.

In 1982, in a territory-wide plebiscite, 56% of the residents of the Northwest Territories approved its division. A boundary line still had to be drawn and approved. In 1984, a settlement with the Inuvialuit, the Inuit in the western Northwest Territories, was ratified, the first comprehensive land claims settlement in the Northwest Territories. In 1992, representatives of the Canadian government, the Government of the Northwest Territories and the Tungavik Federation of Nunavut signed the Nunavut Accord, setting 1999 as the date for the establishment of a new government in the Inuit region of the Eastern Northwest Territories.

Two months after the signing of the Negotiation Framework Agreement between Quebec and the Inuit of Nunavik, the Parti Quebecois defeated the Liberals and Jacques Parizeau became Premier. Parizeau named a Special Negotiator to continue talks with the Inuit on self-government, but negotiations slowed as energies were diverted toward the fall 1995 referendum on Quebec sovereignty.

5

The Kativik School Board – The First 10 Years

As the first Inuit-controlled school board in Canada, the Kativik School Board (KSB) became a model for other boards being created in the Northwest Territories and elsewhere. Responsible for providing educational services in 14 Inuit villages on the east coast of Hudson Bay, along Hudson Strait and around Ungava Bay, KSB was charged with forging a new system out of the existing federal and provincial schools, including reworking the instructional programs and replacing the physical plants. A major asset in the successful creation of the new school system was the James Bay and Northern Quebec Agreement and the extraordinary powers it conveyed to the Board. In 1978, the education provisions of the JBNQA held an untested potential, the reality of which was to be explored through day-to-day operations.

In an October 1990 report prepared for the Nunavik Education Task Force and entitled *General Information About Kativik School Board*, KSB administrators discussed the ways the Agreement had shaped KSB's structure:

> The J.B.N.Q. Agreement gives powers and responsibilities to the Kativik School Board which go far beyond those assumed by southern school boards. In particular, aside from the regular departments found in all school boards, Education Services includes:

1) program development in Inuttitut, French and English
2) a training program for Inuit teachers
3) an upgrading program for Qallunaat teachers
4) a research department that initiates and/or monitors all research projects concerning educational issues.

These areas of responsibility unique to our Board are crucial to the development of a northern education system that will give students the skills to cope in a bilingual and bicultural environment.

Prior to 1978, when Kativik School Board officially started, limited development only had been initiated in the areas of Teacher Training and the development of a French second language program (FranNord). All other educational activities were patterned on the southern system with programs and teaching materials which did not at all reflect the students' cultural background and environment.

It is important to keep this in mind when looking at the work accomplished since 1978. All development had to start from the very beginning – there was no base on which to build!

The tasks facing the Kativik School Board were enormous. School facilities throughout Nunavik were substandard, in some cases unfit for use. Improved and expanded facilities were needed to serve the rapidly increasing elementary school-age population. Education for special needs had to be initiated for the first time. Nor had the federal or the provincial school systems provided for secondary education in the communities. Secondary students had gone south to Ontario or, more recently, to Churchill. Secondary facilities and programming had to be created.

The Board also had responsibility for adult education, ranging from literacy classes to vocational training, in the North and would soon request, and be given, responsibility for encouraging, arranging and supervising post-secondary education for Arctic Quebec residents studying in the South.

Charged with delivering programs in three languages, the Board at its formation had no certified Inuit teachers and few instructional materials. Funding for curriculum and materials development was not normally part of the operating budget of Quebec school boards, and any appropriations for this purpose to the Kativik School Board had to be negotiated with the Ministry of Education in Quebec City. KSB had little lead time to define policy and programs or provide staff training before it began instructing students.

To reflect Inuit values and world view, the instructional

Inukjuak 1950
Augiaq Palliser
writing syllabics
on blackboard.

Margery Hinds Collection
Photo: Margery Hinds
(INDMH05). Courtesy of
Avataq Cultural Institute.

program had to be designed and developed by Inuit. But no Quebec Inuit yet had professional credentials or experience in curriculum development. A new process, culturally based and involving elders as the tradition bearers, was needed. English and French materials had to be adapted to Northern perspectives and realities while sufficiently paralleling Quebec provincial programs to prepare students for post-secondary study in the South. A level of staffing sufficient to offer instruction in three languages was required. Training programs for Inuit and Qallunaat teachers, provided for under the James Bay Agreement, had to be initiated, as did orientation programs for newly elected Commissioners and local Education Committees and on-the-job training for district-level and community administrators.

Language policy was an area of major concern both to the KSB staff and to parents. Inuttitut was still the first language for a majority of the Inuit in Arctic Quebec and the language children entered school speaking, but television's influence was growing. Inuttitut was not yet widely used in office and other professional settings in the North but its expanded use in these settings, as well as its central role in the education system, was seen as important to ensuring its survival. Quebec government policies, while recognizing the use of Inuttitut and English, reinforced the importance of learning French for future employment. Some parents felt their children spoke enough Inuttitut at home and needed to learn English at school. KSB administrators and specialists in language retention and acquisition believed, based on research, that early elementary instruction must be in the mother tongue to build the child's ability to think, resulting in a strong foundation in the child's first language and a greater ability to transfer more easily to a second language.

Another issue facing the School Board was education in the dissident communities. Representatives of Puvirnituq and Ivujivik had been opposed to the James Bay and Northern Quebec Agreement, feeling that it surrendered and extinguished aboriginal rights. The two communities did not sign the James Bay and Northern Quebec Agreement and refused to recognize the authority of the Kativik School Board, a body established under the Agreement. To provide education to these communities, the Quebec government had decided to operate schools directly under the control of the provincial Ministry of Education. Makivik Corporation and the Kativik School Board took the Department of Education to court, claiming that the Quebec government could not set up special schools in the dissident communities when this responsibility was assigned to Kativik through legislation. In July 1982, a Quebec Superior Court Judge declared the Quebec government decree establishing the special schools to be "illegal, null, void, invalid and of no effect" and ruled that the jurisdiction and responsibility for those areas of education in Northern Quebec belonged exclusively to the Kativik School Board.

The School Board subsequently negotiated a series of Management Agreements with Puvirnituq and Ivujivik which permitted the communities to establish school committees empowered to run their schools autonomously to a large extent.

The relationship with the Ministry of Education also

required regular redefinition. An article in the November 1986 issue of the School Board's newsletter *Anngutivik* ("a place to catch up") offered a window to these negotiations. It reported on a May 23, 1986 meeting with the Quebec Minister of Education to discuss the inadequacy of funding, particularly if the School Board was to achieve its existing mandates to train Inuit teachers and develop a curriculum meeting the needs of Inuit children while also addressing areas such as special education, pre-kindergarten and post-secondary education which had not been specifically provided for in the James Bay and Northern Quebec Agreement. KSB administrators cited the difficulty of meeting these needs under the fixed budget established and frozen six years previously, during what had been only the Board's third year of operations. At the same meeting, the KSB proposed a new staffing formula reflecting more realistically the scope of work of Northern teachers. A request for increased construction funding for new facilities and to replace several schools lost to fire was also made. (The full text of the article can be found in Appendix B.)

Structure of the Kativik School Board

Early in its history the Kativik School Board developed a set of objectives to guide its operations. These and the structure of the School Board were summarized in a report entitled "General Information About Kativik School Board" submitted by KSB to the Task Force in October 1990:

Purpose of Inuit Education
- To ensure the survival of Inuit life and lifestyle for the individual, the family and the community.
- To provide each person with the opportunity to develop to the limits of his/her desires and ability.
- To acquire the necessary training to earn a living.
- To acquire [the] interpersonal skills [necessary] to function harmoniously with other people.
- To have a strong sense of self-identity and respect for other societies.

Characteristics of Inuit Education
- It should reflect an Inuit point of view.
- It should enable each person to acquire the skills needed to live successfully in the North.

- It should develop the skills needed to get an advanced Western education.
- It should create awareness and understanding of what it is to be Inuit.

Skills Needed by Inuit
- Knowledge of space, time, energy and matter: their theory and their application to Northern and Western technology.
- Knowledge of Inuit culture, art and Inuttitut, including the history of Inuit in Nunavik.
- Knowledge of the natural sciences.
- Knowledge of the social sciences, including [the] skills [needed] to understand the economic and social structures of Inuit and Western society.
- Knowledge of at least one second language and academic and practical knowledge appropriate to individual needs. (2-3)

KSB is governed by an elected Council of Commissioners composed of one representative from each community and a regional councilor appointed by the Kativik Regional Government. Elections are held every three years in November. The Council of Commissioners meets quarterly, alternating meetings between the KSB headquarters near Montreal and communities in the North. (Note: The structure of the Kativik School Board has changed over time, as have the powers and responsibilities delegated to it under the James Bay and Northern Quebec Agreement and the Quebec Education Act. The information in this book, unless otherwise indicated, reflects these changes through 1996.)

The Commissioners select an Executive Committee from among themselves to meet more frequently, administer Board policy on behalf of the Commissioners, and deal with issues related to the day-to-day operations of the School Board. The Executive Committee is elected annually and is composed of a President, Vice President and two members as well as the regional councillor representing the Kativik Regional Government and the Director General of the School Board. The President's position is currently a full-time, paid position.

Every two years each community elects an *Education Committee.* They then select one member to serve as President. The KSB Commissioner from each community sits as a voting member of the local Committee but may not serve as its President. Non-voting members of the Education Committee

Quaqtaq 1973
Inuit students with
teacher Brian Scully
during a grade six
reading class.

NFB collection, courtesy
of the Canadian Museum
of contemporary
photography.
Photo: D. Bancroft
(ANFB73-5090). Courtesy
of Avataq Cultural Institute.

include the mayor or a designated representative, a representative of Avataq Cultural Institute, two administrators (the
Centre Director and the school principal or head teacher),
and one or more teacher representatives chosen by the teachers of the community school. The powers of the Education
Committee are:

(1) To *provide information and promote consultation*
    among all persons and parties concerning education in
    the community.
(2) To *promote* the participation of the parents with
    respect to the quality and development of their
    children's schooling.
(3) To *promote* input from the parents and the community
    in the development of all school programs.
(4) To *promote* the role of the parents with respect to the
    children's school attendance, discipline and to establish
    with the local school administration rules regarding
    the conduct of the students within the school.
(5) To *provide recommendations* to the Board with
    respect to the selection, hiring, and firing of regular
    full-time employees, including teachers, support, and
    administration staff.
(6) To *provide recommendations* to the Board with respect
    to the school calendar and school organization.

91

(7) To *determine* cultural excursion programs.

(8) To *provide assistance* in determining school facilities needed in the communities.

(9) To *determine* after school use of Board buildings, facilities, and rentals to and from persons or parties outside the Board.

(10) To *determine* local student transportation needs.

(11) To *help process* requests for transfer students.

(12) To *determine* Adult Education courses required.

(13) To *organize* extra-curricular activities, such as school sports exchanges and small fund-raising programs for the benefit of the students and the community.

(14) To *give opinions and recommendations* on all other matters referred to them from time to time by the Board.

The chief executive officer of the Kativik School Board is the Director General, who has responsibility for the management of all the programs and resources of the Board. Management responsibilities include planning, organization, administration, control, and evaluation.

Accomplishments of the First Seven Years

Much was accomplished by the Kativik School Board during its first decade. The Council of Commissioners was elected and its first meeting held in September 1976. Senior staff was in place by the spring of 1977, and control of education in Arctic Quebec was achieved in July 1978 with the transfer to KSB of the students, teachers and property of both the federal and provincial systems.

In the 1978-79 school year, the Kativik School Board had 235 full-time employees, not including adult education staff. A majority of the staff (52%) was Inuit. By the 1990-91 school year, staffing had increased to 451 full-time employees, 54% of whom were Inuit.

The 'Inuitization' of the school district staff is cited by signatories to the JBNQA as one of the most significant by-products of the Agreement. In the *Makivik News* celebrating the 20th anniversary of the signing of the accord, Charlie Arngak, who signed the agreement for the community of Kangiqsjuaq, states: "KSB has improved tremendously also, notably the Inuit teachers which are still growing in numbers and the

Kangirsuk 1973
View of the
settlement.

NFB collection, courtesy
of the Canadian Museum
of contemporary
photography.
Photo: D. Bancroft
(ANFB73-5111). Courtesy
of Avataq Cultural Institute.

better educational facilities. Since the creation of the KSB, a lot has materialized for the benefit of the Inuit; one of them is the fact that Inuit employment is the greatest in this organization."

In the same article, Makivik President Zebedee Nungak, signatory for Kangirsuk and the first Kativik Regional Government Representative to serve on the KSB Council of Commissioners, points out: "Effective control of Inuit lives in the communities by our own people has developed because we no longer have to consult the authorities in Ottawa and Quebec City about the day-to-day operations in our region. Before 1975, we did not have our own organizations that the governments could be accountable to."

One of the KSB innovations in staffing was the creation of the position of Centre Director in each of the community schools as a way to develop Inuit administrators. While the principal or head teacher is charged with overseeing the instructional aspects of the school program, the Centre Director is responsible for all aspects of administration related to education personnel, finance, and equipment, and serves as the primary administrative link between the community, the school, and the head office. The training of the first four Centre Directors began in January 1978.

A teacher training program was created in co-operation with McGill University to provide professional training to Inuit who had worked as teacher's aides in the federal and provincial schools of Northern Quebec. The first graduates of this program became trainers of others, providing teacher education Inuit-to-Inuit for the first time. McGill professor Jack Cram was the force behind the program's initiation and its sustaining support until his untimely death in the summer of 1986.

In an article entitled "Northern Teachers for Northern Schools: An Inuit Teacher Training Program," published in *Education, Research, Information Systems and the North*, the proceedings of the Association of Canadian Universities for Northern Studies (ACUNS) meetings in Yellowknife, April 17-19, 1986, Cram addressed the history and significance of the Kativik School Board program:

> When the DGNQ/CSNQ (the Quebec government authorities in charge of education services in Northern Quebec) decided to offer early schooling in Inuktitut there were no trained Inuit teachers in northern Quebec. Thirty-five competent but non-qualified Inuit, most of whom had been Federal Classroom Assistants, were appointed. They were granted 'tolerance' by the Ministére de l'Education on condition that they follow an authorized in-service teacher training program. A full-time teacher training coordinator was appointed and, early in 1975, the present McGill program director was approached for help in developing a recognized training program ... A tentative program was put together during a workshop involving all 35 Inuit appointees in Great Whale River (now Kuujjuarapik) in the summer of 1975 and the first formal McGill CSNQ course was offered in Fort Chimo (now Kuujjuaq) in the fall of 1975...
>
> In the meantime, economic development plans in northern Quebec were colliding with orderly political development. This collision culminated in the signing of the James Bay and Northern Quebec Agreement in 1975...Chapter 17 of the Agreement created and financed Kativik School Board, a totally Inuit controlled body which assumed all the assets, functions, and responsibilities of its two predecessors, and was empowered to build a system of education appropriate to the Inuit of northern Quebec. Among the extraordinary powers granted to Kativik School Board were the designing of its own curriculum, the

determining of its own calendar and language(s) of instruction, and the training of its own teachers. Kativik immediately invited the CSNQ/McGill teacher training program to become part of its operation as the Kativik/McGill program ... In 1978, the first eight Inuit teachers received provincial certification, 'To teach in Inuktitut in the schools of Quebec', at a ceremony in Inukjuak, marking official recognition of the program...

Ten years after its beginnings as a tentative response to a training need for Quebec Inuit teachers, the Native and Northern Education program has reached relative maturity ... a unique project for the training of Inuit to work as teacher training instructors has been developed by Kativik School Board and the McGill program in Arctic Quebec. Because the amount and level of English used by the Inuit in Arctic Quebec is less than in the Northwest Territories, some way had to be found to offer training

Two young graduates, Jobie Tukkiapik, Mary Tukkiapik, and Allan Gordon of Kuujjuaq receive their diplomas.

Makivik Corporation

95

courses in Inuktitut. With the help of a generous grant from the Ministére de l'Education, a four step process has been developed whereby Inuit graduates of the program learn to develop and present courses in Inuktitut to their confreres without intervening translation to or from English and Inuktitut. This has had a measurable effect on both the morale and competence of unilingual (Inuktitut) trainees who can achieve full certification in their own language. Some twelve Inuit instructors have received this special training and are now recognized as McGill Sessional Lecturers in the Faculty of Education (Cram 1987, 117-19).

By the 1984-85 school year, there were 40 classroom teachers at primary levels and 20 language specialists at primary and secondary levels enrolled in the Inuit teacher training program. Twenty-five of the 26 graduates of the program were working for KSB: three as administrators in Education Services, three as counselors in program development, two as special education counselors, six as teachers and part-time pedagogical counselors to beginning teachers, and 11 as regular classroom teachers.

The beliefs underlying the program are:

- that Inuit teachers have a key role to play in Northern education;
- that the teachers' native language must be respected and courses be accessible to unilingual Inuit;
- that the training system must be adjusted to respect the teachers' family and job responsibilities;
- that the teachers-in-training must be closely involved in the evaluation and revision of course and program content;
- that the teachers-in-training must participate in the development of teaching programs and materials; and
- that graduates must have the opportunity to continue studying toward a higher university degree on a part-time basis, in the North.

To be admitted to the program, candidates must speak, read, and write Inuttitut fluently, be recommended by their local Education Committee and by the Teacher Training Department, and hold a regular teaching position or be a regular substitute teacher. Training includes an intensive session of three to four weeks during the summer in one of the Nunavik communities as well as a week-long training session during the school year. Teachers-in-training work with itinerant or local pedagogical counselors in their schools throughout the year.

Students complete the 45-credit program in four or five years and receive a Provincial Teaching Diploma and a Certificate in Native and Northern Education from McGill.

Another of the most distinctive aspects of the Kativik School Board is its approach to program and materials development. KSB sees as one of its primary missions "pioneering of native people's education management and curriculum development in Canada." KSB program developers felt strongly that translating existing instructional materials from English or French to Inuttitut would not result in effective teaching. Working in teams, they began to build instructional programs for the elementary level from the ground up.

In the General Information prepared for the Nunavik Educational Task Force in October 1990, KSB administrators explained the Board's approach to program development in Inuttitut, French, and English:

> Program development in Inuttitut, French and
> English is a team effort that includes consultants
> from universities, pedagogical counselors, elders,
> and the teachers in the field. Repeated cycles of
> development, experimentation, and evaluation are
> needed to produce programs and teaching materials
> which will meet the needs of our students. This
> process cannot be rushed, nor can existing southern
> programs be translated into Inuttitut. This short cut
> was initially tried, but the results were unusable
> and we are now committed to developing programs
> through a process that involves representatives
> from different areas of expertise and that favors
> development in each of the Board's languages.
>
> The Inuttitut mathematics program for
> Kindergarten, Grade 1 and Grade 2 is a good example
> of this approach. It was started through workshops
> with teachers, elders, pedagogical counselors, a
> linguist and a consultant in mathematics. Together
> this group produced a standardized Inuttitut
> terminology for mathematics...

The School Board's *Progress Report for 1978-1985* detailed its major achievements in Inuttitut program development during the first seven years of operation, including:

- development of an Inuttitut Reading and Writing program for Kindergarten, Grades 1 and 2;
- development of an Inuttitut Mathematics program for Kindergarten, Grades 1 and 2;
- preparation of guidelines for language teachers for Grades 3-Secondary V;
- preparation of guidelines for culture teachers Grades 4-Secondary V;
- development of teaching materials in many areas for use by language teachers from Grades 3-Secondary V; and
- development of a computer system in Inuttitut to help in program development work, to facilitate the development of software in the Native language, to allow unilingual Inuit access to modern technology, and to strengthen Inuttitut in the workplace.

In second language program development, the following progress was reported:

In 1982/83, following a year of severe budgetary cuts which jeopardized program development, programs started to be developed in English and French: Mathematics and Natural Sciences at the primary level, and Ecology, Home Economics and Initiation to Technology at the secondary level. At the same time the tools used to teach French and English, both at the primary and secondary levels, were improved...

Successful discussions have been held with Ministry of Education representatives to amend certain pedagogical regulations in order to recognize Inuktitut as a mother tongue, and for the programs developed by the Kativik School Board for its Inuit pupils to replace, once approved, the government compulsory programs. All Kativik School Board programs must comply with the rules for the provincial certification of studies, enabling secondary students to go on to post-secondary education...

Teachers, with the help of counselors, are encouraged to adapt program material to the requirements of Inuit students for those subjects which have not yet been developed by the school board. Eventually, as more resource people are sensitized to the needs of Inuit students, and more funds become available, a total pedagogical program will be developed which truly reflects the cultural values of the Inuit, while providing sound second-language training.

Simultaneously with staff and program development, a research department of the School Board initiated a number of observational studies to learn how Inuit children learn, to identify the strengths they bring to formal learning, establish norms, and develop diagnostic tools, programs and teaching methods for use in the schools. In 1978-79, COPITT, the Child Observation Project Within Inuit Teacher Training, developed 15 child observation tools for use by classroom teachers in the areas of perceptual, motor, language, and cognitive development.

The secondary school program in Arctic Quebec villages was expanding rapidly. By the end of the first year of Kativik School Board operations (1978-79), secondary schooling was being offered in most of the communities. By the end of the 1984-85 school year, Secondary II was offered in eleven villages, Secondary III in ten, Secondary IV in eight and Secondary V in five community schools.

By 1985, students who had entered primary school in the Inuit-controlled Kativik School Board were in secondary school. Some of the first students to receive their secondary education entirely in Arctic Quebec graduated and began going south for post-secondary training programs or CEGEP. The Kativik School Board developed tutoring and other programs to support them.

Also under development was the Adult Education program, which had increased significantly from 1,993 course hours of instruction offered in 1981-82 to 12,000 hours in 1984-85.

KSB Outreach to Canada and Internationally

From its position as the first Inuit-controlled school board in Canada and as a pioneer in education management and curriculum development by Native peoples, Kativik School Board participated in a wide variety of national and international conferences and other exchanges.

In the early 1980s, staff from the KSB Child Observation Project Within Inuit Teacher Training (COPITT) held workshops in several places in the Northwest Territories, and the COPITT course structure was adopted as the core child development curriculum in the Eastern Arctic Teacher Education Program. KSB also presented COPITT seminars at the Center for Northern Studies in Vermont and at the Inuit Studies Conference held at Concordia University in Montreal.

In 1982, the Special Committee on Education of the Legislature of the Northwest Territories issued the report *Learning: Tradition and Change in the NWT,* recommending changes in the territorial educational system, including the creation of Divisional Boards of Education. The Baffin Divisional Board of Education (BDBE) was to be the first of the divisional boards to begin operations. In February 1985, the KSB Director General, the President of the Council of Commissioners, and the Director of the Board's Inuttitut Culture and Language Department participated with representatives from McGill University "in the writing of goal statements and staff evaluation in school boards, and in discussing what makes Kativik School Board different from other school boards" at a workshop held in Iqaluit to help prepare the Baffin Regional Educational Society to assume responsibility as the Baffin Divisional Board.

Kativik School Board staff were participants in the Canada/ USSR Arctic Science Exchange, beginning in October 1986 with a visit by the KSB Director General and the Coordinator of Inuit Culture and Language to the USSR as part of the official Canadian delegation. A seven-member Soviet delegation came to the Kativik School Board in November 1986. Other visitors in 1986 included a professor from Lulea University in Sweden involved in the development of Sami teacher training programs and management development program trainees from Greenland Telecom. At the Inuit Studies Conference held at McGill that year, KSB staff made presentations on computer technology and on a program for hearing-impaired Inuit students.

A major event during the first years of Kativik School Board operations was Symposium '85, "the first symposium on Inuit education ever to take place in Northern Quebec, and the first such symposium to be hosted by Inuit and conducted in Inuttitut." A May 1985 article in the KSB newsletter *Anngutivik* on the upcoming Symposium stated: "Kativik School Board is the first, and at this time, the only Inuit school authority in Canada. After seven years of Inuit-run education, the time has come to look at ourselves and, indeed, show other Inuit communities where we have gone, and where we are going."

The objectives established by the KSB staff for Symposium '85 were:

(1) To highlight the importance of education for Inuit, both present and future.

(2) To promote a free exchange of ideas and opinions on all aspects of education, including the existing system, with a view to formulating and implementing a comprehensive educational policy for Northern Quebec.

(3) To involve Inuit in educational matters and ensure that future educational policies and programs are of high quality, culturally appropriate, and relevant to the people of Northern Quebec.

(4) To increase parental and student awareness of the curriculum, programs, and teaching methods utilized in the North and to examine the vital role of the parents in the educational process.

(5) To ensure that the system of education will meet all future educational requirements of Northern Quebec by providing training which will allow Inuit equal opportunities to effectively participate in the future economic development of the territory north of the 55th parallel (KSB *Symposium '85 Report*, 1).

The Kativik School Board convened Symposium '85, with students, parents, elders, and leaders representing all Nunavik communities invited to "a forum in which all aspects of education could be openly discussed with the view of providing a broader understanding of the importance of education to Northern Quebec society, and to encourage more active involvement in the development of the system by those who will benefit directly from it" (KSB *Symposium '85 Report*, 9). The 300 delegates also included Inuit educators from the Western Arctic, Labrador, Alaska and Greenland, and Russian delegates responsible for education in the Soviet North.

The November 1985/January 1986 issue of KSB's newsletter *Anngutivik* described the significance of the event:

The flags of the participating nations and the eight-language welcome sign indicated that an event of international significance was in progress ... While Kativik School Board has always practiced and encouraged consultation with the Northern Quebec population, the true spirit of consultation could not have been more evident than at Symposium '85. The exchange of ideas which took place was a far cry from the education system imposed on Inuit for so many years, a system which ignored any kind of input from the people it was serving. And even though Inuit language and culture were neglected, even banned at times, by educators for a quarter of a century, it was evident that Kativik School Board had made tremendous progress in this area. Not only was the Symposium conducted in Inuktitut, but the workshops also were given in Inuktitut by Inuit teachers and Inuit consultants.

Held in the new community school in Kuujjuaq November 8-13, the Symposium's opening ceremony included the federal Minister of State for Mines, representing the Prime Minister, Brian Mulroney, and Gary Mulroney, the personal representative of the Prime Minister, who expressed great pleasure at being invited to this important event for present and future generations of Inuit students. The representative of the Quebec Ministry of Education praised the Kativik School Board for accomplishing a great deal in the seven years it has existed, and congratulated the School Board for holding Symposium '85 during International Youth Year.

Participants from across the Arctic cited KSB innovations and leadership in their presentations during the plenary sessions at Symposium '85: "I'm very impressed that you still retain your language. I'm staying in a home where there are two young boys who speak Inuttitut fluently ... I'm also overwhelmed by the quality of the educational curriculum which has been developed for Northern Quebec." "Listening to the presentations makes me envious of the autonomy that Northern Quebec enjoys within its school system. I am also very impressed by the number and diversity of representatives here, the very presence of which help to strengthen Inuit unity."

6

Symposium '85 and Calls For Change

Symposium '85 took place the same week as the 10th anniversary of the signing of the James Bay and Northern Quebec Agreement. The Kativik School Board had been operating the schools in Northern Quebec for a little more than seven years. While the Board's accomplishments were impressive and it had established itself internationally as a pioneer in Native-controlled education, residents of Nunavik were speaking out for increased control of the schools in their communities. Other regional institutions, most particularly Makivik, had begun to call for a more open review and discussion of KSB policies and operations.

The seed for Symposium '85 grew out of a resolution passed at the 1984 Annual General Meeting (AGM) of Makivik Corporation. Delegates from each of the Nunavik villages come together yearly with the corporation leadership and staff to review Makivik's operations and discuss a broad range of issues relating to the economic, social and political lives of Quebec Inuit. On the last day of the week-long meeting held in March of each year, elections are held for corporation officers, with voting taking place in each of the communities and results phoned in to the meeting site. Delegates express issues of concern through resolutions which are discussed and voted upon on the final afternoon of the AGM.

At the 1984 AGM in Quaqtaq, Resolution No. 1984-M-10 regarding a Special Symposium on Education was moved by Jobie Epoo, and seconded by Zebedee Nungak:

> THAT a special symposium on education and the education system of northern Quebec be convened;
>   THAT this symposium include among its participants a cross-section of leaders of all sectors of

society, including, among others, KSB Commissioners, Education Committee members, parents, students, drop-outs, teachers (Federal, CSNQ, KSB), elders, political leaders, leaders of regional organizations, government representatives, clergy, professional educators, education authorities of other jurisdictions (Alaska, Greenland, Labrador, N.W.T.);

THAT this symposium be held in 1984 under the auspices and sponsorship of KSB, the agenda and contents of which will be prepared by KSB.

The resolution was approved unanimously by the AGM delegates. Fund raising and planning for the Symposium was to delay its convening until the fall of 1985.

The James Bay and Northern Quebec Agreement and the Quebec Education Act recognize the Kativik School Board as the authority having jurisdiction and responsibility for operating the schools in Arctic Quebec. Section 5 of the Makivik Charter also vests that corporation with responsibilities closely related to the mission of the School Board, specifically: "To relieve poverty and to promote the welfare and the advancement of education of the Inuit; to develop and improve the Inuit communities and to improve their means of action; and to foster, promote, protect and assist in preserving the Inuit way of life, values and traditions."

In its *1978-85 Progress Report*, the School Board reported the results of the Quaqtaq AGM: "When the Kativik School Board made its annual presentation to the Makivik Corporation at their general meeting in 1984, the Makivik delegates realized that the people needed to know more about the education system, the progress made so far, and especially about the problems that lie ahead. The delegates recognized that the people must become more involved and actively support the school system. Accordingly, a resolution calling for a special symposium on education was passed."

Makivik Executives Minnie Grey and Jobie Epoo prepared a statement for the upcoming symposium outlining their concerns with the Kativik system and raising the issues they hoped to see discussed. The "Discussion Paper Regarding Education for Inuit of Northern Quebec" began with the Quaqtaq resolution:

Inuit beneficiaries through a resolution at the Makivik Annual General Meeting in 1984 in Quaqtaq,

called for the holding of the present Special
Symposium on Education under the auspices and
sponsorship of the Kativik School Board. It was felt
by the people at that meeting that through the
holding of such a symposium on education, many of
the concerns of Inuit of northern Quebec concerning
their education system and education needs could be
discussed, debated and some solutions found...

Education also holds the key to the success of
any future self-government structures for northern
Quebec. Without an educated and disciplined
leadership, these future self-government structures,
once achieved, will not function effectively...

As well, school drop-outs and excessive
unemployment contribute to social problems in Inuit
communities. These very concerns were raised by
the Inuit communities during an information trip in
February and March 1984 conducted by the Ujjituijiit
(Northern Quebec Task Force on Self-Government).
More particularly, the Report of the Task Force
regarding its field trip (dated May 15, 1984 at page
29) concludes with respect to the issue of education,
as follows: The people view education of fundamental
importance to promoting Inuit cultural identity and
Inuit self-sufficiency. The people expressed their
dissatisfaction with the present education system
in northern Quebec and called for substantial
improvement, especially in the area of curriculum
development. The people suggested that the education
system should be re-designed so that it more
effectively promotes Inuit cultural identity.

Before discussing specific concerns, the Makivik paper emphasized that the corporation had repeatedly conveyed to the
federal and provincial governments that inadequate funding
was severely limiting the ability of the Kativik School Board
to carry out its mandated responsibilities. Throughout, there
is the call for an expanded role for parents in the education,
formal and otherwise, of their children.

Problems raised in the paper include the high percentage of
student dropouts; the lack of adequate discipline, both at home
and at school; lack of student involvement and interest in
their own education; juvenile delinquency; and discrepancies
in the quality of education between Nunavik communities and

105

between those communities and the Southern Quebec system. For those students who do go South for post-secondary schooling, there is concern about the lack of financial, social and other support systems. For all students, there is a lack of job opportunities for Inuit trainees.

Instructional concerns include the quality of Inuttitut language teaching by inadequately trained and inexperienced teachers with few materials; the absence of individualized instruction; and the overall quality of the teaching staff: "Many of the native teachers are unable to demonstrate sufficient authority over the children. Other teachers, both native and non-native, lack a certain degree of professionalism ...To a large degree, quality and discipline of the teachers depends upon the strength of a principal of a particular school." Curriculum development deficiencies are also addressed, as is the absence of parental input into teaching methods and curriculum development: "There is a lack of relevant program material and an overall inconsistency, lack of continuity and lack of structure in the existing curriculum."

In a wider sense, the paper questions the lack of bold, extraordinary, and innovative educational experiences for Inuit students. "Education should not be limited to the school hours and both the school, the families and the community are responsible for ensuring a continuity of educational experience..." Also raised is the role of the School Commissioners and the concern that language barriers and the lack of formal schooling on the part of some of them might result in Commissioners taking action on complex documents or proposals "without fully understanding them."

Recommendations by Makivik included involving parents through "a higher quality of information from the school system concerning the progress being made by their children as well as a clear indication of exactly what their children are taught and why," and expanded roles in determining and evaluating curriculum, selecting teachers and determining the quality of educational facilities for their communities. Other recommendations included an education program for parents to instill in them the importance and purpose of education; establishment of a disciplinary system; training for teachers in how to apply discipline in a small community and small school; establishment of a "set of standards in the school system according to which students' abilities can be evaluated ... application of these standards should result in the failing of students who do not perform"; and counseling on issues ranging from drug abuse to vocational options.

In the area of instruction, the paper recommended collaboration among the various regional organizations to increase the amount and quality of Inuttitut language materials; identification of specific skills and qualifications needed by teachers of Inuit children which could be used in hiring and training; regular meetings and conferences to develop and exchange new teaching ideas and techniques; and consideration of an extended school year to allow for more cultural activities as well as for individualized and 'catch-up' programs.

Overall, there was seen to be a need for coordination and co-operation with other regional organizations, for expanded educational and recreational programming in the communities, and for increased funding and staffing. The discussion paper concluded with the recommendation that a Joint Working Group consisting of Makivik and Kativik School Board representatives be formed to seek solutions for the problems identified at the Symposium.

Symposium '85

The format of Symposium '85 consisted of plenary sessions, workshops, and visual displays. The Symposium was extended from three to four days to allow for more discussion. The extra day was devoted to discussion groups and a general assembly for reports from the small groups and recommendations.

Topics presented at the plenary sessions included teacher training; program development; research projects on Inuit education; language policy and cultural identity; and alcohol and drug abuse. There were 15 workshops presented in Inuttitut by Kativik School Board teachers and administrators with translators available for non-speakers: the Inuttitut reading and writing program; methods in developing school materials; developing creativity through art; the importance of physical education in school; information on special health problems (particularly hearing disorders); learning mathematics in Inuttitut and in the second language; introduction to technology (hands-on mechanics, woodworking and electricity demonstrated by students); creative computing; exploring through science (Kativik elementary science program); the ecology program; culture programs; philosophy of Inuit education; learning in a second language; Adult Education and regional employment strategies; and toward the holistic view of the child (focusing on "external factors which cause children to lose concentration in school").

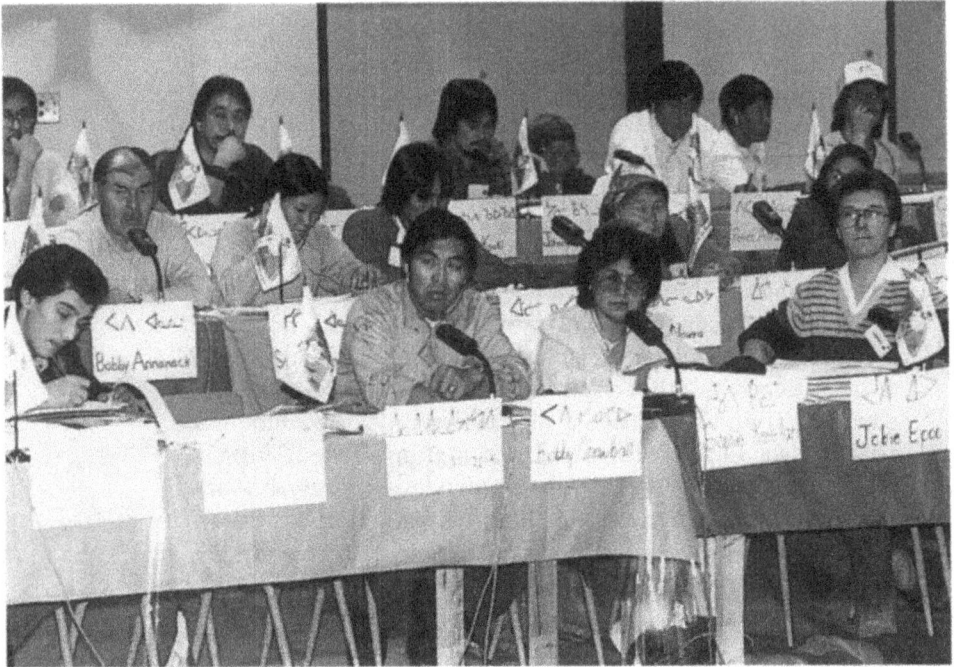

Delegates at the education symposium held in Kuujjuaq 1985.

Makivik Corporation

Nunavik residents began to raise issues of concern during the question and answer sessions following the plenary sessions. The School Board reported these exchanges in *Symposium '85*, a 203-page document published in 1988. At the Plenary Session on Teacher Training, Program Development and Research Projects on Inuit Education, Jobie Epoo, Treasurer and member of the Executive Committee of Makivik Corporation, asked about students who, when their parents moved South for employment or other reasons, found themselves assigned to grades below those they had completed in the North.

Jobie Epoo (Makivik Corporation, Executive Committee): "A grade nine pupil in Northern Quebec is the scholastic equivalent of a grade six student in the South. How do Inuit students' grades in Labrador compare to the average grade level standards in the province?"

Beatrice Watts (Supervisor, Native Education, Labrador East Integrated School Board): "If we compare our students to the Qallunaat grading mode, then the same difference occurs in Labrador as in Northern Quebec."

Gilbert Legault (Associate Director General and Director, Education Services, Kativik School Board): "Students in the North are brought to a level of language competence in English and French. They do not become English or French. As long as they attend school regularly, do their homework and finish high school, they will be able to succeed in college. While their mastery of the second language may never be as fluent, it will be sufficient to enable them to absorb the concepts taught at the post-secondary level."

Following presentations by School Board staff members on research projects, teacher training, and materials development, the time and costs involved in developing Inuttitut curriculum materials were discussed. The exchange also revealed some disputes in the day-to-day working relationship between the School Board and the Quebec Ministry of Education and differences between the KSB headquarters and some communities on the allocation of available funds.

Jobie Epoo: "I'm concerned that if we don't have complete teaching materials, then the education that our children receive also is not complete."

Annie Popert (Director General, Kativik School Board): "When you consider how many years the School Board has been in existence, Inuttitut, English and French production has been substantial, though far from completion."

Doris Winkler (Associate Director, Education Services, and Coordinator, Teacher Training, KSB): "... Today, although we've made a lot of progress in teacher training and program development, it is futile to say that we must complete so many subject areas in Inuttitut by a certain date unless we have the human resources and funding to develop and to use these programs. The Kativik School Board concentrated its initial efforts on creating Inuttitut programs in most subject areas for Kindergarten, grades one and two so that present generations of students would be off to a good learning start. Some subject areas have been developed up to the later primary grades."

Mary Simon (Resource person): "I know that funding has been a problem for teacher training and program development. Has the government changed its policy, i.e., has it responded favourably to School Board funding requests?"

Annie Popert: "It's still a struggle to get adequate money for teacher training and program development from Quebec. We've asked for supplementary funding but with no positive reply to date. We've spent a lot of time documenting our needs to justify our requests. Many presentations have been made to the Ministry of Education by staff and political School Board representatives."

Jobie Epoo: "The Quebec government has been limiting our development of Inuttitut curriculum by lack of funding. The Kativik School Board has the mandate to develop this curriculum, yet the Quebec government seems to be determining whether our programs are acceptable."

Jean-Marie Saint-Jacques (Responsible for the coordination of activities among Amerindians and Inuit at the Quebec Ministry of Education): "In order for funding for Inuttitut program development to be forthcoming from the Ministry of Education, the objectives, the planning calendar, the contents and the available human resources must be supplied with the funding request for the program in question. The value of the program is neither scrutinized nor evaluated by the government."

Annie Popert: "I would like to clarify what was just said. The statement that 'the Kativik School Board has not received extra funding because it has not established goals and objectives' is totally false. We have volumes of documents outlining our needs and objectives and justifications for our requests to the Ministry of Education for extra funding, working countless hours with many different resource people at the Board. Yet the Ministry of Education has not even bothered to acknowledge us. The little funding we receive every year for program development is inadequate, and is indexed very little. It is extremely rare that our requests for supplementary funding for teacher training or program development are approved. The yearly justification for extra funds to the Ministry of Education is like a never-ending nightmare..."

Doris Winkler: "Although government funding has always been inadequate for the development of teaching materials, and although the Kativik School Board has made tremendous progress in program development in spite of this handicap, there is another aspect to developing programs, and that is that teachers must be trained to use the teaching programs at the same time. Due to the high turnover in teachers (especially Qallunaat) every year, teachers must constantly be trained to use the teaching materials and teaching methods appropriate for Inuit students. Training sessions are very costly, and limited funding severely restricts the School Board's ability to hold these sessions as often as necessary. The funding which the Kativik School Board receives for program development is not sufficient to do more than maintain what has been developed, and go on a little bit every year. Now that there are more Inuit trained to work on program development, the progress could be a lot faster if additional funding was available."

Dora Sallualuk (Education Committee member, Puvirnituq): "Puvirnituq and Ivujivik have the same concerns as those of the Kativik School Board, i.e., to develop an education system which enhances Inuit culture and language, and which teaches respect for the land. Two projects are presently under way in Puvirnituq – the compiling of an Inuttitut dictionary and an Inuit history textbook.

"We, the Inuit of Northern Quebec, must set our own education priorities. We shouldn't think only in terms of scholastic achievement. We must determine what values we want to protect, and decide what we want to adapt from western society. If we make the best possible use of funds presently made available to Northern Quebec by setting our own priorities, the funds would probably be adequate. Puvirnituq and Ivujivik have closed their schools to protest against being part of a school board which is under the control of the provincial government. The provincial government is still the ultimate authority over education so that even today, Inuit don't really have adequate control over their education. To fight for this right to determine our own educational values and goals, we are prepared to close our schools in protest once again. We don't feel that our children will suffer, because we consider academics to be a secondary priority."

A major topic at Symposium '85 was the language of instruction. KSB educators feel strongly, supported by research, that students should be taught in their mother tongue during the first few years of school. Discussion during the Plenary Session on Language Policy and Cultural Identity centered on the balance between Inuttitut and the second language, the role of parents, and experiences participants had had in learning and using first and second languages in their own lives. Concern was also expressed about the language competencies of young people and the future of Inuttitut as a working language.

Sandy Saunders (Education Committee member, Kuujjuaq): "When should the second language be introduced?"

Jim Cummins (Language Consultant, Ontario Institute for Studies in Education): "The second language can be safely introduced in the third grade. However, the system which seems to work best is to continue teaching some subjects in the mother tongue until grade six."

Sandy Saunders: "In other regions where school boards are faced with situations similar to ours, who decides which language of instruction will be used in the schools?"

Jim Cummins: "In most cases where children have success-fully developed bilingualism or trilingualism, there has been a partnership between the community and the school board, with the community having a lot of input into the kind of education their children receive. Generally, it's a joint decision between the parents and the school board."

Lizzie York (General Manager, Kativik Board of Health): "When I went to school, only English was taught. The only way I learned to read and write Inuttitut was because my parents taught me. Today, what kind of input should parents have outside of the school?"

Jim Cummins: "Parents have an extremely important role in maintaining the child's mother tongue. If parents don't strongly emphasize the importance of Inuttitut, then children won't see Inuttitut as being important, and won't learn it..."

Jobie Epoo: "Many Inuit youth at eighteen years of age lack elementary skills in reading and writing. Why are we in this situation?"

Jim Cummins: "We must look at how they started school – in terms of the language of instruction used, and how the school system was organized. This was the reason that the Kativik School Board was created – to remedy the inefficiency of past education systems."

Comment from the floor: "Students are not interested in learning Inuttitut because they don't see a future where Inuttitut will be the working language."

Dora Sallualuk: "Even though Inuttitut is taught in the schools, the language will not survive unless the Inuit organizations jointly commit themselves to making Inuttitut the working language in Northern Quebec."

Zebedee Nungak (Co-Chairman, Inuit Committee on National Issues): "Young adults today, like me, who were first exposed to a western-style education under the federal system were obliged to leave our communities to receive that education. Today, we are caught in a dilemma – on the one hand, fellow Inuit depend on those of us who received a southern education for our expertise in certain matters; on the other hand, we are often made to feel as though we betrayed our own status or our sense of being Inuit because of our lack of complete knowledge on traditional Inuit life. After hearing the experiences of other Inuit from around the world, hopefully we've received some inspiration for making the best education choices for the Inuit of Northern Quebec."

In the Plenary Session on Alcohol and Drug Abuse, discussion of the impact of alcohol and drugs on the residents of Nunavik was frank.

Adamie Inukpuk (KSB Inuit Teacher): "Many prominent people in the communities use drugs, as well as many parents, therefore the children have no role models to follow. The drug problem is so prevalent that it's difficult to know how to stop it."

Resolutions and Recommendations

Workshop participants offered their perspectives on what the School Board had accomplished and what needed to be done in the future. Opinions expressed included the continuing importance of the teaching of Inuttitut as a key School Board responsibility; the need to involve parents, the Language Commission and others knowledgeable about the culture in supporting this work; questions about the impact of computers on children's thinking as well as their social and emotional development; agreement that computers could free people to do more interesting and worthwhile work; concerns about whether existing second language programs were adequately preparing students for post- secondary studies in the South; and the need to expand adult education programs in the communities, including improving facilities and providing housing for teachers. (A more detailed report on workshop recommendations can be found in Appendix C.)

Students participating in the Symposium submitted their own recommendations to the delegates. These included the creation of job opportunities within the major Northern organizations; the observation that students appreciate their traditional culture but require help to learn it, not criticism; the recommendation that traditional excursion courses should continue, and should include all the basic information needed every step of the way; that there should be more challenging Inuttitut courses at the secondary level, especially reading exercises; and that there is too much repetition of previously taught material at the secondary level. Students also stated that before entering college in the South, more orientation is needed, including at least one prior visit to the South. They also requested more North-North student exchanges between Northern Quebec and Alaska, the Northwest Territories,

Student Michael Gordon makes a presentation, 1985 during the education symposium.

Makivik Corporation

Greenland, and the USSR. Other recommendations included more Inuit cultural programs on television, and a Northern transfer students' residence in each of the larger communities which accepts transfer students.

Student Lisa Uqaituk advised that "secondary students should become serious about their school-work in the North, otherwise they won't be prepared for the demands made by college in the South ... Teaching methods are so different in the South that orientation in this area alone should be given to students before they go South to study." Student Ida Saunders challenged both students and parents to take more responsibility: "Post-secondary students sometimes don't succeed in the South due to homesickness, drug and alcohol abuse, or poor study habits. These students must persevere if Inuit are to become doctors, lawyers, nurses, etc. Therefore they need the support of their parents, who should encourage them to finish their education in the South."

At the conclusion of the Symposium, resolutions were passed. The first called for the creation of a committee composed of representatives from the Kativik School Board, Avataq, the Inuit Language Commission, Puvirnituq, and Ivujivik to make recommendations to the KSB Council of Commissioners and the Makivik General Assembly on the immediate and long-term needs at the primary, secondary, and post-secondary levels of education with respect to the teaching of Inuttitut, school programs, curriculum development, teacher training, and the preservation of Inuit culture and identity. The resolution also called for the Quebec Ministry of Education "to grant immediately to the Kativik School Board the additional funding already requested by the Board for program development, teacher training, the teaching of Inuttitut and Inuit culture, and the additional number of teachers required."

Other recommendations dealt with funding for facilities for physical education in all communities; funding for programs to detect, prevent and correct hearing problems; and that the alcohol and drug abuse prevention program for Northern Quebec "be given the means to provide culturally relevant information, material and activities to all the communities and be specifically tailored to meet the needs of the Inuit population of Northern Quebec." The final resolution called for co-operation and concentration by Nunavik regional organizations and communities to implement an alcohol and drug abuse prevention program.

At the conclusion of Symposium '85, KSB organizers asked participants to complete an evaluation questionnaire, and results were reported in the KSB publication on the event. Attendees felt the conference was "worthwhile" because elders, and others who didn't go through a formal education system, left with a better understanding of the importance of an education and the way education is imparted to students today; many parents commented that they were made aware of the significant role they had to play; the cross-cultural experiences of the different Inuit circumpolar regions enabled the sharing of cultural and educational concerns. Many of the participants were impressed by the intense desire displayed to maintain and enrich the Inuit culture and language, while at the same time discussing an educational curriculum which would prepare students to participate in the world beyond the boundaries of their communities. They also felt that the Symposium solicited remarks not only on people's present concerns with the education system, but also on their expectations for the future and that it provided a good opportunity to hear the views of the different Northern Quebec Inuit organizations with respect to education. Many participants commented that they left with a fresher and broader perspective of the various roles to be played by everyone who was present.

When asked what they felt was not covered, participants wished there had been more discussions on traditional and survival skills, as well as on Inuit traditions as a necessary part of education. Participants also suggested fewer guest speakers; a shorter agenda, allowing more time for individual topics; fewer delegates; that participants and topics should be strictly education-related; a specific theme related to education; Northern Quebec delegates only; more in-depth briefing concerning agenda beforehand; more time allotted to workshops, and to the Symposium in general; and inclusion of those who didn't attend the first Symposium, and who could benefit from discussions on education.

With respect to priorities, the majority of the participants responded that the most important priority for the School Board was Inuttitut language and program development, with the ultimate goal of making Inuttitut the teaching language at all elementary and secondary levels. Other priorities suggested for the School Board included the provision of education on alcohol and drug abuse and the support of parents in their children's education.

Participants also offered the Kativik School Board ideas to consider in future curriculum and policy planning. These included construction of a Northern college; provision of education leading to obtaining good careers and a better understanding of life; including courses on traditional skills in the teacher training program; compilation of an Inuit history textbook; provision of sex education, and parenthood education; provision of survival training on the land; offering greater support for school dropouts; coordinating the school calendar to correspond more closely with the hunting seasons; developing school programs based on students' needs; a transition program from rural/Northern school to urban/Southern university; provision of on-the-job training for all jobs in the North; sufficient funding for program and materials development, especially for secondary students; more support for traditional skills teachers; more hunting excursions throughout the year; more training for Education Committees, and an improved structure for the Committees to enhance parents' participation and interest in school affairs; developing a religion course; revision of the course on culture, with greater emphasis on family responsibilities with respect to imparting culture; training for non-Inuit teachers so they can integrate more effectively into the Northern school system, including a basic course in Inuttitut; gathering and using school materials

developed in different parts of Northern Quebec; development of Inuttitut, especially technical terminology; implementation of principles on education; evaluation of Symposium recommendations; the teaching of English and French in addition to Inuttitut, so that Inuit can work together with fellow Canadians; and teaching students about the James Bay and Northern Quebec Agreement.

During the education symposium in 1985 held in Kuujjuaq

Makivik Corporation

KSB Follow-Up to Symposium '85

The School Board established an advisory review committee, with representatives from KSB, Makivik, the Kativik Regional Government, the Federation of Co-ops, Inuit Tungavingat Nunamini (ITN), and Avataq Cultural Institute, to recommend on follow-up to the Symposium, including implementation of recommendations and ways for continuing the talks.

In an "Update on School Board Activities Following Symposium Recommendations," which was included in the *Symposium '85* report published in 1988, KSB reported on numerous presentations made on alcoholism and drug abuse; on talks on the holistic view of the child to an Education

117

Committee Council Meeting and a training workshop for student counselors; and KSB Student Services' work with the Northern Native Alcohol and Drug Abuse Program (NNADAP) in setting up a drug and alcohol abuse treatment centre, Isuarsavik, to be opened in July 1988.

The School Board was also working with the two hospitals in the region and with the School of Human Communicative Disorders at McGill to improve detection and care of hearing problems among the Inuit.

In computer education, 75 teachers had taken training in Inuttitut, English and/or French. Modems and computers had been installed in each school, and two schools were teaching computers as a course, with another using them in a business class. Software development was also underway in three languages.

By 1990 every school was to have a gymnasium.

In language and culture, KSB staff had participated in December 1987 in an Avataq-sponsored conference with elders on ways to maintain the richness of the Inuttitut language. School Board staff had completed two books on uncommon Inuttitut terminology in kinship and traditional vocabulary. A male resource person, approved by Avataq elders, had been hired to work on language and cultural material development. Education Committees in some communities had rearranged the school schedule to allow blocks of time for culture lessons. Representatives of the Avataq Language Commission had been hired to work with KSB staff on materials development. However, "it proved extremely difficult getting everybody together at the same time to evaluate and revise the books which were ready to be printed. The School Board Commissioners thus approved reverting to the original system of materials development (i.e., without Avataq) until a viable solution could be found for working together. In this way, production of school materials would not be held back."

The School Board had also initiated in 1986 a major review of funding of Board operations and of program parameters with the Quebec Ministry of Education.

Calls For Change

While Symposium '85 was a gathering of international significance as the first conference on Arctic education convened and conducted by Inuit, it could not meet the School Board's

Tumasi Kudluk of Kangirsuk listening to fellow delegates at the education symposium held in Kuujjuaq 1985.

Makivik Corporation

stated goals of providing a cross-section of Nunavik residents a forum to discuss "where the education system was heading, seek direction on key issues, begin formulating a comprehensive education policy and set new priorities." A three-day meeting, even with a one-day extension, was simply too short a time to explain existing policies and programs, critique them and begin to suggest new directions. Much of the Symposium had been taken up by reports by educators from other circumpolar areas and by KSB presentations on the Board's policies and procedures and workshops detailing its accomplishments. There was not enough time allotted for raising concerns, nor did the format lend itself to goal setting by Nunavik residents. Resident input was random, related to individual workshop themes and the questions on the evaluation form.

In a message prefacing the *Report of the Activities of Kativik School Board 1986-1992*, Director General Annie Popert reflected on Symposium '85: "At the time of the last School Board report in 1985, we were preparing for Symposium 1985. Although the Symposium did not produce all that the

School Board had hoped for, there was a significant accomplishment in the very fact that a large number of people from Nunavik met for the first time to seriously discuss our education system. This forum helped us to realize that continued consultation was necessary as an integral part of the School Board's operations. This Symposium created a better understanding of education among Inuit through sharing of ideas. It also made us realize that Education is not a simple matter. Some recommendations which came out of the Symposium have resulted in the Board taking particular action in the areas that have already been mentioned."

As with any educational system, there were questions about the quality of education being provided. Some of the graduates going south for CEGEP were finding they were not prepared for post-secondary courses. Families moving to Montreal for employment at Makivik and other organizations were being told that their children had to repeat grades already completed in the North. Some of the Inuit leadership and parents were beginning to question whether Inuit-controlled schooling was any more effective than mission, federal or provincial schooling.

Kativik administrators responded that the critics did not understand education or the magnitude of the challenges facing the School Board. Kativik School Board was seeking to develop a comprehensive elementary and secondary educational program from an Inuit perspective, something which no other Inuit-controlled school system had accomplished. Materials development in three languages and training of a sufficient number of Inuit teachers required more time than the few years the Board had been operating.

Much of the conflict seemed to center around who had the right to evaluate and therefore critique the schools.

What is the role of the parents in the business of schools? Mission and federal schools excluded Native parents. Are Native-controlled systems in Canada and elsewhere now doing the same, believing parents don't care or don't know anything about education? This is a temptation for all educational systems, but one which is compounded by the absence of indigenous models for formal education. Are non-Western educators operating from the premise that Western school systems have absolutely defined the methods and purposes of formal education?

What is the role of elders in guiding a system of formal schooling with which they have had no experience? How do parents who did not stay in school or who have bad memories of their own school days relate to the schools their children are attending? Experienced KSB teachers and administrators, both Inuit and Qallunaat, have been trained and certified by Southern institutions. Can they create an approach to education for Inuit communities different from the ones they are familiar with? What Western knowledge and skills are necessary preparation for educated Inuit? What responsibilities should non-Native teachers have for preservation of traditional language, culture, and values?

Like many school districts, the Kativik School Board's response to criticism has often been to list the problems outside the school building which impact school performance. How much of the failure of educational systems is due to societal problems? Are school systems using social ills as a crutch to avoid examining the weaknesses in the design of the educational system? Are schools being asked to do too much? What is the school's role in confronting and meeting social problems? What are the responsibilities of parents and community leaders in creating environments at home and elsewhere which support school attendance and learning?

Many Inuit parents agreed to formal education for their children with the understanding that school would provide the young the skills they needed to deal with the Qallunaat world and would enable them to find jobs at good wages. Yet the jobs are not there. Are the schools failing in their contract with the Inuit or were the expectations unrealistic to begin with? Inuit with university degrees or other experience are beginning to assume professional positions previously held by Qallunaat. Additional positions have become available through the community and regional organizations created since the signing of the James Bay and Northern Quebec Agreement. Small businesses in the service sector (restaurants, stores) and tourism offer employment. But the population is growing far faster than the number of job openings. And young people and their parents are losing interest in school when they don't see education leading to employment or when they have stayed in school but still can't read and write fluently in any language.

Most of the generation currently leading the regional organizations and the municipal governments do not have university training. At the time today's leaders completed their schooling, very few Quebec Inuit had the opportunity, or the expectation, of university degrees. The young look at today's leaders successfully building and running Inuit organizations and question whether a university education is necessary.

It was only 25 years from the initiation of formal schooling in Arctic Quebec to the formation of an Inuit-controlled school board. Does Nunavik have both the unique opportunity and the resources to redefine formal schooling? In Quebec, can the James Bay and Northern Quebec Agreement and the current negotiations on self-government in Nunavik provide the vehicles to redefine the educational system and not just to tinker with the 'givens'?

The start-up of a new school district, particularly one linking together isolated communities, can be chaotic and ad hoc. In Alaska's Lower Yukon School District in the fall of 1976, a National Guard Armory and a pool hall served as high school classrooms while the district built new schools. Teachers cobbled together the instructional programs in the Lower Yukon and the other newly created Alaskan Rural Education Attendance Areas (REAA) from what teachers had taught previously, the books and other materials they found in their classrooms from the State-Operated-Schools or Bureau of Indian Affairs systems that preceded the REAAs, and the graduation requirements and other directives handed down from the district office and the State Department of Education.

There was a lack of funding and time. District and community boards and staff were building the structure while drawing the blueprints. They were aware of some of the problems and mistakes that had preceded them. They wanted to create new, more effective, approaches, but when there was no lead time and little money to do so, they continued with existing systems and pedagogy.

A major accomplishment for the Kativik School Board in the years after Symposium '85 was a review with the Quebec Ministry of Education of funding procedures and levels. In the *Report of the Activities of Kativik School Board 1986-1992*, Director General Annie Popert discussed what was accomplished during the almost three years of review:

> This successful process of negotiations for increased funding consumed much of our time and energy. The demanding process which we followed assured us of a larger number of teachers right away, and established a per capita formula that would allow us to meet our obligations in the future.
>
> The revision of our funding provided us with an

increase in the number of student counsellors such that every community now has a counsellor who is supported by an effective training program to assure a quality service; an increase in special education teachers to better meet the variety of needs in our schools; the establishment of complementary services, which has resulted in work on a variety of topics including substance abuse, sexually transmitted diseases and suicide prevention programs. As well, the Government was made to recognize the need to supply additional resources for program development, which has resulted in the production of many more programs and has greatly increased the use of new technology in our schools.

Although all of the Board's expectations were not realized through this process, it has provided us with an additional ten million dollars yearly since 1989 ... One important result is that our Post-secondary Services now have stable financing on a per capita basis. At the same time, a more stable financing base for Adult Education was achieved...

From 1986 to 1991, the School Board spent more then $23 million on capital projects, including building two schools with gymnasiums, constructing eight residence units, enlarging two schools including gymnasiums, and converting 15 other buildings into residences and an Adult Education Centre. In the area of materials development, KSB staff and consultants completed a science curriculum for elementary levels I to VII with a focus on the Northern environment, integrating Inuttitut and second language development into science activities. By the end of 1988, 38 Inuit teachers had graduated from the Kativik-McGill Teacher Training Program.

The Hunting, Trapping and Fishing (Nunamiigiursanik) Program was initiated in Kuujjuaq for secondary students "to provide students who are not academically oriented or capable with a program which would give them marketable skills within the community."

KSB administrators held a two-day Secondary Conference for teachers and counselors in the spring of 1988 at their offices in Dorval. Its purpose was "to discuss common problems experienced by secondary teachers and counselors and to offer solutions and give new directions." Teachers stated concerns that included absenteeism; students' poor perception of school, homework and studying; insufficient community involvement in the education system; secondary students' lack of motivation; and lack of programs and materials.

In the *Anngutivik* newsletter article (Fall/Winter 1988-89) reporting on the Secondary Conference, a teacher representing the Sautijuit School in Kangirsuk discussed that staff's concern that the KSB secondary programs were "geared to the same goal for all students – to achieve academically. Students who graduate are held up as role models to follow. Students who don't graduate, who have 'failed,' are made to feel left out and inadequate. Among Inuit there was never a feast that was meant just for good hunters and their families."

A participating CEGEP student who had attended school in Salluit, Quebec City and Kuujjuarapik stated that the school system in the North has "too little homework, teachers who are too soft on students, and lack of materials to find information on one's own. She said the thinking was done for you, and she had the impression that teachers thought she couldn't learn or think as well as Qallunaat students."

7

Launching the Nunavik Educational Task Force

Makivik leadership and others were concerned that the dialogue begun at Symposium '85 had not continued and that a process did not exist for substantive input by residents concerned about the quality of education and the operations of the School Board. Makivik Executives Charlie Watt and Minnie Grey asked the KSB to present a workshop on Inuit education as part of the 1989 Makivik Annual General Assembly (AGM) scheduled for March 20-23 in the Hudson Bay community of Inukjuak. After the workshop, for which Makivik had also prepared a discussion paper, delegates passed a resolution establishing an independent Task Force "to identify the educational successes as well as the difficulties now encountered by Kativik School Board."

The resolution cited Makivik's corporate responsibility to "promote the welfare and advancement of education of the Inuit" and the Makivik Assembly's recommendation that the work of the School Board could be strengthened by the information resulting from an independent review of education in Nunavik. Under the resolution, the Task Force was to: (1) be chaired by two people, one from Nunavik and the other "from the outside with expertise in education"; (2) include a "consultation process ... accessible to everyone within Nunavik as well as to other groups involved with, or having expertise about, the development of education for the Inuit of Nunavik"; (3) conduct work through public hearings, written and oral submissions and other means; and (4) submit a final report summarizing findings and stating specific recommendations.

In the resolution, the charges given to the Task Force were to: (1) consider the languages of education, including the "importance of Inuttitut at all levels of education"; (2) examine programs and curriculum for relevance in meeting the needs of the population; (3) suggest ways in which parents, families and other institutions could promote education, including through extra-curricular activities; (4) examine social and economic factors within the communities which might be fostering or retarding students' success; (5) examine ways of encouraging and supporting post-secondary education; and (6) encourage further development of a core of Inuit teachers and examine ways to increase the effectiveness of non-Native teachers in Northern teaching. (The full text of the AGM resolution establishing the Task Force can be found in Appendix D.)

In the Winter 1990 issue of *Anngutivik*, the School Board reported that the KSB had given approval to the AGM resolution of March 21, 1989 and had agreed to contribute half of the Task Force's operating budget, with Makivik paying the other half. (See Appendix E for the full text of the article.) The *1989-90 Makivik Corporation Annual Report* also reported on the establishment of the Task Force as an independent body funded jointly by the Kativik School Board (KSB) and Makivik Corporation. Differences of opinion began to appear almost immediately among the Inuit leaders of the School Board and Makivik and the non-Native technical staff over the style and substance of the Task Force's inquiry.

In early July 1989, Makivik Corporation hired two individuals to begin defining the parameters of the Task Force inquiry and establishing its administrative structure. Bill Kemp was asked to convert the AGM resolution into a draft proposal outlining the specific mandates, organization and other work of an educational task force. Wendy Ellis brought administrative and organizational skills, including experience in report production. Kemp had been employed by both Makivik and the School Board, continuing his involvement with some KSB projects while also working on the Task Force. Ellis had coordinated Symposium '85 for the School Board. The first few months of Kemp's and Ellis's activities centered on designing the Task Force inquiry with input from Makivik and Kativik School Board leaders, particularly KSB Council of Commissioners President George Ittoshat and Makivik President Charlie Watt.

Issues facing the Task Force included sources of funding for its activities; the naming of co-chairpersons; the design of a process for community input; the identification of specialists to serve as consultants; and the timing for folding each of these components into the inquiry. What background and educational experiences should the co-chairs have? How broad-based a community input should be sought? And how should that input be collected – through public hearings or community-based research focused on interviews and questionnaires? Who should solicit input? Researchers from outside the region or residents? Inuit or non-Inuit? At what stage should community perspectives be solicited? Were the issues largely pedagogical and therefore best answered by trained educators? Should communities help frame the problems or should their input be sought after educators had identified solutions or options for solutions?

The scope of the inquiry was a major concern. Should the Task Force accept the present structure of the Nunavik educational system as a given or step outside it in its inquiry and subsequent recommendations? Who had the right to evaluate the schools? Was educational expertise a prerequisite for critiquing the school system?

Underlying specific issues was the question of control. Makivik and School Board executives were providing the initial direction in designing the structure and scope of the inquiry. Could they allow the Task Force independence in its future decisions? Should the Task Force be a co-operative effort, allowing the School Board significant and continuing input to shape the inquiry and its conclusions? What was to be the balance of power between the staff and the co-chairpersons? What should be the role of the co-chairs in overseeing technical aspects of the Task Force work?

By the third week of July, Kemp had drafted an initial Terms of Reference for Task Force operations based on review of the AGM resolution and on formal discussions between the Makivik and Kativik School Board executives held at the KSB offices earlier in the month. The document amplified the specific mandates in the AGM resolution and stated that while the co-chairpersons would be expected to respect these mandates, "they must also be able to expand the mandate in order to include other issues raised during the public hearings."

In examining the languages of education, the Task Force was "to comment on the present program of Inuttitut and second language teaching and, if required, suggest alternatives." While reviewing the school curriculum, the Task Force "must include a recognition that there may be differences within communities and that there will also be differences between the educational, employment and life objectives of different segments of the Inuit school age population within each of the communities." In the area of teacher training, the Task Force was charged to "evaluate the standards and procedures now applied to the development of Inuit teachers including subject matter and teaching methods," and also to "consider the many ways in which non-Native teachers can improve their professional training and attitudes that will make them more effective in the teaching of Inuit." In the examination of post-secondary education, the Task Force was also asked to consider the creation of a university program based in Nunavik.

Technical advisors would support the co-chairs' work with research, and co-chairs would also "be expected to review all relevant documentation that is now, or will become, available on educational issues in Nunavik and to inform themselves on different points of view held by Inuit or other educational professionals about these issues."

The July 21 document called for identifying potential candidates for co-chair through general advertisement throughout Nunavik and through contacting specific individuals identified by KSB and Makivik to solicit their interest in submitting their names for consideration. The KSB and Makivik executives were to select the co-chairpersons responsible for the Task Force. However "once this is made, the two co-chairpersons will be independent from both organizations although they will have a reporting function." Final selection of co-chairpersons was to be made no later than September 15, 1989.

Criteria established by Kemp for co-chairs included "a strong interest in importance of, and recognition of all levels of education within Nunavik; an ability to think and act in an independent manner that is free of predetermined bias about specific education issues; leadership qualities required to demand the attention and respect of northern residents and to provide the creative response to issues and concerns raised by the citizens of Nunavik and by others involved with the development and delivery of educational programs; personality qualities required for holding public hearings that will encourage the statement of concerns and ideas by Inuit and others; the ability to provide direction to the technical advisors in relationship to issues and ideas raised during the hearings; and the freedom to fully commit themselves to this endeavor and to accept the difficulties of time commitment and travel required by the public hearings and other work."

The size of the Task Force staff was to be limited to a secretary, to be hired immediately, and a technical advisor to be selected by October 31, 1989 "from a list of potential

Inukjuak 1950.
At school. L to R:
Allie Samsack,
Johnny Kasudluak,
Johnny Palliser,
Johnny Williams.

Margery Hinds Collection.
Photo: Margery Hinds
(INDMH04). Courtesy of
Avataq Cultural Institute.

candidates suggested by the responsible executives of both organizations in consultation with the co-chairpersons." The role of the technical advisor would be to "provide specific research and technical documents relating to educational or other pedagogical issues as identified by the co-chairpersons; produce technical educational information needed by the co-chairpersons in order to facilitate the public hearing process; and provide writing and editing support for the production of a final report by the Task Force including all of the documentation that must be appended to this report." Additional technical consultation would be sought as needed for specific tasks through limited short-term contracts. The Task Force could also hire part-time secretaries for specific activities or phases of its work.

Inuttitut was to be the language of presentation for all formal documentation and reports, with accompanying French and English translations.

The schedule of work in the July 21 Terms of Reference stipulated that "because of the importance given to this Task Force by the Kativik School Board and Makivik Corporation, the leadership of both groups has firmly stated that the Task Force must not be rushed. This is particularly important during the public hearing stage. The expected completion for this work is twenty months..."

At the same time they were drafting the Terms of Reference, Kemp and Ellis were beginning to have concerns about some of its components. Fund raising was a major concern. They did not want to initiate Task Force work with sources and levels of funding unsure, and they felt that raising funds for this activity from government or private sources would be difficult. They had also begun to favor delaying the selection of co-chairpersons until the structure of the Task Force had been worked out and specific tasks identified. The idea of an orientation program for the co-chairs was also raised for the first time in a July 21 internal staff meeting.

In early August, Kemp met with Makivik President Charlie Watt to explain that he and Ellis felt that the co-chair positions would attract more qualified people if their roles and a time frame tied to specific tasks were set out beforehand. Watt agreed to delay the selection of the co-chairpersons until the Task Force's mandate had been clearly identified, preliminary research on its structure completed, and some of the administrative issues settled.

After more internal staff discussions and meetings with Makivik President Charlie Watt and KSB Council of Commissioners President George Ittoshat, Kemp completed the Revised Guidelines for Task Force operations on August 24. Unlike the earlier Terms of Reference, the guidelines had as a preamble a discussion of "Education and Our Future":

> Education is critical to our future as Inuit. If we are
> to survive as a distinct society within the larger social,
> political and economic fabric of Canada, and indeed,
> of the world, we must once again exercise a direct
> and continuing participation in the education of our
> children.
> In order to obtain a reasonable level of self-
> sufficiency, we, the Inuit of Nunavik, consider the
> development of educational opportunities to be the
> most important factor that will enable young people
> to combine in a productive and satisfying way, the

traditional values and activities that defined our history with the new values and activities that will define our future. Only through a positive integration of tradition and change will Inuit acquire the skills and understandings needed to meet the responsibilities that we must face in the next century. Therefore, Inuit of all ages must be willing to accept the importance of education and to participate in a constant process for improving the objectives, quality and delivery of educational programs.

It was this need for participation and shared control over matters of education that encouraged our negotiators to call for the creation of an independent school board as part of the James Bay and Northern Quebec Agreement that was signed in November 1975. Chapter 17 of this document provided for the establishment of one school municipality for the entire territory north of the 55th parallel under the control of a new school board to be called the Kativik School Board. The Kativik School Board is governed by the provisions of the Quebec Education Act and includes kindergarten, elementary, secondary and adult education. Makivik Corporation also has a responsibility" .... for the advancement of education of the Inuit" which is identified as a corporate objective in Section 5 of the Makivik Charter.

Formal education started about 30 years ago in Nunavik and was at first the responsibility of the federal and then later the provincial government. Although 30 years is but a brief segment of our long history, the development of organized schools has had a major impact on the present-day life of our people. During these three decades we gained our first experience with a way of learning that was much different from the traditional system of educating the young. Although the creation of schools had positive and negative influences on our children and also on adults, the situation was made more difficult for us to deal with because we had no control over any aspects of this imposed system of education.

Since its beginning, Kativik School Board has had to undertake a very broad mandate that included every factor associated with the development of a school system. This mandate included: the need to build and maintain the schools; the need to design a relevant curriculum for all educational levels that could strengthen Inuttitut as a mother tongue as well as facilitate the acquisition of second language abilities; the need to recognize and incorporate Inuit knowledge and values as part of the learning experience in all subject areas; and the need to recruit, train and encourage an Inuit teaching staff as well as to continually protect the quality of non-Native teaching.

It must also be remembered that all of these responsibilities towards the education of our children had to be developed within a population that had very little experience with the purpose or the practice of formal education. Everything was new and untried in the North; directions or outcomes could not be stated with certainty and there was no broad consensus on how formal education could have a long-term positive influence on the life of our children.

Although great progress continues to be made, many questions must still be addressed. It is for this reason that a major symposium on education in Nunavik was convened from November 8 to 12, 1985. It is also why, as an outgrowth of this symposium, Makivik Corporation and Kativik School Board have called for the creation of an independent task force to review the present state of education and make appropriate recommendations...

Under mandates of the Task Force, a responsibility to "comment on how to coordinate the goals and activities of all northern institutions concerned with some form of educational or employment training programs" was added to the examination of the relationship between education and social or economic issues. Instead of the possibility of private schools, the Task Force would "study the role of alternative educational programs and experiences for Inuit students."

The Schedule of Activities reflected the greatest changes. The naming of the Technical Advisor to the Task Force, the identification of the specific mandate and final decisions on procedures and operational guidelines, including the selection of technical studies to be undertaken by the Technical Advisor or consultants, were now to be completed before the co-chairs were named. Added to the schedule was the design and delivery of an orientation program for the co-chairpersons.

The delay of the involvement of the co-chairs until January 1990, the completion of major tasks prior to their involvement, and the creation of an orientation program all signified major shifts in control from the co-chairpersons to the Task Force staff.

Another major change was the substitution of an information-gathering process in lieu of public hearings. Instead, community input was to be gathered through written submissions, a community-based information gathering process including interviews and questionnaires, and other "specific small scale contact with communities."

By the end of September, Makivik and the Kativik School Board had agreed to jointly fund the operations of the Nunavik Educational Task Force. Bill Kemp had been named Technical Advisor and Wendy Ellis Project Coordinator.

On October 10, 1989, Bill Kemp sent a letter to Makivik President Charlie Watt and Corporate Secretary Daniel Epoo discussing his major concerns with the development of the Task Force inquiry and his suggested changes:

> The work needed to carry out this preliminary
> mandate was begun in mid-August and has continued
> throughout September. In the process, it has become
> clear to me, as Technical Advisor, that this process
> has not produced the rapid results that you had
> hoped for ... The time is therefore at hand for me to
> explain as clearly as possible, why I feel that more
> apparent progress has not been made. The following
> points represent my opinion based on professional
> experience and expertise in the field of education but
> also on my recognition of the need to improve the
> quality of education at all levels within Nunavik.
>
> The following six points will identify my major
> concerns and provide an overview of suggested
> changes:
>
> (1) The basic problem is that the resolution passed by
> the AGM sets a fundamentally incorrect direction for
> a Task Force on education ... The original idea of
> co-chairpersons who would head a Commission, based
> on a model of community and other hearings, is
> not appropriate. As a consequence, it is now my
> opinion that a much different structure must be
> created if we are to successfully evaluate and resolve
> the educational problems that have been correctly
> identified in the original resolution.

(2) The central role of Makivik Corporation as the primary body responsible for this process of evaluation and problem solving is not appropriate even if the "Task Force" is perceived to be independent. Independence need not be the primary concern. What must be recognized is that to be successful, the Task Force must become a thoroughly cooperative effort between Makivik Corporation and the Kativik School Board rather than a process that could discredit the work to date of Kativik School Board. Thus the emphasis should be on how to create and maintain a cooperative structure rather than how to ensure independence. The problem is that independence runs a very high risk of isolating the work of the Task Force in a way that would not produce positive results especially in terms of the implementation of its findings.

(3) The original emphasis on the selection of two co-chairpersons to head Task Force work is not appropriate in terms of the complex nature of the problems that must be considered. The level of responsibility linked to the review of information, the evaluation of problems and the creation of solutions places an unfair burden on two individuals...

(4) An emphasis on co-chairpersons even if supported by a "Technical Advisor" fails to recognize the fact that most of the problems under review are pedagogical in nature and require a larger, more balanced group for the discussion of the problems and the evaluation of possible solutions...

(5) The specific problems that are defined in the original resolution are in fact best solved through a process of discussion between selected Inuit and professional educators rather than through a community hearing process. This does not deny the need for information to be gathered from communities but it does reinforce the fact that most of the problems identified in the resolution are best dealt with by individuals with direct educational expertise. Once this step has been taken and either solutions or options for solutions are identified, then the communities can participate with Kativik School Board in discussions and decision -making.

(6) Finally, the cost and time associated with the
Task Force as originally set out must be seriously
questioned ... A revised structure should significantly
reduce the costs and it should also make it possible to
develop and implement solutions much more rapidly...
In recommending changes, Kemp prepared two papers
detailing options for Task Force organization and
operations. The first, entitled "Revised Guidelines:
Option 1," was similar to the August 24 document,
with the addition of workshops on mandates to be
held January through April 1990, community visits by
technical and research staff, and community visits in
the fall of 1990 by co-chairpersons to "discuss, review,
expand and clarify as necessary Task Force findings."

The second document, entitled "Revised Guidelines: Option 2,"
proposed a major change of direction, creating an effort jointly
operated by Makivik and KSB:

The Task Force on Education will be a jointly
designed and operated effort between Makivik
Corporation and the Kativik School Board. In order
to assure that the responsibility for this effort will be
equally shared in all phases of the work, it is proposed
that a joint working group with representatives from
each of the two organizations, along with at least one
outside observer/participant, be established to initiate
the planning process required for this option.

    This joint working group would be required: 1) to
review and revise the mandates now identified in
option 1 and to establish priorities with respect to
these mandates; 2) to create specific procedures to be
followed by the Task Force including the collection
and evaluation of material to produce a report on each
particular mandate; 3) to formalize in this report a
clearly stated set of recommendations and to identify
a procedure for implementing these recommendations;
4) to establish a schedule of activities; and to create an
operational budget including the allocations of funds
by Makivik Corporation and Kativik School Board.
The results of these discussions would be set out in a
formal terms of reference that would define all of the
following phases of the Task Force activities.

After further discussions, Kemp and Ellis completed a summary document containing the Terms of Reference, Schedule of Activities and budget for the Task Force on Education in Nunavik on October 19, 1989. Because of the scope of the inquiry and the estimated workload, the Task Force's governing body was increased from two co-chairpersons to an Educational Review Committee (ERC) of six members. Pedagogical Working Groups were created to examine questions surrounding each of the Task Force mandates, analyze collected information and reach recommendations.

As finalized in the October 19 document, the six issues to be examined by the Task Force were:

> first identified at the Symposium on Education in Nunavik that took place in November 1985. Their importance was reaffirmed during discussions at the Annual General Meeting of Makivik in March 1989.
>
> The Task Force will be responsible [for examining] these issues, to make recommendations for change and to establish a plan for implementing these changes:
>
> *The Languages of Education:* The Task Force will review the debate on instruction in Inuttitut in early education. This will be studied in terms of acquiring fluency in the mother tongue and in English or French as a second language.
>
> *The School Curriculum:* The Task Force will examine the subject matter and specific content of the school curriculum in terms of the questions of languages of instruction, as noted above, and also in terms of the accessibility of quality educational materials in all languages of instruction. It will also examine the relevance of the curriculum for academic and vocational purposes in relationship to northern needs and North American standards.
>
> *The Training of Inuit and Non-Native Teachers:* The Task Force will examine the programs for training both Inuit and non-Native teachers in terms of their knowledge of subject matter, pedagogical skills, and attitudes required to make them most effective in their professional activity.
>
> *Post-Secondary Education:* The Task Force will examine the academic performance of post-secondary Inuit students in terms of their special academic and social needs and in light of alternative programs for

delivering opportunities for post-secondary education.

Adult Education: The Task Force will examine the role of adult education for upgrading academic and vocational skills in terms of both economic development and personal educational goals.

The Role of the Family and the Community: The Task Force will examine the role of the family and the community as part of the educational process in terms of the social, educational and extra-curricular activities of students at all educational levels.

The limitation of the review of languages of instruction to early education represented a considerable reduction of the scope of inquiry.

The Educational Review Committee was to be the primary body responsible for directing the Pedagogical Working Groups and for presenting the results of the research and discussions in a Final Report. This committee would have seven members: three appointed by Makivik Corporation, three appointed by the Kativik School Board, and the Technical Advisor.

The Educational Review Committee responsibilities would be: (1) to review the six mandates; (2) to review the budget and schedule of activities; (3) to establish the Pedagogical Working Groups responsible for each of the mandates; (4) to review on a regular basis the progress of the Pedagogical Working Groups; (5) to review and approve the community-based research project as designed by the Technical Advisor; (6) to advise on the content of the Final Report and to supervise its progress; (7) to report to the 1990 Makivik Annual General Meeting on the progress of the work of the Task Force; and (8) to present the Final Report to the 1991 Makivik AGM, communities, and other interested parties, including educational institutions and governments.

The six Pedagogical Working Groups were each charged with examining one of the Task Force mandates and were each to be comprised of at least three members, one of whom was to be a professional educator with specific expertise on the mandate topic. The responsibilities of the Pedagogical Working Groups would be: (1) to define the issues associated with their particular mandate and to establish the terms of reference for their work; (2) to utilize information from the community-based research project; (3) to identify the technical information required for each mandate and to arrange for acquiring this information through the Technical Advisor or through outside expertise; (4) to present the findings of their discussions and to recommend solutions and identify implementation procedures; and (5) to participate in a final workshop with all working groups to review all of the findings and to discuss the content of the Final Report. The Educational Review Committee would participate in this workshop.

The Technical Advisor was charged with: (1) designing, in consultation with the Educational Review Committee and others, the research program needed to obtain community-based information, to analyze it and to integrate this information for each of the Pedagogical Working Groups; (2) providing specific data and obtaining outside expertise on particular questions when required; and (3) participating in the writing of the Working Groups' reports, interim reports and the Final Report.

The revised Schedule of Activities called for the Educational Review Committee members to be identified by mid-November, and an introductory ERC meeting was scheduled for early December. The field testing of the community-based research project was to take place in November, with the project design finalized in December for implementation in January and February. The introductory Pedagogical Working Groups Workshop was scheduled for the end of January, with final reports of Pedagogical Working Groups due five months later.

On October 26, Kemp and Ellis met with School Board executives to discuss the finalized plan for Task Force operations. Director General Annie Popert commented that the most recent proposal including Pedagogical Working Groups was more in line with what the Board had originally wanted. She recommended that an ERC member should sit on each of the Pedagogical Working Groups.

The following day, Kemp and Ellis discussed the proposed organizational structure with Charlie Watt and Daniel Epoo. While the staff's plan called for Makivik and KSB to each appoint three members to the Educational Review Committee, the Makivik Executives recommended that the two organizations select the six members together. They also felt that the ERC should be composed of Inuit leaders who had gone through an educational system, as well as, perhaps, an elder. Like the School Board, Makivik recommended that each of the Pedagogical Working Groups include an ERC member.

The Naming of the Education Review Committee

In November, KSB and Makivik announced the naming of six Inuit to the Educational Review Committee of the Nunavik Educational Task Force (NETF). The original members of the ERC were Johnny Adams (Kuujjuaq), Jobie Epoo (Inukjuak), Minnie Grey (Kuujjuaq), Josepi Padlayat (Salluit), Mary Simon (Montreal) and Aani Tulugak (Puvirnituq).

Recognized as leaders, each of the ERC members had served their communities and the region in a variety of capacities. A number also operated their own businesses – consulting and translation, a ski-doo shop, and a video arcade, among other things. One worked for Air Inuit, the regional air carrier owned by Makivik, and another in patient services at the Hudson Bay Hospital in Puvirnituq. Mary Simon and Aani Tulugak had worked at various times for both the Kativik School Board and Makivik Corporation, as had NETF staff members Bill Kemp and Wendy Ellis and the KSB Director General Annie Popert. Mary Simon was also President of the Inuit Circumpolar Conference, elected to that position in 1986.

NETF Education Review Committte members, L to R sitting: Johnny N. Adams, Mary Simon; L to R standing: Aani Tulugak, Minnie Grey, Josepi Padlayat

Makivik Corporation

Aani Tulugak had to resign early in the project for personal reasons and was replaced by Elisapee Toolalook (Puvirnituq). Unfortunately, and soon after her appointment, Elisapee found she was unable to continue and was not replaced. Mary Simon tendered her resignation in January 1991, citing an inability "to devote adequate time and commitment to both the Great Whale Hydro Electric Project review and the Education review," and her seat on the ERC remained vacant. The work continued to completion under the direction of Grey, Adams, Epoo and Padlayat.

The initial meeting of the NETF Educational Review Committee took place on December 8, 1989 in Montreal. Bill Kemp had prepared discussion papers on community-based research, Pedagogical Working Groups, and procedures for informing communities about the Task Force's work for review by the ERC members.

In providing the rationale for community-based research, Kemp stated that the original intent of the Task Force had been to investigate educational concerns through a public hearing process. *This approach raised several difficulties. The most important being:*

> (1) that the public hearing process would identify concerns, issues and problems that have already been stated by the Inuit on other occasions. Therefore, the hearings may not have produced new information or insights as required by the Task Force; (2) that the hearing process may not have been able to "bring out" the more specific statements of concerns and problems held by individuals or groups. Therefore, the hearings may not have produced detailed evaluations as required by the Task Force; (3) that the community meetings required for a public hearing process may no longer be the most effective way to involve the Inuit in the consultation required for issues of importance; (4) that the public hearing process is expensive, time consuming and requires an enormous logistical and planning effort. It also requires that the Inuit who will carry out the hearing process must be free to travel for extended periods of time.

Kemp stressed that the decision against public hearings was not meant to exclude the public but rather "to replace the public hearing process with a more practical approach for gathering information from Inuit." As proposed in the October 19 Terms of Reference, the procedure would involve community-based interviews and questionnaires carried out within the structure of a research project designed in consultation with the ERC and administered during an intensive series of community visits. The NETF would also seek submissions from outside sources, and the information collected through these two processes would be analyzed by the staff and made available to each of the Working Groups.

Kemp's second discussion paper proposed the creation of five Pedagogical Working Groups: *Language and School Curriculum*, encompassing the mother tongue, second language learning and "the creation of a curriculum that is relevant to the needs of students as Inuit and as Canadians"; *Teacher Training*, focusing on "a critical issue of educational and cultural development ... the creation of a well-trained and competent Inuit teaching staff"; *Post-secondary Education*; *Adult Education*; and *Family and Community Responsibilities.*

The discussion paper on involving communities cautioned that "if the work is to be successful, both in terms of the community based studies but also in terms of the general recognition of the positive role for the improvement of education that can be played by the Task Force, it is necessary to fully inform the communities ... [The Task Force's] independence from Kativik School Board and Makivik Corporation must also be stressed."

Kemp opened the ERC meeting by stating that planning for the work of the Task Force and the structure to be used to undertake the work had begun with consultation between Makivik and Kativik School Board. Both organizations had approved the Terms of Reference now in use. The Educational Review Committee was now responsible for determining the direction of the work to be done by the Task Force, with the only limits being the budget to some extent and the basic structure of the Task Force.

After discussion, the members "agreed that the work of the Task Force is to review the education system and programs now in place, to identify the successes of the current system, to identify the problem areas, and to recommend solutions as to how the system might be improved – not to evaluate Kativik School Board." They recommended that the Task Force expand its mandate to include a review of the educational obligations of the James Bay and Northern Quebec Agreement in terms of KSB's policies and practices.

Regarding the Pedagogical Working Groups, the ERC recommended that the Working Group on the Language of Instruction and School Curriculum examine cultural and traditional skills programs look at the possibility of implementing a regional current affairs program including the political and historical evolution of the territory and examine what programs were or should be in place regarding sex education. They felt that their work on teacher training should focus on the qualifications of all teachers, Inuit and non-Inuit, and that the examination of Adult Education should include on-the-job training. It was agreed that Minnie Grey would work with Bill Kemp to clarify the questions to be undertaken by each of the Pedagogical Working Groups and then submit these questions for review by the other members.

KSB Council of Commissioners President George Ittoshat

and Makivik President Charlie Watt then joined the meeting to welcome and address the Committee members. Watt emphasized the importance of the work of the Task Force and the benefits the children would receive from it. He pointed out that there was a lot of flexibility in the work of the Task Force and that the only restraints were in the budget and basic structure. If the Committee recognized other elements that should be reviewed, they were to go ahead and do it. Watt stated that the ERC was independent from Makivik and Kativik School Board and had the responsibility to direct the work of the Task Force from this point on. An Interim Report must be presented in March 1990 to the Makivik AGM and the Final Report in March 1991. Watt noted that Makivik has a corporate responsibility toward education which could include a financial contribution toward the future improvement of the education system.

George Ittoshat commented on the importance of education for the Inuit of Nunavik and stated that Kativik School Board was prepared to work in close co-operation when called on by the Educational Task Force. He emphasized the need for the Committee to begin its work as quickly as possible and that the mandate of the School Board for education could benefit from the work of the Task Force. Ittoshat stated that the Kativik School Board had provided funding and that they were prepared to accept the responsibilities connected with this funding.

On January 26, 1990, the Education Review Committee convened its second meeting in Montreal. The Pedagogical Working Groups' responsibilities, as revised by Kemp and Grey, were discussed. The revisions made the Task Force and ERC responsible for defining the issues related to each mandate and expanded the role of the ERC in reviewing the findings of each Group and in approving the recommendations in the Final Report.

It was agreed that, while the ERC members might not be able to be actively involved in the work of the Pedagogical Working Groups, each member should be assigned the responsibility of overseeing the work of one Group. The ERC also approved the Working Groups beginning their work at different times, as completed inquiries on some of the issues could be very useful for the discussions of other Groups. Limits on time and personnel were also factors in this decision. Work would begin with the Language of Instruction and School Curriculum and the Post-Secondary Working Groups.

The ERC members decided that people currently employed by KSB or Makivik should not be invited to be active members of the Pedagogical Working Groups because of potential conflict of interest. However, it was agreed these individuals could be used as a general resource.

After discussion, it was decided that the minutes of ERC meetings should not be distributed to KSB and Makivik. Committee members felt that, since there was a reporting system in place and a willingness to submit additional reports when requested to do so, it would minimize the risk of misinterpretation if the minutes were not distributed outside the ERC.

A conference call among Educational Review Committee members and the two Task Force staff took place on March 9, 1990. The call followed the initial meetings in February of the Pedagogical Working Groups dealing with language of instruction and school curriculum and with post-secondary education. Johnny Adams and Jobie Epoo, the ERC members responsible for liaison with those Working Groups, reported that the Groups had had difficulty in defining the actual work to be undertaken.

Kemp reported on his drafting of the Interim Report for the upcoming Makivik AGM and his belief that the existing educational problems were pedagogical, that real change could be achieved by working closely with the School Board to come up with strong direction and then asking people to comment.

In response to a Makivik request that the Task Force make its Interim Report available to the corporation's Directors prior to the AGM, ERC members agreed but said that, if the Report was given to the Makivik Board, it should also be given to KSB. The ERC felt that the study was being done for Northern Quebec as a whole and that the Report should be presented to representatives of all organizations and the people of Nunavik at the same time at the Makivik AGM.

On 26 March, the ERC and staff met again by conference call to discuss the first draft of the Interim Report and to consider the addition of another Technical Advisor.

Bill Kemp explained that more technical support was required on the Task Force to provide a balance between Inuit and non-Inuit educational expertise and suggested that Sheila Watt-Cloutier be considered. Watt-Cloutier had worked with the Kativik School Board in several capacities, including directing the program providing support to Inuit students studying in the South. She had resigned from that position, citing concerns about the School Board's reluctance to deal with problems within the current system. Mary Simon commented that the ERC had made it clear to both Makivik and the School Board that they did not want to get involved in political in-fighting, and that she felt Watt-Cloutier's expertise would be valuable to the Task Force.

Kemp explained that Watt-Cloutier would work closely with him on the technical side, participating in the design of the information-gathering process, planning workshops, developing questions to be used, and serving as the link between the ERC and the staff and consultants doing the actual work. He felt she could lend credibility to, and a strengthening of, the work to be done. The ERC approved the hiring of Watt-Cloutier.

The Interim Report of the Nunavik Educational Task Force

In its written report to the May 1-4, 1990 Makivik AGM, the Nunavik Educational Task Force stressed that in order to do a good job the Task Force would require the active participation and co-operation of individuals and groups in all communities of Nunavik. To encourage this participation, a newsletter explaining how to make submissions to the Task Force was being sent to every household in the region. NETF hoped to then have a Nunavik-wide call-in program hosted by members of the Educational Review Committee. The Task Force would collect additional information through interviews with students, parents, and others. Staff and consultants would also assemble information about educational policy and programs operating in other Northern areas and elsewhere.

The Interim Report discussed the specific issues and questions that would guide the work of the Task Force in exploring six mandates. With regards to *language of education*, reviewing "all aspects of the language policy and program in relationship to curriculum material, teaching methods, and the values applied to Inuttitut and second language learning" would be the primary role of the Task Force. Another important concern was to be how much strain trilingual instruction and materials development might put on the system. The Task Force would review *curriculum* objectives and content at all levels, including Adult Education. Defining the "quality, commitment and dedication of teachers" as "the essential core of all educational programs," the Task Force pledged to review the *preparation of both Inuit and non-Inuit teachers* and to involve teachers in that review.

Under *post-secondary education*, the focus was to be on engaging students, teachers, pedagogical counselors and others to identify the "conflicts" that were hampering students studying in the South. Regarding *family and community responsibilities*, the Task Force identified four areas of concern: (1) creating a better understanding of the importance of education; (2) giving families the tools to have a voice in day-to-day school operations; (3) providing better extra-curricular and out-of-school learning experiences for students; and (4) the role the schools might play in alleviating social tensions and related problems of drug and alcohol abuse, suicide, violent behavior, and disillusionment. The focus of the Task Force's final mandate on *Adult Education* was defined as meeting "the need for retraining in the rapidly changing work place of today" while still providing "an opportunity for people to improve their academic skills and to pursue their personal development."

Under 'Organization,' the Report explained the roles of the Educational Review Committee, staff, and the Working Groups. Prior to the submission of the Final Report, the Task Force planned to hold a series of workshops and round-table discussions to discuss the findings of the working groups and to develop recommendations and procedures for implementing them. (Fuller excerpts from the NETF Interim Report can be found in Appendix F.)

The April 1990 NETF Newsletter began with a history of education in Nunavik:

> ... Regardless of what educational successes may
> have resulted from either the federal or provincial
> system of education, neither of them enabled Inuit
> to have any measure of control over the language,
> content or objectives of education ... The road leading
> to the formation of the Kativik School Board was
> long and difficult. The creation of an independent
> school board was an important first step towards
> Inuit control over the educational system, but the
> problems that had to be solved were enormous.
> New schools had to be built, a curriculum based on
> Inuit language and culture, as well as on second

language learning, had to be developed, and a group of qualified Inuit teachers had to be established through a program of teacher training. In addition to the mandate for primary and secondary education in the communities of Nunavik, the Kativik School Board also had to develop a program for students wishing to come south for post-secondary education. The meeting of these responsibilities called for an enormous effort and level of commitment by the new school board.

It has become clear, however, that these mandates cannot be properly carried out without active participation from everyone within Nunavik. If this new experiment in education is going to be successful, the people themselves must get involved and be willing to share in the responsibility for the education of children and youth ... The first formal recognition of this responsibility was in Symposium '85, which provided a forum for the people of Nunavik to openly discuss all aspects of education. Although Symposium '85 led to many important recommendations about education in Nunavik, it was felt that the time had come for a more precise review of the educational system.

Like the Interim Report, the newsletter stated that the Educational Review Committee was the primary body responsible for directing Task Force activities and described the Working Groups as the vehicles for carrying out the specific work to accomplish each of the mandates.

The trilingual newsletter included a brief questionnaire and invited readers to comment on all the questions or to limit their response to one particular question. They could also make submissions using a tape recorder or any other means of communication. Community members could also contact the Task Force to request assistance in preparing their submissions. The public was asked to "make your own report card on both the successes and the problems."

The 'Question Box' asked:

What are your concerns or ideas about the value of and need for education? Why and what type of education is important for Inuit? How should the system be changed to better reflect Inuit values and goals?

What are your concerns or ideas about how education is organized in Nunavik? How should control be shared between the School Board and the local school and its teachers? How effective are the local education committees? What other changes do you suggest for the sharing of power and decision-making in education?

What do parents expect from their children as students, what do students expect from their teachers, what do teachers expect from their students? What do parents, students and teachers alike, expect from the Kativik School Board?

What concerns or ideas do you have about the question of Inuttitut? Is, in your opinion, the program now being used by the school board working to produce good Inuttitut speakers? If it is, how could it be made even better? If you feel it is not working, why is this so?

What concerns or ideas do you have about the learning of a second language? How important do you think the need for a second language really is? How can we make sure that the second language will not destroy the use of Inuttitut? What language do you want for the workplace? What other important questions do we need to ask about learning and using Inuttitut, English and French?

What concerns do you as parents have about the school curriculum? Is it providing what you feel is important for your sons and daughters? What needs to be improved and what still needs to be developed?

What concerns or ideas do you have about standards and the need to evaluate grade levels and level of achievements? Should students be tested so that their progress can be compared to other school systems?

What concerns or ideas do you have about school discipline and attendance? What is the role of the school and of the home? How can rules be established and enforced? What should happen when discipline or attendance becomes a problem with individual students?

What do you feel about the role of the school in the life of the community? How should the school be involved in working with families and the community to help deal with problems of drug and alcohol abuse?

What should be the role of the school and the teachers
in creating extra curricular activities including both
social and educational activities for the students and
other community members?

In late April, ERC members made a presentation on the Task
Force and its activities to the Nunavik-wide Youth Conference.
NETF researchers began work in Nunavik communities in
May, and by the end of the month the first phase of community-
based research was completed. Researchers had interviewed
principals, non-Inuit teachers and some Centre Directors and
secondary students. The NETF sponsored a meeting with
selected Inuit teachers from around the region in Kuujjuaq at
the end of May. A few Inuit students in post-secondary programs in Montreal had also been interviewed. Preparation of
research reports had begun with one on Adult Education.

The Education Review Committee and staff met in Montreal
June 5-8 and made some major decisions affecting the future
activities of the Task Force.

The first two Pedagogical Working Groups had not been able
to define the work to be done within their mandates, largely
because the people involved did not have the experience
required for the task. The ERC decided that this approach
had not worked and that a much more efficient use of time
and money would be to contract with individuals with direct
expertise on particular topics to do the work. They agreed that
it was not necessary to hold workshops on each of the mandates as originally intended. However, it would be useful to
hold one workshop in the fall including specialists on each of
the topics, the ERC, and perhaps representatives of Kativik
School Board. This workshop would review all the research
and begin the groundwork for the Final Report.

The ERC also decided that the Task Force should review
KSB instructional programs before looking at School Board
policies. Budget and other limitations sometimes meant that
approved policies were not enacted into programs. The ERC
also approved Bill Kemp's suggestion that the Task Force
review the minutes of KSB Council of Commissioners meetings in order to begin to determine how decisions were made
and policies established. They discussed how far the Task
Force should go in its review of the organizational structure of
the KSB. It was felt that the organization of the Board affected
every issue and that the NETF needed to review KSB's administrative management because there appeared to be problems
there that were directly affecting the delivery of education.

The ERC also saw family and community responsibilities as an integral part of each issue and decided to deal with these responsibilities during the second phase of the community-based research in the fall. It was agreed that the Education Review Committee should do community field trips in the fall, splitting into groups of two, with each team visiting four or five communities and spending two or three days in each community. Because of some complaints received from the communities concerning the first phase, the ERC directed that it review the credentials of all community researchers before they were sent into the communities.

Following the meeting, the ERC met individually with Kemp, Watt-Cloutier and Ellis to review their contracts and decided that Kemp's and Ellis's contracts, originally with Makivik, would be rewritten with the Nunavik Educational Task Force. Watt-Cloutier's contract was already with the NETF.

On June 14, ERC members Minnie Grey and Mary Simon met with KSB Commissioners to bring them up to date, reiterate the mandate of the Task Force, advise them of curriculum materials and other information the NETF would be requesting from the KSB administration, request their support for the community research and field trips in the fall, and make them aware that the Task Force might approach them for additional funds to support their work. They also reassured the Commissioners that "the Task Force was not out to get them."

Following the meeting with the Commissioners, Minnie Grey sent a June 22 letter to KSB President George Ittoshat requesting minutes of all Commissioners' meetings containing resolutions on policy; copies of all established policies of the School Board relating to the development of programs; enrollment statistics from 1978 to June 1990, including the number of dropouts and number of graduates for both the primary and secondary levels; and curriculum programs, including: (1) K.E.S.L. – English primary and secondary; (2) Fran Nord – French primary and secondary; (3) Math Nord – Inuttitut, English and French; (4) sciences – Inuttitut, English and French; (5) social studies (with an understanding that this program was currently under development); (6) ecology – Inuttitut, English and French; (7) math – secondary English and French; and (8) "any other material used in the absence of developed programs."

At the end of June, Grey met with KSB Director Annie Popert with the same requests. By the second week of July, the School Board had sent several boxes of instructional materials to the Task Force.

In a July 13 conference call involving the ERC members and Task Force staff, it was agreed, as Annie Popert had suggested, that after reviewing the materials the Task Force would meet with KSB program developers to ensure an understanding of the philosophy underpinning their programs.

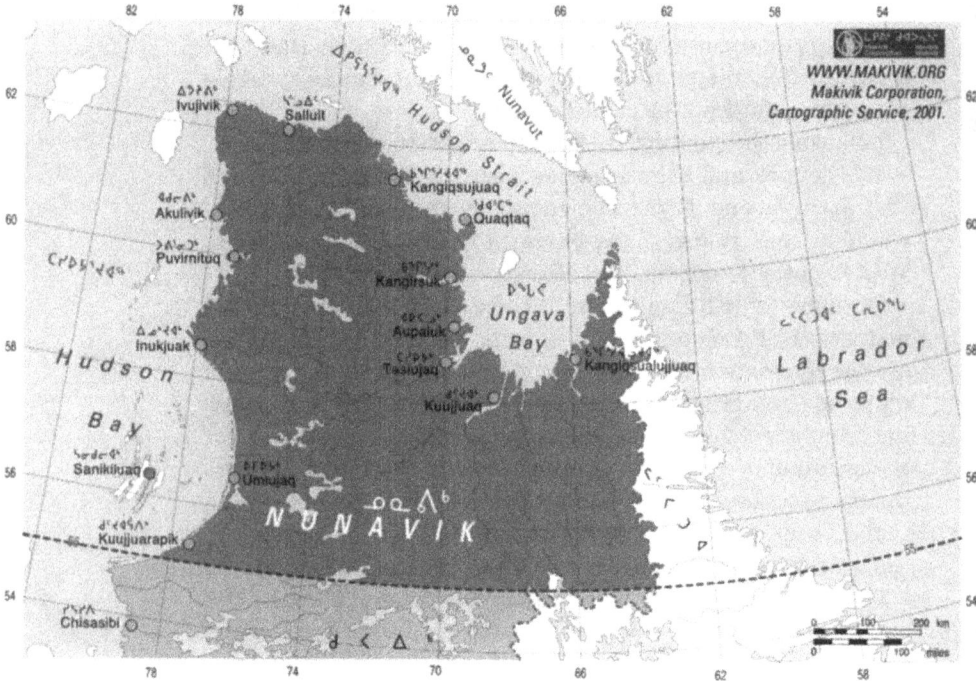

The communities of Nunavik. Inuit also live in Sanikiluaq, N.W.T. and Chisasibi, P.Q.

Makivik Corporation, Cartographic Service, 2002.
www.makivik.org
www.makivik.org/nunavikatlas

8

The Communities Speak Out

We speak at this moment in Inuttitut. We learned
this from our parents who learned from their parents
and so on. This has been our education. We are not
different from the Japanese, Germans and others. We
will pass our language to our children. The people
should not think that the education system we have
now is the only education system. We have elders that
are equal to professors and we can be educated in
Inuttitut ... Since the government started educating
Inuit, the culture has slowly eroded. The passing on
of cultural knowledge has been neglected by parents.
Teaching how to read, write and speak well in
Inuttitut in classrooms is the purpose of the school.
But we have to rejuvenate the teaching of moral
tradition and culture in the home by the parents. This
is part of teaching. My grandmother was teaching up
to the day she died. She talked about family, ways to
keep a good life, respect, and so forth. Just because
children are sent to school does not mean we have
to give up our share of teaching them about life ...
The white man's way is also interfering with our
teaching tradition, for example, when a youth is 18
under the white law he is considered a grown man
and capable of taking care of himself. This creates
disrespect. Under the Inuit way of teaching, an Inuk
was not an adult until he was capable of providing
for the family or the community. If these traditions
are kept alive by the parents outside of school, it can
help us to keep our language and culture. I am talking
about parents' responsibility that seems to have been
thrown at the schools, schools that can only teach the

white way (Statement by resident of Kangirsuk on
January 26, 1991 FM call-in program hosted by the
Education Review Committee).

The Education Review Committee began a series of community meetings in November 1990. When the NETF asked their
opinions on the current educational system and their hopes
for the future, Nunavik residents were articulate and powerful in their responses. Call-ins to ERC-hosted programs on
community FM radio stations began after dinner and continued until sign-off at midnight, sometimes resuming the
following morning at sign-on.

The Education Review Committee, NETF staff and consultants met in the community of Kangirsuk on November 6, 7
and 8, 1990. On the agenda were the October 31 letter from
the Kativik School Board, the scheduling of the ERC field trip
to all of the Nunavik communities, review of the issues to be
addressed by each of the consultants, and discussion of written information provided by the School Board in response to
Task Force requests. The call for individual submissions made
in the April 1990 NETF newsletter had resulted in only a
few letters. The ERC field trip would elicit wider participation through a series of meetings and an FM radio call-in
program in each community. ERC members, working in teams
of 2-4, would tour the entire region between November and
the beginning of February.

While there were not many written submissions by indi-
viduals, those received by the Task Force were articulate.
In his June 25, 1990 submission, Kuujjuaq resident Jobie
Weetaluktuk wrote:

> We have nothing to be ashamed of, even though we
> have shot short of many of our expectations and
> those of others. I appreciate the efforts of the many
> educators, and concerned Inuit and Qallunaat and
> hope the task force will not overlook their efforts. We
> have to have the honesty to give credit where credit
> is due...
>
> First off let's take Inuttitut seriously. Let's not
> forget why Kativik School Board and other regional
> institutions were created. So that Inuit could have
> better self-determination. So that we could make
> our own priorities, based on our tradition, culture
> and language ... We did not get control of our own

Kuujjuaq 1917
Révillon Frères and
Hudson's Bay
Company.

National Archives of
Canada
J. Olus Murie (APA115067).
Courtesy of Avataq
Cultural Institute.

school boards, our corporations, so that we could carry on the philosophies and objectives of the federal administrators of the 1950s. We have the means to promote our traditions, culture, and language, at least within our region...

Assuming that the long term plan for the region is that it is to be a homeland for Inuit, in tradition, culture, and language, all residents will be expected to be proficient in the language of the Inuit, in the same way as Inuit are now expected to be proficient in French or English. Let's get radical.

Kativik School Board started out in a very tough position. Much of the materials it inherited from the CSNQ, and the Federal Day School, were more suited for southern Canada, and in many cases the United States ... Much of the curriculum it has developed is not appealing to students, which should not come as a surprise to anyone. Unfortunately, much of the educational material is not appealing at all, anywhere in the world. KSB had the multiple burden of infancy, and an overwhelming responsibility to teach and develop curriculum at the same time; all of which were and had to be high priority by necessity...

Unfortunately, none of the northern Quebec organizations are going out of their way to promote Inuit into their salaried positions. None of the regional organizations have an apparent recruiting

153

and training initiative for Inuit employees, and certainly have not made any noticeable gain in Inuit presence in their staff population since they were created. The KSB teacher training program is one example, the only one in northern Quebec I can think of off-hand, that is actively promoting Inuit who don't necessarily have the job entry skills.

Success in post secondary education is not only more desirable than ever before, but also necessary. Going into a post secondary education is going into a different world, both figuratively and literally. The first challenge for the student is the access to the many pitfalls of city living. KSB cannot do more than it already has. Perhaps a new approach to keeping students away from city pitfalls is in order ... Being a new student, the greatest challenge is to overcome the difference of previous education with the one unfolding. There is a new vocabulary to learn and new habits to form. Identify and address areas of common difficulty, and possible solutions...

The KSB must study the needs of the region, the manpower needs of regional entities such as KRG, KCRSSS, Makivik Corporation, Avataq, TNI, government agencies in the region, Northern Stores, Co-ops, municipalities, nursing stations, and other services. Then the KSB in conjunction with various levels of manpower could develop programs that will give its students the basis for competition for jobs in these areas ... KSB should put more emphasis on entrepreneurial training, so that our own people can take the initiative to build a living for themselves using the resources we have here.

... many Inuit of working age do not work, because they do not have marketable skills, or aptitude. Furthermore, with over a decade of JBNQA, we find ourselves still dominated by Caucasians in the work force. What ails Inuit most is the inability to help themselves. The adult education section has to shake its traditional image as being the last resort, to a more positive and active position...

Family and community support is a two way street. It is readily apparent that the schools need more community support. That Inuttitut teachers, especially, need community support. That Qallunaat teachers need more interaction with the community in general. That many Qallunaat teachers show interest in the outdoors, but don't get the opportunity to get out with Inuit much.

The school should encourage community and family participation for it to fully tap the family and community support. Most of our communities do not have enough facilities, meeting rooms, or resource centres. Our school board should make a greater effort to meet some of our community needs in all communities ....

Do we expect too much from our schools? The school is not an Inuk tradition. There is no better teacher than the parents, the community and no better school than the community or the outdoors. If the task force finding and recommendation do not offer workable solutions to many of our current problems, then we will be asking ourselves, what is an Inuttitut education?

Simeonie Nalukturak, then Chairman of the Nunavik Constitution Committee and later President of Makivik, wrote on May 9, 1990 from Inukjuak:

The values and tradition of the Inuit elders and parents teaching the young children was sliced and broken off when the Federal Government built and started operating their school. I remember the children being literally picked up from the camps and forced to go with the government officials to spend many months away from their families.

All the skills and training necessary to survive in our environment passed on from generation to generation are all but gone. Young people who would normally be providing for their families now are unable to do so because of the lack of knowledge of lands and wildlife and due to the lack of equipment...

The education system in Nunavik, as I understand it, from beginning to date, uses the southern system as a model. The southern system of education trains its students in the skills necessary to survive in that environment. Our children are being taught the necessary skills needed in the south and very little and not sufficient skills for their own environment.

> Imagine every one of our children going through
> the existing education system, going to college and
> university as we all seem to want them to, and all
> being very skilled and not getting a job in their own
> country. The reality of the situation in my community
> is that there are 954 people and 133 of them have a
> job. In ten years there will be three times as many
> adults as there are now and in 20 years there will be
> twice that many...
>
> It would seem that any creation of jobs and any
> economic development creation in our part of the
> country will have to depend greatly on the skills
> related to the lands and wildlife therefore we must
> include these necessary skills in our education system.

The Education Review Committee field trip elicited a flood
of comments from community members. Following the trip,
transcripts were prepared of all group meetings, individual
interviews, and radio call-ins. Major topics of discussion
included Inuttitut, culture and identity, the role of parents,
the responsibilities of schools, education before the Kativik
School Board, and the KSB system.

Participants spoke about when languages should be introduced and the amount of time that should be allocated to each
in the school program, their concerns that Inuttitut materials and programs be increasingly complex as students moved
into higher grades, parents' rights to select the languages of
instruction for their children, the community's responsibilities
in teaching the Inuit language outside school, how to prepare
the young for post-secondary education and careers, and how
to prevent the decline of Inuttitut.

> I have participated at international conferences, and
> I think education in Greenland is very good. They
> learn with their language not necessarily having to
> learn a second language. Why can't we do the same
> thing in Canada? When our children start to learn in
> a different language, it slows down their education ...
> We are often told that there is not enough money
> to continue teaching in Inuttitut, funds should be
> provided for such (Kangirsujuaq – January 24, 1991
> – FM show call-in).

There seems to be too much emphasis on Inuttitut which is already their life. On the other hand, if there was more introduction to a second language, they would be more challenged and feel more useful. At the present, the kids just feel lost in both worlds and not acquiring proper knowledge in either way of life (Aupaluk – January 29, 1991 – Mayor and Councilors).

Having to learn Inuttitut in school discourages children. At the age of 5 when they can speak Inuttitut well, they learn to read and write, but as they get older they get discouraged because they are ready to learn more and what is being taught them is repetition (Aupaluk – January 29, 1991 – FM call-in).

The Inuttitut program has no principles, no base for the curriculum and no standards. It needs proper recognition from the government and to be used to make textbooks like the other languages (Salluit – January 22, 1991 – Municipal Council meeting).

Parents should have the choice of putting their children in any of the three languages ... We made a mistake when we agreed to teach Inuttitut in the first three grades. Acknowledge our mistake and teach our children in any of the three languages (Salluit – January 22, 1991 – FM call-in).

Inuttitut taught in the schools is not complete and this is the reason why the children are not learning properly ... Children would learn more if their parents would teach them more while they are out camping (Inuit Teachers' Round-table – May 24-25, 1990 – teacher from Puvirnituq).

If children are taught first in their mother tongue, they seem to have a stronger base in their language and know their identity better. If they started school in English or in French, they seem to be caught in between, not knowing their identity. Parents are making the mistake of wanting their children to start in a second language right away (Inuit Teachers' Round-table – May 24-25, 1990 – teacher from Kuujjuaq).

Puvirnituq 1950-60s
Peterhead boats.

Peter Murdoch Collection
Peter Murdoch
(INDPMUR0380). Courtesy
of Avataq Cultural Institute.

If parents gave their support and pushed their
children more, this would encourage students a lot.
There is too much pressure having to deal with three
languages. In Greenland the system runs well without
having to deal with the pressures we face here. We
have to face questions like: What is the future for
students when their education does not go further
in Inuttitut? Will they be able to become nurses
or doctors? Will they have jobs at the end of their
education? If funds are coming from the government,
will the Inuttitut programs be stopped? If we rely on
funds to keep our language, will we lose it if the funds
are stopped? Students need goals for their future; if
not, they will not do well and at the same time we
must teach our children how to survive. The other
reason why we are losing our language is because
it is as if we are not proud of it anymore (Inuit
Teachers' Round-table – May 24-25, 1990 – teacher
from Puvirnituq).

There is no change in Inuttitut. It is always the same
with no levels in secondary. I would rather not take
Inuttitut (Aupaluk – January 29, 1991 – FM call-in).

Students didn't take the Inuit teachers seriously.
Some students feel that since we are Inuit we
don't have to learn it in school (Individual interview
with student from Inukjuak in first year at Dawson
College).

Talking about education and first language ... We
know when we go to the outside world, we know how
to speak Inuttitut. We know how to write it. But who
are we going to apply it to? Who are we going to talk
to from the government? Is he going to speak to me
in my language? No. I'm saying, who are you going
to talk to? To my white boss? Until some Inuk takes
over from him. (Sammy) ... You don't want to lose your
language. (Alisie) ... Yes, but we're losing it because
we can't apply it to nothing. (Sammy) ... We become
those bosses, you know. (George) ... Right now our
language is going out really fast. I see little kids, Inuk
kids, who are talking Inuttitut but there's an English
word in there, or even they don't have an English
word, they're not going to finish a word ... Someone
has to wake up people and make them realize that
we are losing our language fast and there's a lot
of people who don't realize that we are losing
our language (Tunu) ... It's got to come from the
people, from the bottom from the people. Not from
some representative of an organization who starts
talking for the organization saying, "You're losing
your language. You gotta wake up." It's got to start
from the people. (Sammy) (Discussion with Kuujjuaq
youth – November 2, 1990).

Inuit culture and identity was also an area of major interest,
with community members stressing the need for the young to
learn more complex traditional skills, particularly about survival on the land and kinship, expressing concerns that the
culture was being lost and elders dying before they had shared
their knowledge, and stating that culture was not being taught
properly or completely in the existing school culture programs. There were calls for more support of language and
culture teachers by parents, elders, and the KSB Dorval office.
Suggestions were made for college level programs to be developed and delivered in the region. All of the comments stressed
the fundamental importance of learning the Inuit way.

I strongly believe that our way of life should be taught. We grew up in igloos and tents only. When we were hungry and without any food to eat, we ate vegetation off the land ... We did not grow up eating Qallunaat food, sweets, etc. I would like them to be able to find food on the shores, hunt caribou and hunt small game, learn how to make warm clothing, work on seal skins, and learn how to prepare meat. (Tasiujaq – January 31, 1991 – FM call-in)

I feel that there are not enough traditional skills being taught. For example, in the fall when the ice is freezing over. When I was in school, we were not informed enough about safety. They still have to go through experiences where it is important to know safety skills which I feel should be taught as well. (Tasiujaq – January 31, 1991 – FM call-in)

There are not enough camping expeditions for students in the winter and summer. I hope through self-government we will become more autonomous and run our own affairs better. (Tasiujaq – January 31, 1991 – FM call-in)

Culture programs are taught the southern way – working with paper instead of through experience. (Ivujivik – January 17. 1991 – Education Committee Meeting)

Our culture should not be shoved aside ... Success in a different culture is the only one recognized. We cannot afford to lose our culture just to gain recognition. (Salluit – January 22, 1991 – Municipal Council meeting)

We have a 3-lane life and can lean to one way or another. (Salluit – January 22, 1991 – FM call-in)

We are slowly losing our life to the white man. Our traditions – clothing, births, hunting, etc. – can be in our own hands because we are experts about them, instead of letting the white man become the expert on their knowledge of the Inuit. (Salluit – January 22, 1991 – FM call-in)

Ivujivik ca. 1950
View of the Mission
during fall.

Archives Deschâtelets
Collection
Father Chauvel
(O.M.I)(ADES41). Courtesy
of Avataq Cultural Institute.

We just need to improve the program and the material. We cannot keep it simple if we do not want to lose our culture ... The teachers are on their own with no guidelines. Life skills are not being taught such as survival skills in the cold and having proper supplies when going out on the land ... Don't just treat the students with 'kid gloves', but teach them to go out on the land and survive even in bad weather. (Inukjuak – December 3, 1990 – FM call-in)

Throughout history, the white people have had a strong identity, which we are taught. We are not taught our own history and identity. It's no wonder the youth are quitting since they are not being taught their Inuit identity ... The school should use the elders' knowledge. Avataq has material which should be taught to secondary students. If the language is important in kindergarten then knowledge of Inuit identity is important to secondary students. (Inukjuak – December 3, 1990 – FM call-in)

Culture should become part of their knowledge. I want to see our young Inuit have knowledge of both lives. Hand in hand. And learn survival on the land, about hunting and making shelters because our environment

is harsh. If the culture is taught in schools, it should
be hands on, not just through language. For example,
we used to live in igloos, so we should show them
how to build them by doing it with them. Parents are
neglecting to teach their children by not hunting with
them and that is partly our fault. We talk in Inuttitut
with them and we maintain that, but by keeping it
in school, we ensure its survival. But we also need
a second language in order to be competitive and
even more superior ... We cannot survive only on
white education. We need both, our culture in order
to survive in our environment and the white culture
in order to survive in the modern world. (Kangirsuk –
January 26, 1991 – FM call-in)

Most of us who caught a bit of the old life could still
live on the land without the white foods. Inuit have to
set their priorities on what their child should become:
a full-time Inuk, half-time Inuk/half-time Qallunaat
or full-time Qallunaat who acts as an expert Inuk. We,
who were educated by the federal government, took
so much of the white culture, which has influenced us
to think that our children will not become anything if
they do not know the white ways. Instead of teaching
our own culture power we tend to want to use the
Qallunaat power. (Kangirsuk – January 28, 1991 –
FM call-in)

Culture teachers and programs have to be more
dynamic and empowering. Real Inuit teachers are
needed to take over from white teachers – not
just kindergarten to grade 3 teachers, but as math,
English, etc. teachers. (Kuujjuarapik – November 29,
1990 – FM call-in)

Children are learning Inuttitut but cultural
empowerment is lacking. Language is fine but there is
real life history and past that can be taught in order
to instill pride amongst children. This in turn can
help them want to learn more outside things. More
than sewing and crafts and sleds. (Kuujjuarapik –
November 30, 1990 – individual interview)

I feel the students are not acquiring their culture even though they are speaking and writing Inuttitut. There is too much dependency on southern material on their outdoor excursions. They should be taught to go with basics instead of bringing all kinds of sweets. These excursions are also very short and do not give enough time for them to try and eat out of their catch. It would help them to do without Qallunaat stuff. It will get closer to their tradition, i.e. learn not to waste food, learn to survive the real Inuk way ... It would also help if the outings were done during middle of winter, not just in the spring-time. No wonder it does not get to them when we tell them about the olden days. It is because they are not seeing and experiencing it. (Kuujjuarapik – November 30, 1990 – individual interview)

There is a need for a traditional college here in Nunavik, specializing in higher learning in language, traditions, culture, skills etc. It could function like a university or college. This could lead to graduates and expertise in Inuit life, i.e. a PhD in Inuit knowledge ... There are no materials available for culture classes now in the KSB, but these could be developed in the college for use in the school classrooms by the younger children ... We have lost a lot of our Inuit ways now. If we don't do anything about this, we will surely lose our ways. This is outside of language ... We have to act upon this while our elders are alive because they are our experts. All their knowledge has to be recorded even before the realization of a college. (Umiujaq – November 30, 1990 – FM call-in)

I am an Inuttitut teacher, and as a teacher I sometimes feel I have no support. It would be very helpful if the elders would come forward to the teachers to give advice on what they feel should be taught to the children ... We try to teach only with written material. The elders should be resource people to use their knowledge in teaching ... It would be helpful if the teachers attended the elders conferences to gather information from these meetings which could be used for teaching and this would make it easier. (Tasiujaq – January 31, 1991 – FM call-in)

Historical knowledge should be maintained and kept in schools as part of heritage. There should be Inuit ethnographers instead of white university students from the south to record our past. (Kangirsuk – January 28, 1991 – Education Committee and Inuit teachers)

It is important not to lose our language and culture, and while we still have the chance we must start using the knowledge of the elders to retain our language and culture before we lose it because there are not many older Inuit left who can help out. (Inuit Teachers' Round-table – May 24-25, 1990 – teacher from Salluit)

The first seven years of a child's life is the period where they grasp their identity and is an important period in preparing them for their future. (Inuit Teachers' Round-table – May 24-25, 1990 – teacher from Kuujjuaq)

I envy our ancestors who were traditional with strong morals, language, culture and strong family ties. Then came another language and culture which was overwhelming. We now know another language and culture which has changed our way of life leaving us as if not knowing which way of life is better. This leaves Inuit teachers not knowing whether to go on or not. It has become urgent to find ways to not lose our language. (Inuit Teachers' Round-table – May 24-25, 1990 – teacher from Kangirsujuaq)

Teaching Inuttitut should not involve teaching only the language, but also the way of life. There are different teaching methods, in school and at home. Parents teach by example, not by dictation. The problem today is that parents are waiting for their children to learn on their own by watching and doing what their parents do, but on the other hand students are used to being taught in school and having their lessons handed to them. (Inuit Teachers' Roundtable – May 24/25, 1990 – teacher from Kangirsuk)

There is not enough culture in the curriculum. We do not feel it is maintaining our identity. We would

like more hands on in hunting and women's sewing
and food preparations. We feel that knowing where
we come from and who we are will help us be proud.
(Kangirsuk – January 28, 1991 – secondary students)

I mentioned earlier that our language is going pretty
fast. Maybe one of the ways to get it revived a little,
at least try, is to start interviewing an elder, one by
one get a story from them. Ask them questions like
what it was like to live without the white people. Even
my mother remembers seeing a white person for the
first time, remembers seeing a plane for the first time,
remembers going to school. She remembers that. My
mother. She's just the next generation ahead from
me and she used to live in a time where there
was no Qallunaat. Just imagine what happened to
our grandparents. (Discussion with Kuujjuaq youth –
November 2, 1990)

In discussing the role of parents in education, participants
wanted increased discipline at home and less making of
excuses for children. There were concerns expressed about
parents' lack of involvement and their need to understand
more about the goals and purposes of formal education.

We were disciplined properly by our parents and that
encouraged us. Parents today need to be stronger
and when teachers try to discipline the students the
parents should not just feel sorry for their children.
(Inukjuak – December 3, 1990 – FM call-in)

One of the factors interfering with education is lack
of parental responsibility. We depend too much on the
school to take care of our children. Once they're out of
school, instead of relaying our Inuk knowledge we just
allow them to have too much free time. (Kangirsuk –
January 26, 1991 – FM call-in)

We have said this before. The parents are not
involved. There is a communication gap. The school
is open to everybody but hardly anybody shows up.
(Kuujjuarapik – November 29, 1990 – Education
Committee)

Kangiqsujuaq 1951
The new buildings
of the summer.

Archives Deschâtelets
Collection
Photo: (ADES26). Courtesy
of Avataq Cultural Institute.

There is no contact amongst teachers and parents.
The students are what we have in common and we
should help them as much as we can. More counseling
should be done. We need to be friends ... Extra-
curricular activities are nonexistent and contribute to
the gap between teacher, students and parents. These
can help with character skills and empowerment ...
Teachers are not a form of motivation to students
these days. There is no line of communication
between people and the school even if there is an
education committee. We should have more contact,
communication through FM and visits. (Kuujjuarapik
– November 30, 1990 – individual interview)

A part of the problems we experience now is that the
home is not assisting their children by passing on
their knowledge to them. (Kangirsuk – January 28,
1991 – Education Committee and Inuit teachers)

There is not enough encouragement from the parents
in pushing their children through school. Some parents
claim that even without education they are able to
survive and to have jobs. (Inuit Teachers' Round-table
– May 24-25, 1990 – teacher from Kangirsujuaq)

It is difficult to find ways to get more support
and involvement from parents with the school. Is it
because it is not the way of life of Inuit, because they
did not learn in school but at home instead? Maybe

they do not encourage their children as much as they should because they feel their children will not have future employment even if they go to school. (Inuit Teachers' Round-table – May 24-25, 1990 – teacher from Puvirnituq)

Some parents are not involved because they do not understand what their children learn in school, and not because they don't want to be involved. (Inuit Teachers' Round-table – May 24-25, 1990 – teacher from Kuujjuarapik)

Community members placed a great deal of emphasis on formal education leading to employment. The students in particular wanted to see establishment of standards and higher expectations for their performance, more homework, and better preparation for the responsibilities they would inherit as adults. The lack of alternatives for dropouts too young to enter Adult Education was discussed.

More training for community related trades, i.e., we had no phone for three days waiting for a technician. We have to look at these instead of trying to teach them about the stars, moon, etc. We have more use of computers now, they should be taught at school, more practical stuff. Not just language ... So let us teach our children the things that they will put to use so we would not have to depend on outside help. We are teaching too many things which will be useless in the adult world. (Kangirsujuaq – January 24, 1991– FM show call-in)

The School Board should hire field workers who would travel to the communities and teach how the education system should work. There should be counselors also. The role of the parents with youngsters in school should also be taught. (Aupaluk – January 29, 1991 – FM call-in)

Education is very recent in our region. When they are taught two languages without a good base they do poorly in both. The community has to work together. The school is just part of overall education. (Puvirnituq – January 1991 – FM call-in)

We send our children so they can get an education but with no success. (Ivujivik – January 17. 1991 – Education Committee Meeting)

Dropouts need a better route to get back into school. There is a backlog of teenagers that are not eligible to go to adult ed. (Salluit – January 22, 1991 – FM call-in)

We can develop material to prepare our children to adapt to the changes we see and feel ... If we want our children to have jobs, we tell them they have to go to school, but where are the jobs? We must not create false expectations. (Inukjuak – December 3, 1990 – FM call-in)

Graduates who have degrees should have a priority when it comes to jobs. There should be a follow-up by the KSB of all the graduates to see if they have proper jobs. KSB should sponsor these people and push other organizations into hiring people with degrees. (Salluit – January 22, 1991 – FM call-in)

I hit a wall since what we were taught was like play. I would like educational policies to be strengthened. I don't want students who are in the South now to keep hitting the wall. I don't want to lose our language and culture either, so I would want those programs to be strengthened too. (Inukjuak – December 3, 1990 – FM call-in)

There is no discipline and moral teaching in school. No preparation for real life. The students, especially the young adults, should be taught life is not always easy and that there are hard days that will have to be dealt with in a wise manner ... There is no higher curriculum for secondary students. What there is is only boring them and not challenging them. What they felt at an early age is gone by that time because they are not empowered. (Umiujaq – November 30, 1990 – FM call-in)

No matter how hard we work at school in Inuttitut we are losing a big part of our culture due to weak material. Maybe this is a part of the reason why parents are not taking responsibility – making the school try to do too much and taking it away from the parents. (Umiujaq – November 30, 1990 – FM call-in)

I think that self-government and things like that
should be introduced to school, like we have to know
what is going on too to have an idea what to expect
when it is our turn. It's kind of hard to learn when
you are 20 years old and you're trying to pick up
everything just by scraps. (Discussion with Kuujjuaq
youth – November 2, 1990)

Then they say, "You don't know how to do this" and
that's when they say, "Oh, a white man is needed for
that job." And then there's another problem we have
too – all the jobs going to white men because we don't
have the qualifications and that's when school comes
back full circle. (Discussion with Kuujjuaq youth –
November 2, 1990)

Parents who attended school before KSB remembered their
schooling as more disciplined, with particularly positive experiences at Churchill. They saw today's student as having
too many distractions outside school. Earlier teachers were
recalled as spending more of the year in the communities and
having more after-school interactions with residents.

Discipline is a part of the Inuit way. It is passed on
from parent to parent and to the children ... It is
not only white people that discipline. The Inuit did
not tolerate rampant youngsters ... Inuit were strict
disciplinarians. Discipline was one of the important
aspects of learning ... It is no wonder that the
teachers have such a hard time today with children.
The children have no more respect because of lack
of discipline. They answer back whatever they feel.
In our days we were not allowed to answer back.
(Aupaluk – January 29, 1991 – FM call-in)

The ones who had gone to Churchill are able to
skin animals, make igloos, know how to preserve and
ferment meat properly, are able to interpret and do
office work. (Aupaluk – January 29, 1991 – FM call-in)

The first people that went to school in English did
well and have done good for themselves ... They did
well because there were not many distractions in
those days like there are today. If there were less
distractions today, Inuttitut would not be in the way.

There are too many things that interfere with the
schools these days. (Aupaluk – January 29, 1991 –
FM call-in)

The young people no longer want to be reprimanded.
It must be clearly understood that this is part
of disciplining them. If we made mistakes or did
something that was not right, we were brought up
to respect the corrective measures that our parents
took upon us. Thinking back to those times we took
scoldings and such, we appreciate that because that
is what kept us in line. Young people today should
not just get angry with their parents because they are
only trying to make a better future for them. We must
give them the love they need, do not just feel sorry
for them and side with them all the time. We were
brought up respecting our elders and what was told to
us. (Tasiujaq – January 31, 1991 – FM call-in)

I'll use an example. The Education Task Force
members are well off because their system was better.
KSB has no goals right now. (Salluit – January 22,
1991 – FM call-in)

I was one of the first to go away to school
in Yellowknife. I was taught vocational, in heavy
equipment, and half days in English. Then I was
sent South to do on-the-job training. This is when I
grasped most of my English related to the job. It is
easier to learn English while hands on. I was able to
survive in the South and work side by side with white
employees. I was able to get income and provide for
myself, and have my own place. I have gone through
the experience from being an Inuk to living amongst
white people. This is the purpose of education. You
have to look at your future, getting a job and earning
money. I have done both ... I also learned from my
father about the Inuit culture. The Inuit way of life
is surviving on animals. We learn from listening and
watching. Having had the opportunity to live both
ways of life, I like the Inuit way of life. It is a good
life. The wisdom of the Inuit is worth keeping ... We
have to keep our way of life because it will be all we
have when the money and the white men are gone.
(Kangirsuk – January 26, 1991 – FM call-in)

Killiniq ca. 1960
A bay with summer camp.

Rosemary Gilliat Collection
Photo: Rosemary Gilliat
(INDRG13). Courtesy of
Avataq Cultural Institute.

The Churchill experience was not only academics, vocational training was included as well. I would like to see a similar program. (Kuujjuarapik – November 29, 1990 – individual interviews)

Teachers in the late 1950s to the 60s did not have so many trips and stayed with the Inuit. Nowadays the teachers have too much time off – ped days, Easter, Christmas besides their summer holidays. This does not promote good relations between them and the community. (Umiujaq – November 30, 1990 – FM call-in)

In discussing the Kativik School Board, several people stated that Inuit were not really in control of the system. Concerns were expressed that all power was centered in the head office in Dorval and that the system did not readily accept either criticism or suggestions from the communities. Inuit

171

teachers asked for more sequencing in the teacher training program and lamented the amount of time they had to spend developing their own teaching materials because system-wide programs had not yet been developed. Students wanted more textbooks, less reliance on photocopies, and more writing, reading, and speaking of English or French.

The reluctance to try new things and defensiveness to any criticism is ruling our education. (Kuujjuaq – February 1. 1991 – Education Committee)

We should be sharing resources with the other regions instead of trying to do our own little thing. (Kuujjuaq – February 1. 1991 – Education Committee)

Inuit are not in charge. They are just used as rubber stamps ... Complaints – legitimate – have no place in the system. We have nowhere to turn to even if we have suggestions for improvements. (Umiujaq – December 2, 1990 – Parent Interview)

It seems like the students overall have slowed down. We weren't prepared when we took over the system – no materials, etc. (Salluit – January 22, 1991 – FM call-in)

Policies or organizations took on the old ways of the government. They say Inuit are in control, but we are just costumes disguising the new system. (Inukjuak – December 3, 1990 – FM call-in)

The Education Committees have no powers, only on paper. We cannot make our own decisions for our education and only have administrative powers ...Dorval has too much power over what is happening in the communities. (Inukjuak – December 3, 1990 – FM call-in)

People calling for change for betterment are considered enemies. There is too much defensiveness when we try to ask for improvement. (Inukjuak – December 3, 1990 – FM call-in)

Myself and others have had to repeat the same courses over and over. We are mixed in with beginners in the same class. The person who gives the training is in too much of a rush. (Tasiujaq – January 31, 1991 – FM call-in)

The Qallunaats have many materials all ready. The Inuit teachers have to spend hours preparing our own teaching materials ... It is no wonder that we have problems to find people who are willing to teach because of all the work involved in having to prepare our own material. (Kuujjuaq – February 1, 1991 – Inuit Teachers)

As teachers, we have to constantly come up with ideas and produce teaching materials ourselves suited for the different levels we teach and we spend many hours working and making copies. Then what we have just spent hours in making is finished in no time once we start teaching our classes. Curriculum produced in the south is very slow. Most of the material produced in the south (by the KSB head office) is for the lower grades and hardly any for the higher grades. (Inuit Teachers' Round-table – May 24-25, 1990 – teacher from Kuujjuaq)

Another problem I see as an Inuk teacher is that I have to train non-Inuit teachers when they first come to our community. I tried applying to become a head teacher and have been told that I am not qualified or experienced enough for the position. (Inuit Teachers' Round-table – May 24-25, 1990 – teacher from Aupaluk)

Most of our work is photocopy material ... There is hardly any homework now ... There are no lab experiments even though we have the equipment ... In religion, we just sing, kneel and read the bible with no discussions. No moral teaching. (Tasiujaq – January 30, 1991 – secondary students)

There is no discipline, no detention, no textbooks, lots of photocopies and copying from blackboards. We would like more homework ... We are using the same materials year after year ... If we were in charge what would we change? We'd have whole new textbooks, strict teachers qualified to teach their subjects, we'd learn current affairs and have the JBNQA part of

Kuujjuaq 1960
On the way to
establish a summer
fishing camp on the
George River.

National Archives of
Canada
Photo: Rosemary Gilliat
(APA145042). Courtesy of
Avataq Cultural Institute.

the curriculum. (Kuujjuarapik – November 29, 1990 –
secondary students)

There are things I hear. You know, "He's an Inuk boy,
be good to him. Don't give him him too much hard
time." … You take a person from Japan. You take a
person from Canada. They don't know anything and
you start applying them and teaching them. They can
learn, anybody can learn, it's all [if] you want to. You
know they say, "Their culture's different. Don't give
them so much work. Be good to them." No. Be equal
to everybody because everybody has a mind and can
learn if they want to. It's all up to us – if we want
to. You understand that. (Discussion with Kuujjuaq
youth – November 2, 1990)

9

The Education Review Committee Takes Control

Between the late summer of 1990 and the issuing of its report in February 1992, the Nunavik Educational Task Force chose to consider and define an entirely new educational system involving all of the regional organizations, not just the School Board. These new directions resulted in changes in technical staff and growing disagreement with the School Board over the scope and style of the inquiry.

In addition to Kemp and Ellis, the Task Force engaged a number of consultants for specific tasks. This included reviewing curriculum materials and reports submitted by the Kativik School Board; researching educational practices in other parts of North America and identifying innovative programs; analyzing the content of KSB Council of Commissioners' meetings; making research trips to Nunavik communities; preparing status reports on KSB adult education, vocational education, and teacher training programs; and making recommendations on dropout prevention, academic requirements for Inuit students entering post-secondary education or advanced technical training, and methods for linking Nunavik's educational system with regional and community economic development.

One of these consultants was Ken Low, founder, president and chief researcher of the Action Studies Institute (ASI), a Calgary-based think tank "focused on adaptive intelligence and the human capacity for self-control and creative action, especially in changing difficult or uncertain conditions." Sheila Watt-Cloutier first became aware of Ken Low when she happened to see a portion of *Powers and Becoming* on television. This award-winning documentary on "the skills and environments required for healthy independence and the conditions that create dependence" was written and hosted by Ken Low for the Alberta Alcoholism and Drug Abuse Commission.

After discussing Low with the Task Force staff and ERC Commissioners, Watt-Cloutier contacted Low to request more information, and in August flew to Calgary to visit the Action Studies Institute. On September 16, Low came to Montreal for a week of meetings with NETF and to conduct interviews with senior administrators and pedagogical staff at the Kativik School Board. Additional interviews by Low were scheduled for the October Pedagogical Days ("Ped Days") in Kuujjuaq, an annual week-long in-service for teachers from all KSB schools.

On September 19 and 20, Low led a workshop for the Education Review Committee, NETF staff and consultants on Strategic Learning, a framework and training program created by the Action Studies Institute "to help individuals and organizations develop the pioneering skills required to deal with high levels of change and uncertainty." As defined by ASI, strategic learning is "the process that underpins the ability to create, develop, refine and abandon action plans. When internal or external uncertainties and resistance are too great for strategic planning the only effective fall back is strategic learning ... Strategic learning is based on three things: (1) an understanding of adaptive power and how it operates, (2) what effective learning is and how to make it happen, and (3) the barriers and decay processes that keep effective learning from occurring. Strategic learning is based on a systems perspective of the interactions between individual, organizational, cultural and biological levels of control, and is equally applicable for personal, corporate or cultural development."

That same week, the Kativik School Board replied to the Task Force's July 24 request for more financial support. In July, ERC Chairperson Minnie Grey had written to George Ittoshat, President of the Council of Commissioners, that "the request for additional funding is based on the fact that we now have a much better understanding of the scope and complexity of the Task Force mandate, and therefore of the activities and personnel required to accomplish this mandate. From January to June 1990, the ERC spent much of their time identifying the critical issues and underlying problems that had to be addressed by the Task Force. From these discussions it became clear that we needed to reorganize our work, assign new responsibilities to the ERC members, and hire an additional Technical Advisor. At the same time, however, we had to continue the collection of information on each of the six mandates originally identified in the resolution of the Annual

General Meeting." A similar letter was sent to Daniel Epoo, Makivik Corporate Secretary. Both the School Board and Makivik Corporation agreed to provide additional funds to support the Task Force operation.

Internal discussions on the direction and priorities of the Task Force inquiry came to a head in mid-October with a letter from Bill Kemp to the members of the Education Review Committee:

> ... My concerns on both approach and content
> focus on three areas. The first area involves the
> general principle of cooperation vs. a more adversarial
> position with respect to how the Task Force will
> interact with KSB during the last phase of our
> work. The second area involves how the Task Force
> can organize and carry out the activities defined by
> their mandates and which are required in order for
> the ERC to have adequate information for reaching
> conclusions and making recommendations about the
> state of Education in Nunavik. The third area
> involves the need to re-evaluate the responsibilities
> and expectations of the technical advisors and
> other researchers that are involved with the design,
> collection and analysis of information...
>
> Although the original call for a Task Force on
> education may have assumed that it should have
> been entirely independent from KSB, it soon became
> apparent in the early stages of discussion with
> Makivik Corporation that it would be better to create
> and proceed within a cooperative framework. In order
> to keep the record completely straight it should
> be recognized that I favoured this fully cooperative
> approach including joint funding between Makivik
> and KSB. My decision to act as a technical advisor
> was based on an anticipation that this principle would
> function throughout the life of the Task Force.
>
> Problems with respecting the principle of
> cooperation have arisen for two reasons. The first is
> that in recent months a different and legitimate point
> of view about the value or purpose of cooperation has
> been raised within the Task Force. This view states in
> part that cooperation cannot be really accomplished in
> this type of evaluative situation and as a consequence

it tends to act as a control over legitimate activities of the Task Force.

A second reason that it has been difficult for the principle of cooperation to be applied is because we established this principle but did not create an appropriate mechanism that would allow it to operate effectively. Perhaps some would argue that the ERC is, in fact, this mechanism. My feeling is that the ERC is a component of this mechanism but that we still need to define a more workable structure. I would suggest that such a structure would have to operate at both the political and technical levels. At the political level it may be possible for KSB to have a representative on the ERC. At the technical level it will depend on the type of work being undertaken but through some method it would be helpful if KSB interests could be expressed in the design stage of the research.

It should also be recognized that there is a legitimate concern with making sure that the Task Force remains independent of outside influence. Hopefully we can define a reasonable means for expressing an independence, that will allow for cooperation without control. Although it is not always easy to maintain independence within a framework of cooperation I think that it will be very difficult for the Task Force to complete its mandates and to implement its recommendations. As a consequence the ERC should perhaps question the advantages that may be gained from an even greater degree of participation once a cooperative structure is defined and implemented...

In work of this type, it is probably inevitable that a great amount of time is spent on a continuous discussion and re-evaluation of objectives, principles and concerns. I do not advocate that the ERC should stop these important discussions, but I do feel that the time has come for decisions to be made that will allow for the more technical aspects of Task Force work to proceed in a somewhat independent manner...

I hope that this letter will be of help for your discussions. I have tried to be open and honest in my expression of concerns but I would like to repeat that it is my opinion and that you should feel perfectly free to question my assumptions and conclusions.

On October 17, 1990, a previously scheduled meeting of the Education Review Committee convened in Montreal. Kemp restated his concerns as detailed in the October 15 letter, and lengthy discussion followed on the current status and future direction of the Task Force. Feeling that the ERC members did not agree with him, Kemp submitted a resignation letter the following day, effective immediately. He was to return to work with the Task Force as a consultant in the spring of 1991 to conduct a review of the KSB-McGill University Inuit teacher training program.

In a November 20 letter to the ERC, Sheila Watt-Cloutier presented her perspectives:

> ... This way of thinking (cooperative *versus* adversarial) prevents people from considering other solutions and alternatives and tries to make people assume that if I and/or the Task Force question the policies/ philosophies of the Kativik School Board in a certain way that we automatically assume the adversarial position and should therefore be considered as wrong. This approach helps to separate people from one another and keeps people confused and indecisive, believing they must choose between a rock and a hard place.
>
> What I am trying to say is that just because Bill Kemp chooses what he calls the cooperation route we must not assume that the only other way is adversarial. In fact being adversarial has not been an issue for me or any other member of the ERC that I have spoken to. It goes without saying, however, that the direction/approach taken by the Task Force has, on a number of occasions, been interpreted as adversarial by certain staff of the Task Force and Kativik School Board. It must be recognized for what it is, as *their interpretation* and *not* as *our intention* to be adversarial.
>
> I have expressed on occasion that I felt the cooperative approach as defined by Bill Kemp was not workable at this stage of the work. My reason for this is that I feel the Task Force should work as independently as possible during this review of the system ... Rather than come to grips with the issues, [KSB] has on a number of occasions become extremely defensive and chosen to attack people who

have something to say about the system...
I would like to conclude by saying that the only
directions that I have observed as having changed in
the Task Force is the power shift from Task Force
staff to ERC members, which is where it belongs...

The Kativik School Board was not pleased with what its top
administrators perceived as major changes in the scope and
style of the Task Force inquiry. In an October 31, 1990 letter
to the Nunavik Education Task Force, with copies to the
Makivik Board of Directors, KSB President George Ittoshat
summarized the School Board's concerns:

Had the original concept of working groups been
realized, they would have facilitated the necessary
dialogue and information gathering so that ultimately
the recommendations would have taken all
information necessary into consideration. In the
absence of the working groups, we have resorted
to writing extensive documents including statistical
information. This time consuming exercise delays the
process of providing other information necessary in
order to complete the comprehensive study the Task
Force is supposed to achieve.

The Kativik School Board deems it very important
to consult with parents and the general public to give
them an opportunity to voice their opinions and have
some input into the recommendations of the Task
Force. This in turn would strengthen the proposed
solutions. Unfortunately, considering that the final
report would have to be completed for the Makivik
Annual General meeting, it does not appear that the
Task Force could realistically conduct a thorough field
trip and deal with the complex issues which must be
addressed. This leads us to conclude that the Inuit
will feel they have been left out of a process the
results of which will affect directly the education of
their children.

As you are aware, one of the areas to be looked into
by the Task Force is the socio-economic situation and
the effects it has on the development of Education. To
our knowledge this important area has been looked
at minimally, perhaps not at all. We feel that this
area must be addressed in a comprehensive in-depth
study because no matter how good the quality of

Education is, if the socio-economic situation is not
looked at and solutions found, Education on its own
won't work.

Ittoshat also raised questions about the qualifications and
style of Task Force consultant Ken Low. Some of the School
Board staff Low interviewed found his approach overly aggres-
sive, feeling, according to Ittoshat, that Low "lectured them
with strong preconceived convictions which included statements that, in his opinion, the School Board programs were
not culturally relevant and that they are inadequate as well
as the regular programs of the Ministry of Education."
Low addressed the School Board's concerns, as well as the
broader issue of the role of consultants and non-Inuit staff
in the evaluation of Nunavik schools, in an October 29, 1990
letter to Minnie Grey:

> After the week I spent in Dorval and Lachine, it
> was clear to me that the most critical priority was
> E.R.C. task ownership, but this was going to be
> difficult given the dependence on technical advisors
> and consultants. By this action, the E.R.C. has clearly
> stated its intention to be independent. Now the
> challenge really begins, but I have no doubt that you
> can handle it.
> Since I am a consultant too, I am in something
> of a bind. When encouraging others to accept task
> ownership and express their powers it is hard to know
> when to step in and when to hold back. One thing that
> is clear is that this must be your "bridge". It is very
> important that you design and build it yourselves.
> I can share with you what I know about building
> bridges that stand up, but the design and construction
> must be your own. To put it another way, my concern
> is less with the bridge than with the skills and
> insights of the bridge builders.
> The high level of personal sensitivities and conflicts
> in this situation make progress more difficult. It is
> essential to work through some of them at least,
> to see whether they are part of a larger systemic
> problem. I am still trying to sort out what is
> strategically significant and what to ignore. Some
> patterns are emerging and I will say more about this
> in my report ... Some hostility is inevitable whenever
> outsiders are "chartered" to examine an organization's

181

performance. However, beyond a certain point, the hostility becomes a marker that reveals something about the organization's problems and insecurities. Of course this assumes that the outsider is qualified and knows what he or she is doing. If this is not so the hostility is justified. Who wouldn't be hostile to an ignorant and possibly destructive intruder? As a result, if there is any way to do it, the organization's first line of defence in these situations is usually to cast the outsider as an ignorant, offensive outsider. In this situation it is easier to do because my background is not reassuring to those who believe in conventional education.

For the 20 years that I have been professionally involved in education I have been openly critical of the institution's lack of interest in really empowering youth. I have been dismissed as a radical by some and openly supported by others. In recent years my work has become more acceptable to the mainstream, not because of anything I have done, but because more people are doing similar work and saying similar things. Yet it remains a frontier and there is still much resistance to asking questions about how empowerment works and what keeps it from happening...

I agreed to work for the Task Force because you have a core of people who are asking significant questions about empowerment even though there is stiff opposition. In my view, what you are doing is part of a larger struggle that goes back a long way in history and is repeated every day somewhere in the world. I see the educational situation in Nunavik as an extension of a much bigger human problem. This may be one of the reasons why some people have expressed the concern that I have already made up my mind.

There is some truth to this. I am not a neutral observer who only reports what is there. I also interpret, analyze and judge. The framework I use is the empowerment of children to become effective, independent learners. I don't hide this framework, nor do I claim to have the only worthwhile analytical perspectives on how empowerment is achieved. I can say with certainty however, that much of what educators and parents accept as normal education does little to empower children and may even do the reverse. In this sense I have indeed made up my mind. I remain open to new information and perspectives, but I am also very cautious about accepting educator's claims at face value. Education has many self-serving myths, and things are often not what they seem to be.

The members of the Education Review Committee were not unaware of Low's sometimes controversial style. Among the letters NETF received from Low's references was one from Michael Crelinsten, who had hired Low in his capacity as National Learning Programs Manager for the Federal, Secretary of State National Youth Development Program, Katimavik, from 1982-85:

At that time, Mr. Low was one of a six-member team, convened from across Canada, to develop innovative and integrated experiential learning curricula for the Katimavik program. Mr. Low's specific responsibility focused on the work skills agenda, but his overall frame of reference became the conceptual matrix within which the other learning programs were considered and developed.

Mr. Low is, in my opinion, singularly qualified to recommend to yourselves with regard to the potential for human empowerment and learning ... [he] has carried out what I believe to be amongst the most advanced work in North America with regard to the ways in which systems can enhance and support the development of human capacity to act.

Mr. Low's work with regard to competency and skill development in contexts of rapid change, is a conceptual benchmark in understanding the nature of innovative learning and experiential education. He is also a leader in understanding how learning and educational systems will need to evolve, given a context of rapid cultural change, post-industrial cultures and an overriding need for adaptability. Mr. Low has developed an innovative set of skill inventories and curricula which I believe to be widely adaptable to a broad range of contexts. He shows an unusual capacity to understand the subtle tension and interplay between the necessity for cultural adaptation juxtaposed with the need for the sustaining of strong cultural identification...

Mr. Low's credentials are difficult to evaluate in the context of our traditional measuring mechanisms ... Mr. Low has invested his professional life in what I believe to be a highly successful articulation and implementation of techniques that are an alternative to mainstream educational methodologies. Consequently, it is inevitable that traditional educational credentials will be limited in their ability to describe effectively Mr. Low's skills and value as a consultant...

Outside consultants often play a catalytic role in educational change. As outsiders they can sometimes function more freely than staff or Board members, having no prior institutional or personal politics to consider in making recommendations or taking action. They can serve as "hired guns," performing tasks which insiders cannot or will not undertake. Change will inevitably cause conflict. Criticism aimed at an entire project or at local leaders may be aimed indirectly at outside consultants because they are safer to attack than insiders.

The hiring of staff and consultants shapes any endeavor because of the experiences and perspectives those people bring with them. How much did Ken Low and other outsiders shape the Task Force inquiry? Did the ERC hire consultants who could effectively verbalize the ERC's concerns or did the consultants and non-Inuit staff lead the Task Force to the advisors' own biases? The same question arises with the Kativik School Board. Did experienced Qallunaat educators shape the system to their vision instead of defining an Inuit one? To what extent did the Task Force and KSB hire outsiders who reinforced the directions toward which the Inuit were already heading and to what extent did those that were hired redirect the Inuit?

Following the ERC field trip, the Task Force convened a February workshop in Montreal to review and analyze the Kativik School Board curriculum materials. The review team included ERC member Johnny Adams; NETF Technical Advisor Sheila Watt-Cloutier; NETF consultants Ken Low and Ida Watt; G. Gerald Auchinleck, Former Director, Instructional

Services, Protestant School Board Greater Montreal and Past President, Canadian Association of School Administrators; Baruch Aziza and Pierre Sicard, Consultants French Second Language, Protestant School Board Greater Montreal; and Dr. Milton McClaren, Professor, Simon Frasier University Faculty of Education, Director SFU Tele-Learning Center and Science Educator.

The Inuit members provided a knowledge of Inuttitut and Inuit culture. Auchinleck's background included MEQ instructional systems, administration, and instructional supervision. Aziza and Sicard brought expertise in French second language programming at the elementary and secondary levels. McClaren knew curriculum design, science, and math education and instructional systems development. Low provided a knowledge of instructional design processes, high order skills, dependencies, and experiential learning. Over a two-day period the team scanned or reviewed over 300 KSB documents, with special attention to handbooks and program guides.

In his written review appended to the summary report of the curriculum analysis workshop, Gerald Auchinleck stated:

> No other School Board in Quebec enjoys such
> freedom in the curriculum section, development
> and implementation of programmes and teaching
> materials. Kativik School Board has unique
> jurisdiction over certification. Within Quebec
> regulations pupils are not subject to MEQ evaluation
> and the Board is fully responsible for implementation
> and training of staff.
>
> Conscious of the fact that pupils are expected to
> feed into the Quebec post secondary system and the
> reality of Quebec society the Board has used as
> its base the structure of the system of the MEQ
> and the credit system of secondary education, which
> delivers an MEQ Diplome D'Etudes Secondaires at
> completion of Secondary V on an assessment based on
> the schools, not the MEQ.
>
> Notwithstanding the quality of the MEQ Régimes
> Pédagogiques programmes, the Kativik School Board
> has missed a golden opportunity to improve upon the
> MEQ programmes and to develop adaptations and/or
> new programmes which reflect more current thinking
> in instructional design.
>
> Many of the adaptations indeed represent a return

to older traditional approaches and the accompanying materials are home grown and lack the attractive quality of materials used in schools in Quebec. Sometimes the appearance of change is in the documents, but close attention to the activities reveals that the programme is not leading to the objectives outlined in KSB documents...

Dr. McClaren wrote in his review:

In many of the materials I reviewed the approach to instruction seemed to emphasize *teacher* activity more than *student* learning. Work sheets, drill cards, fill in the blank exercises are often liked by students precisely because they don't have to think. They just go through the motions...

Research has shown that many students fail or do poorly not because they lack ability, but because they are not taught even the basic ideas about how to learn. This becomes very important when students come from families where few have been to school or where many did not do well at school in the past...

Many of the curricula contained lists of topics and detailed objectives. What they lacked was a clear statement of the big ideas or major themes which students need to make sense of the curriculum ... The greatest lack in the whole review was the absence of an overall framework for this curriculum...

I should also say that I had two days in which to review a large number of documents. I reviewed the intended curriculum, or written curriculum, not the curriculum as taught or delivered. I am fully aware of the difference between a written guide or activity book and the curriculum as taught and experienced in classrooms. Nevertheless, written curriculum is an important expression of thinking about purposes, teaching, learning and social organization...

After reviewing the KSB French Second Language Programmes for Primary, Sicard found a "strong discrepancy between the KSB programme for French second language and the teacher's guides. The programme emphasizes a communicative approach (teaching functional French) but the teacher's guides put an emphasis on learning language structures."

Aziza's review of the French Second Language Programmes for Secondary concluded that "most of the material is not reflective of the new MEQ programme and its philosophy of language acquisition, and most of the material is French mother tongue, not French second language."

In the summary workshop report to the ERC, Ken Low wrote:

> Not all of the materials raised concerns, some were reviewed quite favorably. However, the overall pattern was that the materials suffered from all the deficiencies that are likely to occur when adapting traditional narrow focus institutional materials into a community base program with no guiding framework, no vision of human potential, no wholistic framework ... The current framework, or more precisely, lack of one, makes it very difficult to create an integrated approach where the second language instructors can work closely with the Inuttitut instructors...
>
> One of the clearest deficiencies in the whole KSB operation is the lack of effective needs assessment...
>
> The KSB programs are generally below accepted North American standards and the adaptations of the MEQ curriculum materials have not been successful. There is a lack of an organizing framework and integrating vision to drive the instructional development system. The Inuttitut teachers and programs have made a good start, but further progress will depend on the system acquiring an integrated vision and new framework. There is little instructional design capability in the system. It does not know how to respond to the immediate, pressing educational needs. The system is willfully parochial and has resisted learning from outside sources. The problems are systemic and can only be solved by a major restructuring of the organization...

1991 Makivik Annual General Meeting

By the end of February, the Task Force had completed the ERC field trip, concluded most of the community-based research by technical consultants, received and reviewed the research reports it had commissioned on the status of education in Nunavik and elsewhere, and analyzed the KSB curriculum materials. During the first week of March, ERC members, NETF staff and consultants met to review the progress, discuss the findings, and plan the preparation of the Preliminary Report to the upcoming Makivik Annual General Meeting in Kuujjuarapik.

The relationship between the Task Force and the Kativik School Board had become increasingly tense since the fall of 1990. Growing discussion of the need for systemic reform instead of change within the existing school system added to the concerns of KSB staff. The School Board continued to provide funds for the inquiry and to respond to requests for information, including preparing a number of special reports for Task Force review.

The members of the Education Review Committee presented the NETF report to the Makivik AGM on March 20, 1991, and began by recognizing the many years of hard work by the Kativik School Board. The School Board had, however, adopted too much of the Quebec Ministry of Education curriculum, and where adaptations had been made the effect had been to water down the academic requirements. The Task Force had determined that the initial scope of work proposed for the inquiry was too narrow, and efforts to broaden it had met with stiff resistance from the KSB. Differences with the School Board had come to a head with the resignation of the Task Force's first Technical Advisor.

The Task Force was now confident of its direction and focusing its efforts on "hear[ing] the voices of the communities." The communities were saying there were problems with KSB, and the School Board was saying many of the causes of these problems lay in the communities. The Task Force acknowledged that the communities were not without problems, but after consultation with experienced educators "with proven track records" the Task Force had concluded that there were "serious structural problems" with KSB and that the education being delivered was "well below North American standards." The NETF final report would include specific recommendations for dealing with these problems. The ERC members expressed strong confidence in finding the "tools, understanding, and perspectives out there" which could support the people of Nunavik in solving these problems.

Appended to the Preliminary Report were comments from students, post-secondary students, parents, Education

Committee members, teachers, KSB administrators, and consultants extracted from NETF-collected interviews and research. (Fuller excerpts from the NETF Report to the 1991 AGM can be found in Appendix G.)

On April 16, KSB President Putulik Papigatuk wrote to the ERC members on behalf of the Executive Committee, with copies to the Makivik Executive and Board of Directors:

> This is a response to your proposal to hold a general meeting in June to discuss the final report of the Nunavik Education Task Force. After a study of the preliminary report submitted in March, the School Board, in the spirit of the Makivik General Annual meeting resolution creating the Task Force, feels that a better dialogue has to occur between the Task Force members and the School Board. We feel very strongly that this dialogue must occur before the tabling of the final report to a general assembly, in order to eliminate unnecessary confrontation which could jeopardize the overall objective of the Task Force and therefore miss the opportunity to use the Task Force findings in assisting in improving the quality of Education in Nunavik.
>
> It is incomprehensible to us, that a report of such importance be tabled without verifying with the School Board the accuracy of the facts that form the basis of the study and consequently the recommendations. Unless there are face to face discussions between the School Board and the Task Force members on the issues which the Task Force is addressing, we will not be able to properly review the findings to ensure the accuracy and integrity of the final report.
>
> Consistent with the above the Kativik School Board is requesting that the final report be submitted to the School Board as soon as it is completed. The School Board will then require six months to review the report with all individuals and bodies concerned with the delivery of Education Services in Nunavik.
>
> We feel this will lead to constructive dialogue at the general meeting and will ensure that all recommendations will be given due consideration. The process will also guarantee that planning for implementation of the recommendations will be mutually agreed upon by all parties concerned.

Considering that the report will be submitted to
the School Board some time in June, as indicated
previously by the Task Force members, we would
expect that the general meeting would be held
sometime in January of 1992 ... We would like to
meet with you on April 26, 1991 at 10:00 a.m. in the
School Board's Conference room to discuss this matter
further.

ERC Chairperson Minnie Grey responded:

We acknowledge your concerns and understand where
those concerns may be coming from, we however
have fundamental differences in the perceptions of
the situation. These differences of perceptions have
clearly been evident since our work began with the
review. We would like to assure you that there is
no attempt on our part to deceive anyone and that
all individuals and bodies of Nunavik concerned will
have full opportunity to examine the issues in regard
to our findings and the final report.
　We agree that a meeting must be held where
this issue, along with other issues such as
the implementation process and the educational
conference, would be discussed. Directions must be
set and decisions made surrounding these issues. We
are organizing a meeting to be held on April 29,
1991 at 10:00 a.m. to which we are inviting the
KSB Executive members, the Makivik Corporation
Executive members and the Education Review
Committee members...

The members of the Education Review Committee, Makivik
Executive, KSB Executive, KSB Director General, and
Secretary General met in Montreal on April 29. The KSB
Council of Commissioners met on May 2 and passed a
resolution repeating its stand that KSB could not accept any
proposal for a General Meeting to deal with the Final Report
of the Task Force unless the report had been presented to the
School Board at least six months in advance.

KSB's Perspective on Program Development

As the Task Force began planning the Final Report, it continued to contact other organizations and programs which might
serve as models for education in Nunavik. In early May, visits
were made to the MicMac Learning Centre in Halifax, Nova
Scotia, and to schools and technology institutes working on
Native language programs in British Columbia. Consultants
Ken Low and Ken de la Barre served as general advisors
to Sheila Watt-Cloutier and the ERC in identifying and
researching potential resources and in beginning to draft recommendations for the summary report.

The Task Force had earlier agreed that, after reviewing
the KSB materials, it would meet with the Board's program
developers to ensure an understanding of the philosophy
underpinning their programs. In mid-June, a 2 1/2-day workshop involving KSB program developers, ERC representatives,
and NETF consultants was convened in the KSB boardroom
in Dorval. KSB staff had also prepared a written report in
response to a list of questions submitted by the Task Force.

In the oral presentations and the written response, the developers explained how needs were usually identified by Inuttitut
language teachers, culture teachers and primary teachers.
Other suggestions come from local Education Committees,
pedagogical and other counsellors, at Commissioner's meetings, and through meetings of other regional organizations
such as Makivik and Avataq. A few suggestions also come from
parents. The initial requests for a Northern history program
and the alcohol and drug abuse prevention program came
from Education Committees.

Data is provided by individual experts and resource people,
usually elders; through teacher workshops; and by adapting
NWT, Alaskan, and Greenlandic materials. Counselors from
all the communities meet once or twice a year to go through
the list of priority needs, read first drafts prepared by KSB
technical staff, or create first drafts. Elders participate in
these meetings to ensure the quality of the Inuttitut language,
the proper use of terminology, and the cultural relevancy of
the program.

After these meetings revisions are made to the first drafts.
Consultants are involved as needed. They are usually non-
Inuit who specialize in various fields and are hired for specific
projects on a contractual basis. Teachers help to correct and
revise the final draft; create activities and teaching ideas; help

to categorize the work into levels; and evaluate and try out pilot versions with their students.

Program developers introduce teachers to new materials either at training sessions or during the annual Pedagogical Days. They also present developed materials to the Commissioners in an annual report, to Education Committees at their meetings twice a year, and to Centre Directors at their meetings. Overall production takes one to two years.

The developers cited the Inuttitut math programs and reading programs as particularly high quality parts of the curriculum. In the written response to the Task Force's questions, KSB staff described these programs as "developed with the respect of Inuit perceptions and concepts of time, space, seriation (relationship between things) and the world in general, as well as their language which reflects the same, plus their values, beliefs, practices and standards (which are very different from Anglophone and Francophone language and culture, and may in fact be contradictory at times)."

The program developers described how "Inuit teachers used to teach Inuttitut the way they were taught ABCs by their non-Inuit teachers when they were themselves in school. Around 1980, they voiced their concern of how by the end of the third year of their instruction in Inuttitut, their students weren't acquiring fluency in the reading of syllabics. So they stated the need to develop a reading program at the primary level with a non-Inuk reading specialist [who] was chosen for the task and worked on development with the help of Inuit teachers. She had to look at the approach teachers were using, at the strengths and weaknesses of Inuit children as they enter school, which could influence how they learned to read Inuttitut syllabics."

At the high school level, the presenters explained that "since our objective is to give a real Secondary V to our students, we have no choice but to follow MEQ standards and objectives in our programs. Objectives are one thing but content is another one and this is where adaptation comes into place. MEQ programs need to be adapted to the situation which is second language learning and a cultural environment that is different from that of southern Quebec."

They cited culture programs in response to the Task Force's question on programs or pieces of curriculum in serious need of improvement.

Everyone agrees that Inuit culture cannot be taught indoors, certainly not in a couple of hours a week at a time. It is a lifelong journey to learn and acquire one's culture, especially that of the Inuit because we are very outdoors oriented and still 'nomadic' people to some extent. Outdoor traditional skills and knowledge include being able to survive on the land and the sea, in the harshest climate, with the rawest of materials. Inuit culture includes all things that make it different from other cultures ... Elderly Inuit are quite shy and feel uncomfortable and guilty doing these activities inside classrooms. These activities are done outdoors or at home, or they smell up the whole sanitized schools with very sophisticated and sanitary-conscious Qallunaat all around...

Not too many able Inuit men and women will stay in a community to do one hour a day of teaching (for they are all fishermen/women, parents, grand-parents, hunters, carvers etc.), unless the school is big enough for these hours to add up to days. For these reasons, we've had our schools choose the way they schedule cultural activities and most communities have chosen to bulk the hours into half or full days a week ... Some communities would have a cultural week (1 or 2) rather than hire culture teachers by the lesson.

Education Committees select the culture teachers. Understandably, they select the candidates who are most knowledgeable in their culture. Those are usually Elders or elderly, who naturally teach in the way they were taught – that is by demonstrating and showing one-on-one how to do the work. Our students today are used to being taught not only visually but to be motivated through audio-visual, kinetic and tactile methods ... So ... some students are often not motivated and would cut classes...

Everyone's attitudes and statements in regards to education strongly influence our students' performance in school. Strong statements pushing for our schools to provide education in English and French only because they hold the key to a successful future economically, indirectly, but in very subtle ways, discriminate against Inuttitut and Inuit culture.

Our students' self-identities are threatened when they are put into situations where they have to choose between their mother tongue and the second language. They are made to feel confused because they are Inuit. They like being Inuit, but when community members claim that Inuttitut has no room in our schools nor in our future today, they get awfully hurt and so they reject the second language. Some would say that it is true, that we have lost a lot of our language and culture and we will not go back to the old ways, so why bother to learn the language and culture. These students dream of coming down to Montreal for further studying in the second language, so they cut culture classes. And still some say inwardly "O.K. You reject my language, but in rejecting it you reject yourself." They lose the desire to learn the second language. Either way a bias on 1st or 2nd languages have proven to have detrimental effects on lots of things and people (language and culture teachers, our Inuttitut program developers, our students and their own future).

There are some students who fear Inuttitut and culture is at its last generation. They don't feel strong enough to pass them on to the next generation.

Culture teachers are the group we have had the most problem with in providing the support from which other teachers benefit. Principals provide pedagogical support to the teachers, but they are very aware of their absolute ignorance of the Inuttitut language and Inuit culture so they pass along the responsibility of pedagogical support to Centre Directors who, in turn, are very aware of their lack of pedagogical and Inuit cultural knowledge and background. So ... there is no pedagogical support from the administrators for our culture teachers. Our pedagogical counsellors all have a background in primary instruction. They are also very aware of their lack of knowledge of Inuit culture and the rich and strong language culture teachers use. We've had very few travelling counsellors available to travel and help these teachers: unfortunately very, very few want to take on this job. You have to be single with no children to take on such a job but almost no Inuk falls into that category...

Culture is what makes us different from others. It is the most important area for us ... Culture teachers are the most knowledgeable group on our culture. We

haven't been able to fit some of them into our little
school buildings ... They may pretty well be the group
who holds the key...

In late June, NETF representatives met with Quebec Ministry
of Education officials to discuss the historical and working
relationship between the Kativik School Board and the
Department of Education.

In the spring, Bill Kemp also completed his review of the
Inuit Teacher Training Program. In introducing the report,
Kemp reviewed his own history of involvement with the
Kativik School Board, including the teaching of courses in
Northern ecology and Northern history; work on curriculum
materials; and participation in the primary grade social stud-
ies group with elders, teachers, and KSB staff.

He cited as strengths the strong commitment felt by KSB
Inuit teachers to the training program and their belief that it
was directed toward their needs and backgrounds and "without it there would be few if any Inuit teaching in the Kativik
schools at this time." In Kemp's assessment, the program
enabled the School Board to meet key pedagogical objectives
– having the first formal educational experience of Inuit children occur in Inuttitut under the guidance of Inuit teachers.

In meeting with Kemp, Inuit teachers had made two primary
recommendations for change in the program: a strengthening
of the summer program focusing on teaching methods and
a restructuring of the subject area content courses (history,
ecology, science, etc.), including distribution of well prepared
materials prior to the courses and follow-up after the completion of winter workshops. While the teachers felt that an open
admissions policy was important, they did request different
levels of courses reflecting teachers' prior coursework and the
students they were teaching.

In looking to the future of the program, Kemp raised questions and advised changes:

It is certain that courses are improving, that the
qualifications of teachers are being upgraded, and
that the Inuit who now regularly teach certain
courses are becoming more competent. But I do not
think that the evaluation and review process has any
formal structure or specific objective.

My primary concern here is not as much with the
internal Kativik process, but rather with the process

that would allow the program to be discussed by the McGill people who are directly involved...

The question now to be considered is whether or not the strategy formulated over 10 years ago is still, in spite of certain revisions, adequate to meet the present day practical needs. It is time for the program to "come out of the closet" by defining what it is, how it functions, why it is important and what possible new directions might be taken. What, for example, is the continuing role of KSB with respect to the program? How important is the concept, or reality of, "KSB ownership" of the program? Would it be possible to address the very particular academic backgrounds of Inuit participants or the special pedagogical needs of Inuit students if it was not "owned" or at least very strongly influenced, by KSB values and objectives?

The Development of the Final Report

As the Task Force came to the end of its inquiry, it was clear that the publication of a Final Report could not reconcile the differences of opinion among the residents of Nunavik concerning the present and future of the region's schools. Implementation of recommendations and reconciliation of differing views would have to occur after the release of the report. The ERC members, staff and consultants began discussing the structure and function of an implementation committee to be created when the Task Force completed its work.

Based on a telephone conversation with the Director of Strategic Planning at the Calgary Board of Education, Ken Low suggested that consideration be given to a performance audit of the Kativik School Board by an outside agency independent of Nunavik organizations. A candidate for this review might be Fenwick English, a professor at the University of Cincinnati College of Education, who had formerly been with the American Association of School Administrators (AASA). In an April 30, 1991 fax to NETF, Low described Dr. English's experience in investigating educational systems:

He used to do about 50 audits a year. He now teaches others how to do it through the AASA and he only does a few every year. He has investigated very large and very small school districts in USA

and elsewhere in the world. He has had some
experience investigating systems on native reserves.
The performance audit is especially useful where
there is a combination of political, leadership and
educational problems ... Educational audits are
based on generic standards that apply to all
human organizations. The application of these generic
standards may vary from culture to culture, but the
general principles are universal and there has been no
trouble applying them in different cultural settings.
The investigators are trained to be sensitive to local
contexts and different cultural priorities...

In a May 10 fax to Minnie Grey, Low described curriculum
auditing as another evaluation tool:

I have been studying Fenwick English's book on
Curriculum Auditing ... Curriculum auditing is
relatively new, and it hasn't made much of an impact
in Canada yet, but it is a strategic development
that the Task Force cannot afford to ignore ... The
curriculum audit approach is compatible with what
the Task Force and its consultants have already done,
although 'auditing' is more structured and narrowly
focused. Despite the title, curriculum auditing has
more to do with administrative competence than
curriculum. The primary focus of the audit is the
school district's quality control mechanisms. A full
audit of this type would throw a bright spotlight on
the specific leadership problems at KSB. I don't think
that it is necessary to go back and do a full audit this
at this point ... it is useful to have this option as a
"strategic reserve".

At the end of July 1991, the Education Review Committee met
in Kuujjuaq with the Task Force staff, Low, and de la Barre
to review the first draft of the Final Report. The group met
again in August in Montreal to review completed sections and
proposed layout and to settle on a production schedule. They
discussed implementation options, including establishment
of a "core working group" to be composed of five representatives appointed by Makivik, the Kativik School Board,
Kativik Regional Government, Avataq Cultural Institute, and
the Nunavik Constitutional Commission. Another follow-up

Zebedee Nungak speaks on the topic of the Constitution of Canada at the Makivik Corporation Annual General Meeting in Puvirnituq, March 1992.

Photo Stephen Hendrie/ Makivik Corporation

option was a region-wide educational conference to be held after release of the Report and funded out of Makivik's education budget.

Preparation of the Final Report, entitled *Silatunirmut/The Pathway to Wisdom/Le chemin de la sagesse*, continued through the fall and early winter. Prior to its general release, portions of the report were presented by the Task Force to regional organizations, including the Makivik Board of Directors, Kativik School Board Commissioners, executives of the Kativik Regional Government (KRG), representatives of the Nunavik Constitutional Commission, and the Mayors of Nunavik. At a January 16, 1992 meeting on self-government for the region, ERC members decided to release the entire English version of the report to the Executives of Makivik, KSB and KRG, and others involved in negotiations with Quebec on the form and function of Nunavik government.

On February 27, 1992, Minnie Grey formally transmitted the Final Report of the Nunavik Educational Task Force to the Kativik School Board with a letter to President Putulik Papigatuk: "What is expressed in this report comes from our people and the recommendations it makes are based on what was found during our research. Education is a major component of our future within self-government and we feel this report makes a significant contribution towards that end ... We hope this report is received in the spirit in which it is intended – as a working document that will lead to the continuing improvement of educational policies, programs and services for the people of our communities ... I would like to thank the Kativik School Board for all their support throughout the course of our work."

The School Board requested copies of the Task Force-sponsored reports and research listed in the report's annotated bibliography. These were forwarded to Annie Popert in mid-March, except for reports where those interviewed had requested confidentiality.

Makivik Corporation delegates attending the 1992 Annual General Meeting in Puvirnituq, March, 1992.

Photo: Stephen Hendrie/ Makivik Corporation

Copies of *Silatunirmut/The Pathway to Wisdom/Le chemin de la sagesse* were delivered, free of charge, to each community by First Air and Air Inuit and distributed to each household through the mayor's office.

The Makivik Annual General Meeting took place in Puvirnituq during the last week of March. ERC members presented a summary of the Task Force report to the delegates, but most people had not read the detailed report – over 100 pages in each of three languages including 101 recommendations and a 26-page annotated bibliography. The Spring 1992 *Makivik News* stated:

> ...the report was bold in scope. Perhaps a little too bold for some, initially. The head of the Kativik School Board loudly defended the work of his organization. Putulik Papigatuk spoke in tones that did not need much amplification about the uphill struggle the Kativik School Board has been engaged in for the past 13 years ... In response, many of the people in attendance spoke passionately of their own experiences with education. The topic was not exhausted on Thursday evening, and continued into Friday morning ... In the end it was generally agreed that when delegates returned to their communities they should urge everyone to spend time reading the document, thick as it may be, for the sake of future generations.

The AGM concluded its consideration of the Task Force Final Report with the passage of a resolution:

Resolution No. 1992-M-3
Re: Report of the Nunavik Educational Task Force

WHEREAS   the Nunavik Educational Task Force (the "Task
Force") was created in 1989 at the Makivik Annual
General Meeting by Resolution No. 1989-M-22;

WHEREAS   this Task Force has now tabled its Final
Report (the "Report" entitled "Silatunirmut – The
Pathway to Wisdom") to the Makivik Annual
General Meeting;

WHEREAS   this Report has important implications for the
future of the education system in Nunavik and for
the future of Nunavik as a whole;

WHEREAS   there is not sufficient time here at this meeting
to undertake the review and evaluation which this
report requires;

On motion by Daniel Epoo, seconded by George Koneak, it was
hereby resolved:

THAT   Animation for discussion on the Task Force Report,
SILATUNIRMUT, take place in the Nunavik
communities as soon as possible by co-operation
among Municipal Councils, Education Committees,
KSB Commissioners and any others;

THAT   Members of the N.E.T.F. conduct a field trip to all
Nunavik communities to further consult the people
on the contents of the report SILATUNIRMUT;

THAT   An All-Organizations Meeting be convened by late
spring/early summer to absorb the results of the
above mentioned animation/field trip, and to plan
for a Special Assembly on the Education Task
Force Report and that each organization is to bear
individual costs of participating at the meeting;

THAT   A Special Assembly on the N.E.T.F. Report,
SILATUNIRMUT, be convened by late summer/
early fall to fully discuss and debate the contents
and recommendations of the said report.

Unanimously approved.

Following the 1992 AGM, staff organized the Nunavik Educational Task Force records into archival files, updated the annotated bibliography, computerized the report distribution list, completed summary financial and administrative reports, and closed down the project. Makivik established an internal budget to support costs associated with implementing the resolution, including field trips by Josepi Padlayat and Sheila Watt-Cloutier to explain the report to the communities.

Makivik Corporation delegates attending the 1992 Annual General Meeting in Puvirnituq, March, 1992.

Photo: Stephen Hendrie/ Makivik Corporation

Images of Nunavik

Leah May Grey,
Kuujjuaq, 1992.
Photo: Michael Westgate.

Lichen-covered rocks
Kuujjuaq, 1992.
Photo: Michael Westgate.

205

Kuujjuaq in July
Photo: Gordon Cobain

Ivujivik waterfront,
in January 1991.
Photo: Ann Vick-Westgate

Early spring in Nachvak
Fjord (Quebec/Labrador
area), 2001.
Photo: Gordon Cobain.

River landing strip at
hunting camp, 1991.
Photo: Ann Vick-Westgate

Ouside of a hunting
camp, 1991.
Photo: Ann Vick-Westgate.

Heading back to town, 1991.
Photo: Ann Vick-Westgate.

Tent at night, near
Kangiqsualujjuaq, 2001.
Photo: Gordon Cobain

Sunset at Torngat.
Photo: Gordon Cobain

First Air landing at
Kuujjuaq, 1992
Photo: Michael Westgate.

Puvirnituk waterfront,
January 1991.
Photo: Ann Vick-Westgate.

210

The Emataluk family
in Tasiujaq
Photo: Gordon Cobain

Tasiujaq in June with
caribou in foreground.
Photo: Gordon Cobain

Community of
Kangiqsujuaq, 2000.
Photo: Gordon Cobain.

Pingualuit Crater inland
from the communities
of Kangiqsujuaq and
Salluit.
Photo: Gordon Cobain.

10

Coming Together
– Task Force Report and School Board Response

The Nunavik Educational Task Force's Final Report recommended a major restructuring and refocusing of the education system in Nunavik, emphasizing new approaches which differed from the existing educational framework.

Silatunirmut/The Pathway to Wisdom/Le chemin de la sagesse began with a discussion of the purpose and history of education in Arctic Quebec:

> Education is the means of learning, the way people prepare themselves for life. The effectiveness of education is measured by how well it prepares people to handle the problems and the opportunities of life in their own time and space. For thousands of years our people had a very effective education. We knew how to prepare our children to handle everything they would face when living on the land. Then things changed. The path of education we had followed for countless generations could not prepare us for all these new things.
>
> We had no experience with the southern institutional way of doing things ... We inherited an institutional system of learning that was designed and controlled elsewhere ... The system never had enough program development capability to design and produce effective programs. What it provided was a watered down version of the official Quebec curriculum. Creating an education system is a necessary step to self-government in Nunavik ... The restructuring of our education system in Nunavik is part of our learning and development as a people...

The report recognized the Kativik School Board's achievements in rapidly creating a basic educational system for communities poorly served by federal and provincial authorities and acknowledged the intense effort required to press for adequate financial support from the governments during the first six or seven years of School Board operations.

In assessing the current system, the Task Force concluded that KSB was not meeting the needs of Nunavik residents and that, while the administration of KSB acknowledged that serious problems existed, "they were mainly seen as being external to the system. The administration sees a lack of commitment to formal education and the social difficulties of northern life as major barriers to the system."

While the report affirmed the School Board's policy that a solid base in students' mother tongue helped second language learning and stated that "effective bilingual education is not only possible, it is normal," it determined that "the language issue has been such a huge one for KSB that it has just about swamped every other pedagogical concern." KSB was found to lack system-wide curriculum standards, consistent evaluation systems for instructional programs, or effective measurements of student achievement, resulting in "a serious mismatch between what the system offers and what would actually be useful to the students – especially at the secondary level".

Silatunirmut concluded that:

> By accepting the MEQ Régime as the basic
> instructional plan, KSB locked itself into a framework
> that made it almost impossible to pay any attention
> to the communities' real needs ... Our analysis of
> the KSB Commission meetings eliminated all doubt
> about whether our Commissioners have ever been
> able to control the Board. They have not. They have
> been swept along by the operational details of the
> institution, and largely forced into responding to other
> people's agendas.
>
> One problem is that there are currently four
> regional organizations with educational
> responsibilities, and the James Bay and Northern
> Quebec Agreement created a power distribution that
> is basically unworkable. This leads to conflict and
> isolation instead of cooperation and integration.
>
> Another problem is that KSB has no independent

vision, and is highly dependent on MEQ for
its program structures and operating guidelines.
A further problem is that KSB operates in an
isolated, inward-looking fashion and it does not learn
from high quality education and training programs
elsewhere. KSB's meager resources are spread too
thinly over too many responsibilities and it does not
have the operational capability to initiate and follow
through on program development initiatives. Finally,
KSB is far removed from the communities.

The Task Force expressed confidence in the residents' ability
to confront and correct the weaknesses in the educational
system: "There are great challenges ahead of us, but in
Nunavik we may be closer to solutions to this problems than
most other people. We are small in number, pioneering in
spirit, do not have the inertia of long-established institutions
to contend with – and, perhaps most of all, we still have a
natural respect for wisdom."

Following the February 1992 release of *Silatunirmut*, the
KSB Council of Commissioners, acting on a resolution of the
Education Council, formed an Internal Review Committee
with representation from teachers, counselors, centre directors,
principals, education committees, students, Commissioners,
and central office administrators. The Commissioners mandated the committee "to review the Report from the Task Force
on Education, to look at other issues which were not addressed
in this Report, and to recommend action to be taken." Through
a process of consultation and discussion, they were to "determine which of the Task Force recommendations are valid,
create a method and timetable for the implementation of
recommendations, and study and make recommendations on
social and related issues which affect education but which were
not fully treated in the Task Force Report." KSB administrators
installed a toll-free phone line in the Dorval office "to ensure
that the general public as well as the School Board personnel
have direct input into the work of the Review Committee."

In October 1992, the Internal Review Committee invited
members of the Task Force to a meeting in order to explain
the follow-up the School Board was conducting concerning
the Task Force recommendations. They also prepared and
released a *Report of the Activities of the Kativik School Board
1986-1992*, which, like *Silatunirmut*, stressed the upcoming
responsibilities of self-government:

The people of Nunavik have been working for
many years to establish our own self-government.
Aside from our responsibility to ensure that our
programs properly equip our students to operate this
government, the School Board must play an active role
in determining the eventual organization of education
within the self-government structure. The system that
we have been able to build must be used as a basis for
any future organization of education in Nunavik.

In the "Message from the President" which led the *Report of
Activities,* the Task Force Report was criticized for completely
reorganizing the structure of education in the region, providing "little that can be used directly to improve educational
services" and taking "little or no interest in the innovative
programs that have been developed by many of our schools
and Adult Education Centres."

The *Report of Activities* included a section on each community school emphasizing the unique nature of each village and
its leaders. On a regional level, the report reviewed the School
Board's accomplishments in negotiating with the Quebec government revised budgetary rules and funding levels and
amendments to the Education Act subsequent to the James
Bay and Northern Quebec Agreement. Also highlighted were
KSB's commitments to children learning a second language
while at the same time having supportive teaching for their
mother tongue (addictive bilingualism); to teaching from an
Inuit perspective; to the team approach to program development; to co-operative learning; and to individualized paths of
learning. The Teacher Training Program was cited for bringing the total number of legally qualified Inuit teachers in
Nunavik to 46. Under "Members of a Worldwide Community,"
it was noted that during the previous five years, 18 members
of the pedagogical staff had attended a total of 105 conferences worldwide, given 54 talks to educational institutions in
Canada, and submitted 14 papers for publication in pedagogical journals.

In March 1993, the Kativik School Board issued the *Review
of the Report of the Nunavik Educational Task Force,* based
on the findings of the Internal Review Committee. The review
dismissed a majority of the Task Force's criticisms and
recommendations, particularly the redesign of the existing
system. In addressing specific components of *Silatunirmut,*
the School Board review concluded that the Task Force's work

on curricula was the least helpful part of its entire report and charged that the NETF had only looked at curricula, programs, teaching materials, and the teacher training program in a very cursory manner. (A detailed comparison of each of the Task Force's 101 findings with the School Board response can be found in Appendix H.)

The Internal Review Committee stressed the negative impact of socio-economic problems on school performance:

> The highly unfavourable conditions for education
> in Nunavik that we have described are very
> controversial. These conditions seem so overwhelming
> that they might be seen as preventing educators from
> setting high standards ... However, the only reason
> for analyzing conditions in Nunavik is that these
> conditions are a necessary context for understanding
> the evolution of education in Nunavik, realistically
> assessing the performance of the School Board, and
> the setting of realistic goals for the future.

The internal review report did promise greater autonomy at the community level:

> Many of the improvements in education during the
> upcoming years will be made by the individual
> schools themselves. To do this effectively, and as
> the task force suggests, they must develop into
> strong community schools. With this in mind the
> School Board has committed itself to developing a
> strong system of community schools, rather than the
> centralized restructuring as was suggested in the
> task force report ... While the Board will remain
> responsible for the setting of standards, and the
> determination, through consultation, of core skills
> which students should be taught, the schools will
> be given greater autonomy in deciding the types
> of services they will offer, and the style of those
> services ... The Board has begun to identify those
> budgets which can eventually be transferred to the
> communities so that they might control the resources
> they will need to effectively develop novel, locally-
> based solutions to the educational problems they
> must face.

The School Board response to the Task Force Report concluded with KSB's commitment in the immediate future to:

> 1) Engage recognized experts to carry out a formal audit of all of our teaching programs, with a view to finding what changes must be made and in what areas, and to planning a curriculum that will meet all of the needs of the children; 2) Organize a formal independent review of our teacher training program to better build on its strengths and to correct its possible weaknesses; 3) Continue our current research study of how social and economic problems impact on the success of our students, and how we, along with our partners, might better help to alleviate them; 4) Strengthen cross-cultural training for our teachers; 5) Begin a program of decentralizing more resources and responsibilities to our schools; 6) Make the internal review process an ongoing component of the Board so that there is a consistent and formal method for evaluation, review and reporting of developments in education. In addition, the recommendations of the task force judged to be beneficial, and not currently in place in the school system, will be implemented through the internal review process; 7) Continue to support the development of self-government, both through our educational programs and through institutional support for the Nunavik Constitutional Committee; and 8) Carry out a continuing process of consultations with the local communities.

On March 4, 1993, the Education Council of the Kativik School Board passed a resolution, with 41 members voting for adoption and four abstaining, endorsing the conclusions of the Internal Review Committee and its analysis that "the radical change of structures proposed by the Task Force ... would in no way solve the various problems and issues in Education raised by the Task Force and ... would have a destabilizing effect with serious consequences for Education in Nunavik."

The resolution included a plan of action that called for the Kativik School Board to:

> 1) continue to support the development of self-government, both through Kativik School Board

educational programs and through collaboration with the Nunavik Constitutional Committee; 2) make the internal review process an ongoing component of the Board so that there is a consistent and formal method for evaluation, review and reporting of developments in education ... 3) continue the Kativik School Board current research study of how social and economic problems impact on the success of Nunavik students, and how Kativik School Board, along with its partners, might better help to alleviate them; 4) [implement] the recommendations of the Task Force which Kativik School Board considers to be beneficial, and currently not in place in the school system ... ; 5) carry out a continuing process of consultation in each of the communities; 6) begin the Kativik School Board program of decentralizing more resources and responsibilities to its schools; and, 7) formalize the working relationship between Kativik School Board and Avataq [the regional organization charged with preservation of Inuit culture and history] for the development of traditional cultural programs. The second part of the action plan specifically called for engaging recognized experts to conduct a formal audit of all KSB teaching programs "with a view to determining if changes are necessary to ensure that the curriculum will meet the needs of all the children in Nunavik" and for a formal independent review of the KSB Teacher Training Program.

The 1993 AGM

When Makivik's Annual General Meeting convened in Kuujjuaq in the last week of March 1993, delegates were familiar with both the Task Force's report and the School Board's internal review published in response. On the third day of the meeting, discussions centered on self-government for Nunavik. Representatives of the Nunavik Constitutional Committee read to the delegates a recent letter from the Quebec Minister of Native Affairs regarding the appointment by the Quebec government of a special negotiator to work out with the Inuit of Nunavik a draft agreement "governing the reorganization of existing structures implemented pursuant to the James Bay and Northern Quebec Agreement. Essentially,

Makivik Corporation
Annual General
Meeting
Kuujjuaq, Nunavik
March 1993

Photo: Stephen Hendri/
Makivik Corporation

the special negotiator's mandate would focus initially on the creation and implementation of a form of self-government in Nunavik and on a sweeping reorganization of existing institutions, which would fall under the jurisdiction of the proposed autonomous government."

Discussions of the future form of Nunavik government focused the next day on education and the differing visions of the Nunavik Educational Task Force and the Kativik School Board. Makivik News reported on the events as follows:

> If there was a storm brewing at this assembly, it erupted on Thursday afternoon, live on CBC Northern Service Radio across the Arctic. For listeners in faraway Tuktoyaktuk, or Resolute Bay, the radio program may have sounded totally out of context. However, for observers of the political process in Nunavik over the past several years, the hours spent on this topic on Thursday March 25th, were cathartic, to say the least ... The Introduction and General Response [of the KSB Review of the Task Force Report] were read aloud to the assembly and radio audiences followed by the resolution passed by the Education Council [on March 4]. Contained within the resolution was a sentence that caused considerable commotion. The Education Council resolved, "That any attempt by Makivik corporation to create, authorize or control

any aspect of education in Nunavik be rejected and shall be opposed." The Education Council also rejected recommendations 1, 2, and 11 of the Silatunirmut report, recommendations that would have restructured the education system with Makivik as the head in the transition period of self-government...

The debate that followed was passionate indeed. All speakers told of the difficulties their children faced in the education system. Many wondered specifically why their children dropped down a few levels when they wanted to pursue their studies in the South after graduating from High School. Tillie Kliest of Kuujjuaq asked why this was so. Annie Popert, Director General for KSB, explained the situation, "Some of the major reasons are: they feel the education is too heavy when they leave their homes and study down south. Language is another barrier. Up North they have English as a second language, but down south they have to use it as a first language. Also students have little self-control when they go down south. They're not used to doing their homework. They want to make money, they want to play hockey in a new building, they get pregnant, they need baby-sitters, drugs and alcohol abuse, confusion about what they want to do in the future, immaturity, not wanting to deal with their studies."

Testimony like this was not easy to take for some of the young people in the room, or those listening at home. The youth of the AGM left the meeting momentarily to appoint speakers. When they returned, George Berthe of Kuujjuaq spoke, "There are a lot of comments that were given to me from the youth reps. Kativik School Board has a review committee, and there is Silatunirmut. It seems that you are fighting in our eyes. We know KSB has to be improved. It's not really that bad either. We heard a lot of bad things about KSB, why there are too many teacher dropouts. Why there is only one Inuttitut class per day. Why there are so many student dropouts. Graduation ceremonies are bad because some students actually have failed. In culture class we fix ski-doos and small qamotiks [sleds]. There is not enough home-work, sometimes only at the secondary level, and only if they ask. The students are going to be the ones who lose out if you go too slow. Makivik Education Task Force, and KSB, you should have met each other. I think you two have to meet, because the losers are the young people when you are fighting each other like this."

Other youth gave equally gripping testimony. Billy Meeko from Kuujjuarapik said that when he went to study in the South, he had to work twice as hard. He advised the commissioners to ask more questions to the students. Harriet Keleutak of Kangirsuk, Makivik's newest and youngest Board Member, spoke as a youth. She told of her experience in the South, "I was one year behind in math, chemistry, and physics. I asked my councilor why am I behind, he said because I'm Inuk, and he didn't explain. I'm not saying KSB is bad, but you made a fool out of me." There was a great deal of honesty in the testimony. Inukjuak Mayor Jobie Epoo, who was part of the Education Task Force Committee, was very frank about what was happening in the room: "It seems like we are trying to outdo each other. We are trying to figure out which document will prevail, and people are trying to figure this out."

Much later, after the CBC radio program was over and the delegates had gone for supper and returned, the discussion continued. Zebedee Nungak, who chaired this part of the meeting, kept asking for solutions when people spoke, not just criticism. Governor Lazaroosie Epoo (a member of the Board of Governors, the council of elders created by Makivik in 1993 "to provide wise advice on the matters at hand") reminded the assembly, "This is not the first time we have gotten angry at each other. We have had meetings where we were shouting at the top of our lungs at each other. I want people to be patient working towards self-government." And indeed it was with the Nunavik Constitutional Committee that a solution was found.

In the space of less than half an hour, it was agreed to amend the KSB Education Council recommendation which objected to the participation of Makivik Corporation, and the Makivik AGM was temporarily adjourned in order to convene a special public meeting. This took place at 10:25 p.m. At the

public meeting a resolution was passed to extend the
mandate of the Nunavik Constitutional Committee
until a successful outcome of the negotiations [was]
achieved, and that "the NCC appoint negotiators
to represent the interest of Nunavik in all these
negotiations, such negotiations to include two members
of the NCC and two members from each of the
following organizations: Kativik School Board, Kativik
Regional Government, and Makivik Corporation."
Once the resolution was passed, the public meeting
was adjourned, the Makivik AGM was reconvened, and
then closed for the night. (Spring 1993, Issue 26)

AGM delegates created the Nunavik Education Implementation and Planning Group (NEIPG) by a unanimous vote.
The resolution passed at the Kuujjuaq AGM acknowledged
the role played by the youth in moving the adult delegates
toward co-operation:

Whereas the members have heard during this
meeting from the youth representatives of Nunavik,
who eloquently expressed their opinions concerning
the deficiencies of the present education curriculum
standards in Nunavik; Whereas these deficiencies
result in Nunavik students having significant
difficulties in adjusting to southern school or college
curriculum; Whereas youth representatives from
Nunavik have also expressed in this meeting the need
for the cultural content of the KSB curriculum to
be more relevant and more oriented toward lifeskill
apprenticeship; Whereas the members have clearly
expressed the importance to work toward resolution
of differences of views instead of maintaining an
adversarial approach. Therefore ... it is hereby
resolved...

Each of five regional organizations – Makivik, Kativik
School Board, Kativik Regional Government, Avataq Cultural
Institute, and Nunavik Constitutional Committee – would
have two members on the NEIPG, and each organization
would bear the costs related to its participation. Under the
resolution the NEIPG was mandated "to examine in depth all
the recommendations of *Silatunirmut*, taking into account the
Report of the KSB Internal Review Committee, with a view to

implementing them and in particular prioritizing those which can be implemented in the short and long term; to address the concerns raised by the youth during this meeting in regard to KSB curriculum standards deficiencies in order to find remedial solutions to alleviate the negative effects on students going south to pursue their education; and to examine problems identified by the youth concerning culture and curriculum."

The process which had begun with Nunavik leadership very far apart, now had settled on a partnership approach which had resulted in a coming together.

The first two meetings of the NEIPG, chaired by NCC Chairman Simeonie Nalukturuk of Inukjuak, concentrated on the questions of curriculum review and curriculum auditing of the Kativik School Board. Dr. Francis Jones of the Piedmont Triad Horizons Educational Consortium and Dr. Virginia Vertiz of the American Association of School Administrators (AASA) met with the NEIPG delegates and recommended the group review the recommendations of the Task Force report and the KSB response before commissioning other studies. An initial decision, as reported in NEIPG newsletters, was to "work with curriculum experts to create a single curriculum framework so that the essential elements of objectives, teaching methods and testing are working in the same way." The group also decided that Sheila Watt-Cloutier would serve as a full-time coordinator for the NEIPG.

In January 1994, the National Curriculum Audit Center (NCAC) of the American Association of School Administrators completed an NEIPG-commissioned analysis of the Task Force recommendations.

The National Curriculum Audit Center Report grouped the NETF findings into 12 major themes: (1) redesign organizational structures; (2) revise certain policies, beliefs; (3) recruit and train teachers and administrators; (4) redesign staff evaluation procedures; (5) establish a collaborative curriculum design plan; (6) develop and communicate student outcomes, standards, and specific programs; (7) design program and student assessment procedures; (8) provide training for various constituents; (9) change certain delivery systems; (10) establish specific programs through which to deliver instruction; (11) provide equitable learning opportunities; and (12) establish fiscal efficiency and adequacy of support base. NCAC found that the Task Force had placed most of its emphasis (78 of 101 recommendations) in five areas: establishing specific instructional programs (18 findings dealt with this area), developing and communicating student outcomes, standards, and specific programs (16), providing training for various constituents (16), redesigning organizational structures (16) and changing certain delivery systems (12). (A more detailed analysis can be found in Appendix I.)

The NCAC Curriculum Management Audit has five established standards for school districts: (1) demonstrated *control* of resources, programs and personnel; (2) establishment of clear and valid objectives for students (*direction*); (3) demonstrated internal consistency and rational equity in program development and implementation (*connectivity and equity*); (4) use of results from district-designed or adopted assessments to adjust, improve, or terminate ineffective practices or programs (*feedback*); and (5) improved *productivity*.

The consultants found that most of the Task Force recommendations related to connectivity and equity, followed by control and then direction. They found few NETF recommendations related to feedback and only one in the area of productivity.

The NCAC analysis also keyed the responses of the School Board's Internal Review Committee to the Task Force recommendations, indicating whether KSB had agreed, disagreed or been unclear in its response. The NCAC concluded that KSB had accepted 35 of the 101 recommendations, disagreed with 15 of them, and had not been clear in its response to the other 51 Task Force suggestions. The School Board position was not clear to the NCAC when: (1) the response did not address what was felt to be the essence of the recommendation; (2) the Board did not agree with the delivery agent; (3) the Board responded it was already doing what was recommended; or (4) the meaning of the response was not understood by the consultants. (See Appendix I for more details.)

The NCAC report concluded that "clearly, the Nunavik community has identified many areas of school improvement that might be considered. At the same time, there are many other areas which are normally addressed through the Curriculum Management Audit which were not discussed from a systemic perspective in the Task Force's report. It could be that these areas are being adequately handled in the communities and were therefore not identified or it could be that they simply were not considered. These issues should be raised as those with vested interest work toward improving the schools."

In March 1994, the Makivik AGM convened in Salluit. Some of the delegates expressed concerns about the slow pace of school reform, and they passed a resolution urging the leaders of the five organizations participating in the NEIPG to do what they could to help the work move at a faster pace.

Executives from Makivik, KSB, KRG, Avataq and NCC met in May 1994 "with the intent of furthering the spirit of openness and co-operation in improving the education system for Nunavik. Both pedagogical and political issues were discussed and dealt with. Among those political topics was the use of $2.5 million which had been received from the federal government which Makivik has set aside for educational purposes. All participants were reassured that the interest from this invested money would continue to be used for educational purposes and managed by Makivik. In terms of education, the leaders present stressed the importance of implementing the recommendations in a reasonable time frame" (NEIPG Newsletter, October 1994).

More work needed to be done to clarify the issues and to build a consensus on what needed to be done to improve the educational system in Nunavik. As the primary tool for this clarification and consensus-building, the School Board adopted a new, more inclusive process for consulting with the communities about the kind of education they wanted for their young people. The process was called *Satuigiarniq*, an Inuit word meaning reclaiming.

The Satuigiarniq Process

In late April 1994, the KSB Education Council held an expanded meeting in Umiujaq, with each Nunavik community invited to send two Education Committee members, a teacher, a student, the teacher training and student counselors, the principal, Centre Director, and KSB Commissioner. One hundred and fifty people came together at Umiujaq, representing all 14 communities.

Specific issues discussed at the meeting included participants' visions for education in Nunavik in the year 2000; time, human resources, training, and other support required for culture and language teaching; skills and attitudes needed by high school graduates; teacher skills and attitudes; the role of parents in supporting education; the role of communities in creating job opportunities for high school graduates; and alternative requirements for learning paths, diplomas, and certificates.

Development of a set of learner outcomes which would allow students, parents and schools to know what is expected of them and also facilitate the development of programs and materials in a well-aligned curriculum framework was a major topic for discussion. Participants emphasized the importance of consultation at all levels of the community – learner outcomes were not to be drawn up solely by professionals at the Board level.

In a report to the communities entitled *Focusing on the Future: A Report on the Education Council Meeting – Umiujaq, April 19-21, 1994*, Kativik School Board staff stated:

Our idea of education now is much more than filling up children with facts, ideas and skills. We realize that children do not come to us empty, ready for filling, but rather as whole, unique human beings who have already learned from their parents and their community when they come to school ... To date in Kativik School Board we have concentrated most of our energy on one learning path and on one diploma: that is the set of courses that leads to the Quebec High School Diploma. Because it leads to CEGEP and college entrance, it has been seen as the most desirable path for children to take in order to gain the skills to become future Inuit leaders. However, many children do not receive this diploma, or they may remain in school and complete their Secondary V only to find out that they are not interested in the few options for which they've been prepared.

In the communities of Nunavik, there is no common, agreed-upon standard of what a child must know before going on to a certain job or role in the community. If the school and community together could decide on what is needed to be successful in a certain employment or a certain role in the community, together they could design a path of learning and a diploma that would indicate the child is now ready to do that work or take on that responsibility. This could be in the field of hunting or traditional skills, or in caring for children, or in being the clerk or the manager of a store or running a small business such as hairdressing or appliance repair. When we start to match the learning paths and the diplomas with the natural talents of children and with the needs of the local or larger community, then the schools will be able to serve the community and the children as they must be served. As long as we have only one or two chosen paths of learning with only one or two diplomas or certificates, we will continue to lose children from the school system and we will continue to not prepare children to take on all the roles that they and their communities want and need...

In *Focusing on the Future,* KSB staff also reported that the teaching of Inuit culture and language had "generated the most reaction of all the topics discussed, from Elders to students. The general demand was for longer hours and more funds to be devoted to the teaching of culture. If the teaching of culture is part of our mandate, and therefore a priority, more funds and teaching time must be accorded it. While there was unanimous acknowledgement that youth must be prepared for self-determination, there was also a unanimous desire to keep the Inuit traditions, and thus the heritage alive... "

They concluded the report with a discussion of the Community Consultation Process, which was to be initiated region-wide with the return home of the community teams who had assembled in Umiujaq:

In the last three Education Council meetings, questions concerning what is taught in the schools and how it can be improved have been discussed by all the participants, and the staff has gained a direction in approaching improvement of the curriculum of the School Board. One thing has become clear: in carrying out the dual mandate of the School Board, there must be one set of educational objectives which provides teaching goals for all subjects taught in Nunavik ... The parents must know what is being taught, and what level of achievement is being accomplished by their children...

In Nunavik, we are going to the communities to ask you what these learner outcomes should be. We are asking you to say what role you expect formal education to play in building the kinds of communities you want to live in ... The final goal is to put in place a single curriculum framework with goals that everyone agrees on, and to create the tools and materials to teach it and evaluate the learning such that everyone can continue to be a partner in the process of education...

This consultation process will not end this year. If we are to continue building the best education system possible, this is only the start of a continuing active dialogue on education which will be used to analyze, plan, and evaluate on an ongoing basis. It is now time for the communities to assume the leadership, and to carry out the next stage of the community consultation on education in Nunavik.

In December 1994, KSB staff reported to the KSB Council of Commissioners on the development of the community consultation process. To facilitate the process, the staff had created a Central Committee which included NEIPG Coordinator Sheila Watt-Cloutier. In October the Council appointed three of the Commissioners to participate in Central Committee meetings. The process was now called *Satuigiarniq,* to reflect more accurately the scope of the task and the intended result – "to redefine, strengthen and reclaim a holistic education system in Nunavik in partnership with, and with direction from, the people of Nunavik."

The 17-member *Satuigiarniq* Committee [formerly the Central Committee] began meeting in the fall of 1994 with trainers from Axiom Consultants to organize training workshops for community leaders. They reported to the Commissioners that these meetings helped them to redefine their goals: "What we have gained from [Axiom] is the knowledge that community involvement and empowerment will come only from the development of a sense of ownership of the process. Our aim is not to do the consultation for the communities but rather to help them develop the leadership skills necessary to design and conduct their community's consultation and to develop the attitude of self reliance and a level of competence which will truly lead to their community's reclaiming of the education system..."

In November 1994, the *Satuigiarniq* Committee asked each community Education Committee to select two people to serve as leaders to oversee the local *Satuigiarniq* process. In most communities the Centre Director was one of the leaders. A meeting of the local team leaders and *Satuigiarniq* Committee members was held on November 30 and December 1. The local leaders then began to put together a team of people to work on the succeeding phases of the consultation process. In January 1995, a week-long training session was held in Kangiqsualujjuaq.

In a 1995 report to the communities, *Satuigiarniq: The people of Nunavik reclaim education*, the School Board stated:

> The people of Nunavik are not alone in demanding that our education system meets the standards which will ensure that our children will become productive members of society once they finish their basic education. We are also demanding that our students finish school with a strong sense of self-identity and self-worth, and guided by a strong sense of cultural values. Nunavik is not waiting for someone else to come and solve its educational concerns. We are addressing those very concerns now in a process called Satuigiarniq.
>
> Satuigiarniq is an Inuit word meaning reclaiming, and it's the name that's been given to the process we have already embarked on. The Kativik School Board is going to you, the people of Nunavik, to ask what kind of education you want for your children, and for yourselves. We want to encourage those with a vested interest in education (and that includes everybody in Nunavik) to participate ... What's at stake is more than just gathering data. Satuigiarniq is asking you, the people of Nunavik, to reclaim the responsibility for the education of your children, to redefine and strengthen your education system, and infuse it with the Inuit spirit...
>
> The communities will have total control over the Satuigiarniq process. Each community will conduct the consultation according to the goals agreed upon locally, and using the methods that best meet local needs.

In the same report the Umiujaq *Satuigiarniq* Committee stated:

> The Satuigiarniq Consultation Process is a suitable follow-up to Silatunirmut which now has made some room to listen to others and perhaps begin to adopt new ideas without hostility. This is essential because this younger process [Satuigiarniq] is basically inviting the population of Nunavik to be involved in formulating all kinds of ideas to begin to implement a more relevant education system in Nunavik.

In an article entitled *"Satuigiarniq*: Reclaiming Responsibility for Education" that appeared in the Summer 1997 issue of the *Journal of Staff Development* (Vol. 18, No. 3), KSB Director General Annie Grenier, Director of Education Services Sarah Bennett, and Staff Development Counselor Elaine Armstrong revealed more fully the behind-the-scenes dynamics of launching *Satuigiarniq*:

> ... For 18 years, the Kativik board had worked hard to develop and improve its services and to fulfill its dual mandate: "To develop a curriculum that embraces native traditions, culture and language, and to prepare students for active participation in the modern world." But in 1992, a Regional Education Task Force Investigation (Nunavik Educational Task Force, 1992) reported that many people were dissatisfied with the education being delivered. The time had come for the Kativik School Board to consult the people of Nunavik in order to renew and improve the education system...
>
> The Kativik board assembled a central committee of 17 educators and political representatives to begin the project. This was a professional body of organizers, predominately non-native staff members from the board office, and not Inuit from the communities. With the best intentions, members organized themselves as they had always done, preparing to take charge ... Had we continued to use this plan, the proportion of Satuigiarniq involving stakeholders would have been small and the central committee would have controlled and owned the project...
>
> Based on their work with the consultants, the training subcommittee embarked on a goal-setting exercise with the central committee, hoping to clarify this committee's purpose and help members unite for a common purpose ... The central committee consisted of 17 individuals with strong and deeply held opinions. Most of these individuals had operated autonomously within the Kativik board for many years. Emotions flared during the three-day workshop as these distinctive personalities debated each and every word...
>
> The process has not ended with the completion of [community] consultations. Instead, it has become

a way of doing things throughout the board and
the communities. Many communities feel they have
just begun their consultation and will continue to
dialogue with stakeholders as they explore issues
in more depth and refine ideas and comments into
solid recommendations. The communities' oral reports
to the Education Council in spring 1996 included a
strong message that the local leaders would not simply
hand over their data and back out of the process.

Toward Self-Government

The 1975 James Bay and Northern Quebec Agreement marked
the initial steps toward reclaiming Inuit sovereignty in
Northern Quebec. The Inuit of Nunavik and the Government
of Quebec began discussing the form and function of Inuit
self-government in their region in 1983. A redefinition of the
purpose and the delivery system for education is part of this
process.

In November 1983, at Parliamentary Commission hearings
in Quebec City, Premier René Lévesque indicated that his government would be prepared to negotiate self-government in
Northern Quebec if the region's Inuit residents could present
a unified position. The following month Paulusi Sivuak, the
President of Inuit Tungavingat Nunamini (ITN) – an organization formed in 1976 to represent residents of Puvirnituq,
Ivujivik and Salluit opposed to the signing of the JBNQA
because of provisions providing for surrender and extinguishment of aboriginal rights – wrote to Lévesque committing ITN
to work with other Quebec Inuit in creating a meaningful and
effective self-government structure for the region. In January
1984, ITN, Makivik, the Kativik School Board, the Kativik
Regional Government, and the Fédération des Cooperatives
du Nouveau Québec (FCNQ) decided to form a task force on
self-government (*Ujjituijiit*) composed of two representatives
from each of the five regional organizations.

They began their work with a field trip to the Inuit communities. The *Ujjituijiit* summarized what they had learned in a
report issued on May 15, 1984. While cautioning that the trip
was only the initial step toward defining needs and that the
information contained in the report was neither complete nor
conclusive, the report did offer some general observations. And
education was integral to the discussions of self-government:

The people view education [as being] of fundamental
importance to promoting Inuit cultural identity and
Inuit self-sufficiency. The people expressed their
dissatisfaction with the present education system
in northern Quebec and called for substantial
improvement especially in the area of curriculum
development. The people suggested that the education
system should be redesigned so that it more
effectively promotes Inuit cultural identity ... Over
and over again the people expressed concern with the
lack of adequate consultation by the regional entities
with the population. This lack of consultation, the
people suggested, results in the regional entities not
being responsive to the needs and aspirations of the
people, namely that they want to protect their culture,
they want to be self-sufficient, they want a good
education system and they want a better form of self-
government ... Many people felt that until we set our
goals and objectives as a people, there is little point
in creating new structures because the structures will
not give us direction. In other words, many people felt
that our needs and our goals and objectives should
determine what structures we need rather than the
other way around as we may have done in the past.

In their major recommendations based on the consultation trip,
the Northern Quebec Task Force on Self-Government stated:

Inuit must be ready to take control of our own self-
government, otherwise there can be no true self-
government. We see education as playing a major
role in preparing Inuit for this purpose and without
properly educating our future leaders, any new self-
government structures will be meaningless and will
fail ... We recommend that the education system
for northern Quebec, specifically programming,
curriculum development and promotion of Inuttitut,
be rigorously examined to determine the problem
areas. We feel that one way to begin this review of the
Kativik School Board is through the upcoming Special
Symposium on Education...

In fall 1987, a referendum was held in Nunavik for residents to
select the process to be used to develop a constitution providing

for self-government in the region. The Fall/Winter 1987/88 issue of the Kativik School Board's newsletter reported that:

> 62% of the population participated in the referendum, voting between two groups who, while both in favour of the creation of a Self-Government, differed on the creation process for this government. The "Citizens for a Responsible Government" led by Harry Tulugak, manager of the Puvirnituq Co-op, maintained that the work group to write the constitution should be elected through a universal vote and financed by a special tax. The "Timiujuit (Organizations) Group" led by Simeonie Nalukturuk, maintained that the work group mandated to draft the constitution of the future regional parliament should be made up of and financed by the following established Inuit organizations, since "the people who work within the organizations are familiar with and understand government structures": the Makivik Corporation, the Kativik Regional Government, the Kativik School Board, the Federation of Co-ops of Northern Quebec, Inuit Tungavingat Nunamini, and the Avataq Cultural Institute.
>
> The "Citizens for a Responsible Government" won, receiving 1,111 votes to the 983 votes of the "Timiujuit Group". Spokespeople representing both options will work together from now on to establish procedures for electing a work group which will draft the constitution of the future Self-Government.

On April 10, 1989, 63% of the eligible voters in 14 communities elected 6 representatives from 13 candidates to develop a constitution. After community meetings and a review of earlier self-government efforts, the Nunavik Constitutional Committee (NCC) completed a proposed constitution. Advised by experts in constitutional law, the NCC worked through several drafts of the constitution before returning it to the communities for endorsement through direct vote by the people. The format decided on was a non-ethnic regional government involving all residents north of the 55th parallel.

In July 1991, the Nunavik Constitutional Committee and the Quebec government signed a Memorandum of Agreement (MOA) committing Quebec to negotiate a form of self-government for Nunavik, based on the Constitution NCC had tabled earlier. National constitutional considerations, including the Charlottetown Accord and a failed constitutional referendum, dominated much of the next two years. In May 1994, the Quebec government appointed a special negotiator to work with the Inuit in defining a Nunavik government.

Three years after the signing of the MOA, a Negotiation Framework Agreement was signed by Nunavik and Quebec officials. The Agreement contains 17 sections outlining the objectives of the negotiations and the negotiation process and providing for funding for the negotiations to come from Quebec, Canada, and Nunavik organizations. Special Negotiator for Quebec Francis Fox said about the July 21, 1994 signing of the Agreement: "There is no other part of Quebec where the government is considering setting up a Regional Assembly. It's certainly a radical departure, and I think it's the result of the government listening closely to the requests of the people living north of the 55th parallel, and coming to the realization that the problems of the Inuit communities, and what they face are indeed radically different from those that exist in other parts of the province" (*Makivik News*, Fall 1994).

With the defeat of the Liberals and the election of the Parti Québécois under Jacques Parizeau in September 1994, discussions on sovereignty for Quebec itself came to the fore. The new government named a new special negotiator to continue discussions with the Nunavik Inuit, and agreement has been reached on financing the new regional government through a block funding transfer and a share of the taxes Quebec obtains from the Nunavik territory as well as a portion of the revenues that come from developing the region economically.

In November 1999, following the signing of a Political Accord between the federal government, the provincial government and Makivik Corporation, a commission was created to propose a form of regional government for Nunavik. The eight-member Nunavik Commission, including three Inuit leaders, released its report in March 2001 and proposed that the new government be operational by 2010. After further negotiations between the three parties to the Political Accord, residents will approve or reject the finalized format for the regional government in a 2003 referendum.

Through the processes of negotiating and implementing the James Bay and Northern Quebec Agreement and regional self-government, the Inuit of Arctic Quebec have the opportunity to radically redefine and reform fundamental governmental structures to meet their needs, including education and the schools.

Since 1989, residents of Nunavik have been engaged in the Task Force review, the School Board response, the formation of the Nunavik Education Implementation and Planning Group (NEIPG) and the subsequent launching of the *Satuigiarniq* process. The School Board has made a number of the recommended changes, and *Satuigiarniq* and other activities are gradually moving the region's residents closer to community-based definitions of knowledge and education in an Inuit context. The self-government process will guarantee that the issues of educational reform and redesign will stay in the forefront.

In its 1992 report and recommendations on the status of education in the Inuit communities of Northern Quebec, the Nunavik Educational Task Force identified the importance of the relationship between the control of schools and Arctic self-government and summarized the challenges facing Arctic residents in education:

> The education system in Nunavik should be
> restructured and refocused to make it work for us,
> to ensure that it prepares us to handle the problems
> and opportunities of living that we actually face – not
> just the ones the school board has been mechanically
> structured to deal with. We are not asking someone
> else to create this system for us. Creating it ourselves
> is a necessary step to self-government in Nunavik.
> Self-government and education go hand in hand just
> as independence goes with wisdom. The restructuring
> of our education system in Nunavik is part of our
> learning and development as a people. There are
> many challenges ahead of us, but we have many
> advantages. We are small in number and are not
> burdened by a heavy load of inflexible institutions.
> We have the potential to be world leaders in
> education, not for the recognition, but because it
> is in us to do.

11

Indigenous Models for Educational Change

The education debate in the early 1990s among the Inuit of Quebec centered on the purposes and future of the public schools in their fourteen Northern communities. What were the strengths of the Nunavik Educational Task Force Review and the Kativik School Board's response? What remains to be done? What can the Nunavik experience teach other communities, both Native and non-Native, seeking to improve the education of their young? Which aspects of indigenous education might be incorporated into the theory and practice of educational change for all schools?

The endeavor undertaken by the Nunavik Educational Task Force was ambitious and its pursuit guaranteed to be difficult. Change threatens those in control of the status quo and is particularly threatening if it involves in the process organizations external to the system being evaluated. Conflict is inevitable. "Substantial change involves complex processes. The latter is inherently problem rich" (Fullan 1993, 27).

Change without debate and temporary loss of equilibrium is superficial. Educator Ted Sizer cautions that "to pretend that serious restructuring can be done without honest confrontation is a cruel hoax." Yet, to get beyond recommendations into implementation, a change effort must move toward achieving agreement among most participants that improvement is necessary and that they must attempt proposed solutions.

Furthermore, the proposed solutions must themselves be subject to review and change in the future. Educational systems need to continually mutate to adequately prepare students for the dynamic societies they will be entering. "We are not dealing with problems that, once solved, do not have to be solved again and again. The American Constitution was not a solution. It was a blueprint of values, aims, and institutional

arrangements that the writers knew would require inter-
pretation, reinterpretation, and change. That provision was
made for an amendment process was not fortuitous ... [The
Founding Fathers] knew that the Articles of Confederation
were inadequate and potentially lethal to the growth and
security of a fledgling society. As long as they allowed themselves to stay within the confines of these Articles, the major
problems would be intractable to remedy. Confronting that
intractability, they entered history" (Sarason 1990, 179).

The process begun in 1989 has opened the Kativik School
Board to external evaluation and to increased participation
by all residents, not just School Board employees and elected
representatives, in setting the goals for elementary, secondary, and post-secondary education in Arctic Quebec.

Some of the major factors which have contributed to educational change in Nunavik are:

• *the mandate provided by the James Bay and Northern
Quebec Act and the Quebec Education Act.* At a time when
Quebec was establishing provincial control over education and,
for the first time, instituting strict controls over languages
of instruction and content of curriculum, it was legislating
for the Inuit extraordinary powers to design and administer
education in their own communities. While the enabling legislation granted powers, it was up to the Inuit to assume and
exercise these powers. The evaluation process brought more
open discussion of the options available to the Inuit and prod-
ded the School Board leadership toward greater independence
from the Quebec Ministry of Education.

• *political clout.* School districts rarely rush to initiate comprehensive evaluations or to open their doors to external
change agents. It is particularly hard for a school district
with a national and international reputation for innovation
like the Kativik School Board to confront internal problems.
Because other Nunavik institutions in addition to the School
Board were legislatively and politically charged with educational and social responsibilities for Nunavik residents, they
were able to bring pressure to bear toward school change and
to move an initially reluctant School Board to participate.

To accomplish more than a polite inquiry, the Task Force had
to ultimately exert the political leverage it had and assume
a confrontational stance with the School Board. From the perspective of Seymour Sarason: "But of one thing I am certain:
any effort at reform has to have as its goal a change in existing

power relationships in the system. That, I hasten to add, is no guarantee of success, but it is a pre-condition for other alterations in the system" (Sarason 1990, 46).

Even then, real movement toward implementation of the Task Force's recommendations only began to occur after more political pressure from constituents began to be felt, most dramatically in the alliance of the elders and students at the March 1993 Annual General Meeting of Makivik Corporation. Political leverage enabled the Task Force and the constituents to ask hard questions. And change at the community level required the development and adoption by the Kativik School Board of the *Satuigiarniq* ('reclaiming') process of community consultation.

• *money.* During the 2 1/2 years of its inquiry, the Nunavik Education Task Force expended more than one million dollars provided by Makivik Corporation and the Kativik School Board. This figure does not include in-kind contributions, KSB staff time preparing reports for Task Force review, or subsequent costs related to the Nunavik Education Implementation and Planning Group or *Satuigiarniq.* Having the resources, and the will to allocate them for educational reform, was critical to the success of this undertaking.

• *the ability to step back beyond formal schooling to traditional values and processes of education.* Formal schooling is very new to the Inuit of Canada's Eastern Arctic. As Zebedee Nungak points out in the Foreword to this book, "our grandparents, the first generation of Inuit to observe their grandchildren (us) being herded into unilingually English Federal schools, were the last of countless previous generations to leave the nomadic lifestyle. Even our parents' generation, for the most part, never saw the inside of a classroom." The institutions called schools did not evolve out of their own society. And Nungak's peers, in his words, "the first Inuit generation to 'benefit' from formal education, [were] put through several wrenching wringers ... several systemic cataclysms which can be oversimplified into the Federal/Provincial/Kativik School Board periods."

Many of the Inuit of Nunavik do not think that education must be limited to a predetermined box called "school." As the chapter "The Communities Speak Out" vividly illustrates, the Inuit feel free to criticize the existing parameters and to define new purposes for education. And because they are still close to the values in their traditional society, they can readily integrate these values into their educational philosophies.

These perspectives give them an advantage in conceptualizing new approaches to education. "First, you must understand and digest the fact that children, all children come to school motivated to enlarge their worlds. You start with *their* worlds. You do not look at them, certainly not initially, as organisms to be molded and regulated. You look at them to determine how what they are, seek to know, and have experienced can be used as the fuel to fire the process for enlargement of interests, knowledge and skills ... As long as you start the reform effort with that unreflective acceptance of the culture, traditions, and organization of classrooms and schools as we know them, the implications of the first point will not surface. If you take that first point seriously, you will find yourself asking: if we were to start from scratch, what would schools look like?" (Sarason 1990, 164).

• *a willingness to question the status quo and existing institutional frameworks.* The Inuit of Quebec were unwilling to accept the system they had inherited from federal and provincial authorities as the only way to do education. Perhaps more importantly, they were willing to review and change the system they themselves had built since 1978.

• *a willingness of residents to participate in evaluating the schools and to speak out on difficult issues.* Nunavik's population is just over 10,000. Staff members and elected representatives of the Kativik School Board, Makivik Corporation and other local and regional organizations are often related to each other and/or have worked for the institutions they are now criticizing. The young had to speak out while still showing respect for their elders. The current leadership had to make way for new perspectives and succeeding generations. Those who criticized had to accept criticism. The challenge will be to sustain this level of participation, to keep the institutional doors open to outside view, and to make internal and external evaluation an integral part of the Nunavik educational system.

• *their positive experiences in 'Inuitizing' Western models, particularly that of co-operatives.* In their book on *Between Past and Future: Quebec Education in Transition*, Norman Henchey and Donald Burgess discuss the power shifts brought on by the Quiet Revolution and subsequent developments in Quebec education: "... the role of the Church in Quebec education was considerably diminished during the reforms of the 1960s and, as a result, a vacuum of power was created ... The government is a secular rather than a religious institution.

The school boards, the schools, and certain other structures, however, continue to exist within a confessional framework. This has resulted in dissonance between the legal authority for education, on the one hand, and the educational structures on the other ... The teachers and parents, that until the 1960s could be thought of as silent partners in the educational enterprise, have since emerged from comparative obscurity to demand what they see as their own share of power, influence and control" (Henchey and Burgess 1987, 192-93).

Comparable shifts of power have taken place in Native Quebec. It was through the co-operative movement that the Inuit first began to assert control economically and politically in the new settlements. While the idea to start the co-operatives and the initial funding came from outside, the co-operatives developed into truly Inuit-controlled institutions, owned and run by village residents for their own purposes. The Inuit had begun to take back control of their own lives and communities.

Another Western institution adopted and modified by the Inuit of Arctic Quebec is the corporation. Unlike the 1971 Alaska Native Land Claims Settlement Act (ANCSA), the land claims agreement with the indigenous peoples of Arctic Quebec addressed education, health and social services, administration of justice and other economic and social development issues in addition to land ownership and financial settlements. Makivik Corporation, the legal entity created to receive and administer compensation funds under the JBNQA, is charged with generating revenues for economic and *social* development. While investing its assets in profit-making ventures and creating subsidiary businesses, Makivik cannot have revenue generation as its only purpose.

What allowed or caused this Inuitization of co-operatives and corporations? Since the Second World War, Quebec Inuit language and culture have been under tremendous stress. Every aspect of Inuit society – governance, resource allocation, education, health care – has been impacted by a foreign model intended to replace the Inuit form. At first the Inuit were overwhelmed by the rapidity and totality of the change. But as Inuit familiarity and facility with the Western models increased and as these structures failed to meet social and economic needs in the communities, Inuit confidence in running the show grew. They began reshaping Western forms to include Inuit perspectives and values and questioning the status quo even where elected and appointed leaders were Inuit.

• *the decision to look both to the communities and to external 'experts' for answers.* In his book, *Promoting Change in Schools: Ground Level Practices That Work*, Jon Wiles observes that "outside assistance (consultants) are valuable in creating disequilibrium and in establishing a process or 'way' of changing" (Wiles 1993, 36). The Task Force recognized that community input had to be combined with a perspective on 'the state of the art' in schooling. Involvement of outside specialists added credibility to the Task Force's work in the eyes of KSB professionals as well as those of the larger educational community and government officials. "Connection with the wider environment is critical for success. The best organizations learn externally as well as internally" (Fullan 1993, 22).

Outside expertise and resources will be needed to continue improving the educational system in Nunavik, but each community must first identify the needs, develop and sustain the commitment to attack problems at the local level or the attempts at change will fade away and fail.

Unfinished Work

What remains to be done? As Nunavik residents facing the challenge to continue the educational change begun in the 1990s into the next millennium, they should:

• *keep the focus on reculturing.* Michael Fullan cautions those involved in educational change that "to restructure is not to reculture, but to reculture is to restructure" (Fullan 1993, 131). One strength of the Nunavik Educational Task Force's recommendations is their multi-institutional, holistic approach to meeting the educational needs of youth. Another is their focus on education from early childhood through adulthood. The Kativik School Board's reaction to this sweeping vision was in line with that of most school districts under similar circumstances – they rejected it and said the Task Force had not answered the questions asked. The School Board's desire to limit the number of people with real decision-making power about the system is an expected institutional response, but it does not have to be accepted.

Because the NETF recommendations deal with who has decision-making powers and with redesigning the purpose and function of schooling, they are particularly threatening.

Most educational change efforts deal only with changing the curricula and/or instructional techniques:

> Actually, the route to real reform pointed in a very
> different direction. America's national inadequacies,
> which we sense and which we attribute to our failing
> schools, have arisen not because our schools have
> changed, but precisely because they continue to do
> what they always have, in the same ways they always
> have. The authors of *A Nation At Risk*, like most
> of the reformers that their report has inspired, have
> failed to understand that genuine reform is not about
> repairing the dilapidated structure of traditional
> schooling. Instead, it is about discerning a new vision
> of what it means to educate and be educated in a
> world that is fundamentally different from the one
> our schools still believe themselves to inhabit ...
> Unfortunately, by urging reformers to address these
> symptoms of educational failure instead of to search
> for its true causes, the report sent our national reform
> effort off in the wrong direction. As a result, our
> crusade to reform U.S. education has itself become
> mired in crisis ... (Wilson and Daviss 1994, 4).

School change cannot just be the business of Nunavik's School Board. It must become the business of all Nunavik institutions. Unless educational functions are reflected in the ongoing staffing, budget and operations of institutions such as Makivik Corporation, the Kativik Regional Government and the Avataq Cultural Institute, the process will be too dependent on special funding and the initiative of individuals. When an individual sparkplug leaves an institution, too often the initiatives they began do not continue.

• *deepen the dialogue on educational change and continue to construct a shared reality.* "... complex changes in education sometimes require active (top-down or external) initiation, but if they are to go anywhere, there must be a good deal of shared control and decision making during implementation." (Fullan 1997, 31-32). The NETF community hearings and the subsequent *Satuigiarniq* ('reclaiming') process of community consultation were powerful vehicles for engaging all sectors of Nunavik society, not just elected leaders and professional educators, in discussions of school change. The challenge is to find ways to continue this real engagement and communication and, because the process is now in the hands of the Kativik School Board, not to fall back into the already accepted model of formal schooling, limiting input to the Commissioners, advisory boards, and staff.

The Nunavik educational system has not yet been brought fully under Inuit control. To do so will mean redefining education even if it puts Inuit at odds with the experts who 'know' the existing educational system. It will mean creating Inuit vehicles instead of focusing the debate about educational change within the parameters of that foreign format. Can the Nunavik government, and its educational arm, break the existing molds and design new approaches to education, combining Inuit values with economic sophistication and political savvy born of a new perspective on institutional form and function? They must if the needs of the young are going to be met.

• *tie school change to student and graduate success.* Traditional Inuit education 'worked' because its methods and purposes were clearly understood by all members of the community and because it effectively prepared young people for the pre-established roles and responsibilities they would inherit as adults – roles which have changed in contemporary Inuit society. Does schooling meet the region's, the community's, the individual's needs? Parents and children won't 'buy into' education until they see graduates succeeding. Are societal roles – parent, citizen – sufficient motivation to stay in school? Not if the education received is unrelated to those roles. Not if at the end of all that education there is no employment.

The difficulties Inuit face in creating employment opportunities in small Arctic communities with rapid population growth cannot be underestimated. But Inuit are taking over governmental and teaching jobs previously staffed by Qallunaat. Village economies are diversifying and employment opportunities are expanding beyond the public sector into private business, including retail, restaurants and hotels, entertainment, and tourism. Technological change is providing new opportunities. Web pages and related e-commerce will soon be able to operate out of Nunavik as well as New York.

"In every community, the daily lives of our youth must be the central focus of our labor in schools. Adults working within institutions and systems serving youth and their families must begin to communicate with one another to collaborate more fully in creating conditions for education success. The resilience of our youth should be celebrated and nurtured within the daily settings of families, schools, and communities, and also within the systems of health, justice and social welfare" (Swisher and Tippeconnic 1999, 302).

• *continue reflective engagement by all parties.* Inertia – keeping things going the way they are – and nostalgia – emphasizing how things were better in the past – both impede change. Nunavik has an advantage because of the youth of its system and the residents' ability to step back *before* formal schooling. But inertia and nostalgia develop very rapidly. In his book on promoting change in schools, Jon Wiles discusses sustaining the momentum of change:

> Most failed changes in education result from lost
> momentum. Since most change in schools originates
> from the idea of an individual or a source of funding,
> the driving force for changing is personality or money.
> Take away either of these items, and most educational
> change grinds to a halt. Most educational innovations
> last eighteen months, and our school culture is
> characterized by continuous unsuccessful change ...
> As a rule of thumb, I always feel that coming back
> with a bigger idea is a good tactic when anything
> small interrupts change. Also, use of outside resources
> or influence (e.g., a corporation) will normally override
> internal impediments. In short, if sidetracked, open
> up the field of play ... Once an expectation for positive
> change becomes institutionalized, change itself will
> become a professional task. (Wiles 1993, 191-92)

• *consummate regional self-government.* As the Inuit of Nunavik negotiate self-government with Quebec, the form and function of the regional education system is on the table for discussion. In its Final Report, the Nunavik Education Task Force chose to define an entirely new education system for the region. The March 2001 Report of the Nunavik Commission calls for the consolidation of existing regional institutions into a new government. If the Kativik School Board wishes to retain responsibility for the schools under the new regional government, it has to convince residents that it can provide quality education. If it does not, it can and should be replaced with a different vision for education.

In 1988, the Assembly of First Nations released a nationwide review of First Nations' education. That study found that while the Canadian government had endorsed the concept of Indian control of Indian education, it had "consistently defined

'Indian control' to mean merely First Nations' participation in and administration of previously developed formal education programs." The authors of *Tradition and Education: Towards A Vision of Our Future* identified as some of the requirements for genuine control of education by an indigenous community: adequate financial and human resources; training of education authority members; community, and particularly parental, involvement at all phases of the transfer and delivery of education; the presentation of educational options to the community; the development of an education philosophy, long-term plans and evaluation procedures at the beginning of the process to guide its implementation; policies and procedures consistent with the stated philosophy; hiring of qualified staff; sufficient administration and teacher preparation; language and culture-based curriculum development and programming; and access to, and utilization of, technology.

Using these criteria, the Quebec Inuit have achieved a great measure of authentic 'Native' control of education in their communities. But vigilance and a healthy skepticism is required to retain and support what they have accomplished. And determination and creativity will be needed to complete the task.

The Potential Impact of Indigenous Models on Western Schooling

How transportable is the Nunavik educational experience to other communities, Native and non-Native?

European and other colonizers have tended to justify their treatment of indigenous peoples by emphasizing the deficiencies in Natives' cultures. In an essay on "The Unnatural History of American Indian Education," Karen Cayton Swisher and John W. Tippeconnic III describe how teachers in federal boarding and other Indian schools "turned to stereotypes of Indian emotional and physical 'deficiencies' to explain student behavior and to justify federal reshaping of Indian emotional life and expression" and the application of "specific pedagogical methods ... needed to overcome deficits in mental, moral and physical characteristics" (Swisher and Tippeconnic 1999, 17,19). What had been termed 'deficiencies' in the 19th and first half of the 20th centuries was relabeled 'disadvantaged' in the more politically correct 1960s and 1970s. Both terms rested on the need to impose Western approaches over indigenous approaches.

In a larger context, Native communities do have contributions they can make – rooted in traditional values – to the redesign of schooling in the 21st century. Recognition of these innovations will require moving away from the 'deficiency' model which has dominated education of indigenous people to one based on cultural strengths.

Indigenous people are creating their own educational systems. In the United States, recognition of tribal sovereignty provides the opening for innovation. "Numerous studies and reports have concluded that tribal/local control of formal education in schools is absolutely necessary if education for American Indians is to improve significantly ... Local or tribal control is also a basic principal inherent in the sovereignty status of American Indian tribes. The current federal policy of tribal self-determination, supported by legislation, provided the administrative mechanism for tribes to assume greater control over their own affairs, including education" (K. Tsiaina Lowawaima in Swisher and Tippeconnic 1999, 34). Self-governance in Nunavik will expand the rights and responsibilities acknowledged in the James Bay and Northern Quebec Agreement. The Inuit don't have to do it the way it was done in the schools they themselves attended.

Native communities should have confidence in what indigenous educational practices can contribute to, and in some case reinforce in, the theory and practice of educational change for all schools. Specifically:

• *learning based in a profound connection to societal roles.* Traditional Inuit education 'worked' because all members of the community clearly understood its methods and purposes and because it effectively prepared young people for the pre-established roles and responsibilities they would inherit as adults. Formal schooling is too often divorced from the societies it operates in. "When I say that schools have been intractable to reform, I mean that for the large majority of students, including most from non-poverty backgrounds, the declared aims of schooling are empty rhetoric that bears little relationship to their social experiences" (Sarason 1990, 4).

• *an emphasis on performance-based assessment.* In the traditional Inuit lifestyle, education was part of day-to-day living. It was not something you studied, it was something you did. The essence of education was getting ready to assume adult life roles. The pace varied with each child – there were no set ages for acquiring skills or precise paths which had to be followed. A child began to learn a skill when he or she began to pay attention, to notice how an adult did something, and to try to imitate those actions.

Young people demonstrated successful learning through performance. A boy showed he had learned to hunt by bringing in game, by feeding the community. A girl became a woman when she could preserve food for the winter's meals, when her boots kept her family's feet dry, when she trimmed the wick on the oil lamp so that it provided the amount of light and heat needed in her home.

• *multi-generational input.* Authentically engaging the consumers in defining – and achieving – the end goals is one key to school change. This is where most formal systems fail and the traditional ways succeeded. It may not be easy for parents to verbalize what they want from education, and their own negative experiences with schooling may also impede the process. But it is essential to involve them. Engaged students have the clearest of goals and are the least encumbered with institutional or community politics and agendas.

Indigenous cultures have traditionally honored elders and acknowledged their role as keepers of history and values. Their perspectives, their grounding in cultural strengths, are needed most particularly in times of pervasive change, when societies fear they have lost the old trails and have not found the new. Western cultures are tempted by change for change's sake. Youth dominates marketing and media, diminishing the role of older citizens and denying society their contributions.

• *teaching through coaching.* Indigenous cultures traditionally teach by example and apprenticeship. Adults do not lecture children; they model the skills needed to accomplish tasks. "Few teachers have been shown that effective teaching is itself a higher order skill. Most have never seen it practiced as such, and virtually none have been taught to coach students towards mastery instead of to teach it by information transfer" (Wilson and Daviss 1994, 84).

• *education rooted in values.* In a recent book on research and practice to advance Indian Education, Gregory Cajete, a Tewa from Santa Clara Pueblo in New Mexico, articulately describes the grounding many Native students have in traditional values: "A Native student's constellation of values has ancient and well-developed roots in the tribal social psyche. It is because of these deep-rooted values that unconscious aspects of Native American social personalities remain so durable and relatively visible through layers of acculturation ... Research from a variety of sources supports the notion that an insightful, well-integrated, and consistent cognitive map and worldview leads to a healthy concept of self and positive social adjustment. The opposite condition is usually apparent when chronic inconsistencies and conflicts arise between the internal constellation of values and those of the external social environment" (Swisher and Tippeconnic 1999, 137). The knowledge of what matters can give indigenous communities an advantage in designing their educational systems.

This does not mean that Western school systems ought to adopt indigenous values for their own but rather that they should acknowledge the importance of grounding education in more than content area knowledge and academic skills. "If we took this scenario [of designing a home] into education, the routine would be very similar. But instead of styles of houses, the educator would speak of philosophies that are formal statements of values and other foundational undergirding. If such values and priorities were clear, the development of an effective educational program would be a simple logical and deductive process. If, on the other hand, the client had no clear idea about what is desired in schools, he or she would probably react to the environment and select from those choices perceived as available. Unfortunately, much of the change in schools is of the 'selection' variety, and such a pattern over time will lead to chaos" (Wiles 1993, 9).

• *co-operative/collaborative orientation.* Indigenous societies emphasize learning and working co-operatively in the context of the community. Teachers have long observed that Native students prefer small-group, collaborative work to whole class activities or working in isolation. Research is increasingly supporting this approach as effective instructionally:

> *One* major conclusion that can be drawn from
> this research literature is that where co-operative
> learning is implemented, classrooms do not become
> disorganized, disorganizing, and chaotic places ... A
> *second* conclusion is that the level of student interest
> and motivation is far higher than in the usual "whole
> class" method of teaching. A *third* conclusion is that
> using the criterion of academic achievement, the
> co-operative, small-group approach is as effective as
> the conventional one and, more often than not, is
> superior. A *final* conclusion is that, depending on the
> particular focus of the research study and the outcome

measures used, the small-group method changes racial and ethnic attitude in a desirable direction" (Sarason 1990, 89-90).

• *concern for future generations*. Just as respect for elders is a core value in traditional Native communities, so too is concern for the impact of today's actions on the next generation and the one that follows it. Indeed, consideration is frequently given to the needs out to the seventh generation. Authentic school change requires putting the needs of the next generation ahead of those of the system.

• *viewing the world holistically*. Traditional indigenous peoples see the world holistically. Change in one part impacts every other. In the words of Onondaga elder Audrey Shenandoah, "There is no word for 'nature' in my language. Nature, in English, seems to refer to that which is separate from human beings. It is a distinction we don't recognize. The closest words to the idea of 'nature' translate to refer to things which support life" (Wall and Arden 1990, 26).

In an essay on "The Imperative for Systemic Change," Indiana University Professor Charles Reigeluth lists the major differences between the Industrial Age and the Information Age that affect education (Reigeluth and Garfinkle 1994, 6):

Industrial Age	*Information Age*
Adversarial relationships	Cooperative relationships
Bureaucratic organization	Team organization
Autocratic leadership	Shared leadership
Centralized control	Autonomy with accountability
Autocracy	Democracy
Representative democracy	Participative democracy
Compliance	Initiative
One-way communications	Networking
Compartmentalization	Holism
(Division of labor)	(Integration of Tasks)

Reigeluth also contrasts the emerging features of an Information-Age educational system with those of the Industrial Age school system (Reigeluth and Garfinkle 1994, 8):

Industrial Age	*Information Age*
Grade levels	Continuous progress
Covering the content	Outcomes-based learning
Norm-referenced testing	Individualized testing
Non-authentic assessment	Performance-based assessment
Group-based content delivery	Personal learning plans
Adversarial learning	Cooperative learning
Classrooms	Learning centers
Teacher as dispenser of knowledge	Teacher as coach or facilitator
Memorization of meaningless facts	Thinking, problem-solving skills, meaning-making
Isolated reading, writing skills	Communication skills
Books as tools	Advanced technologies as tools

Indigenous ways of teaching and learning echo many of the features Reigeluth proposes as necessary components of Information Age educational systems.

• *adaptability and willingness to adopt what works and supports survival.* Throughout their history, the Inuit have adopted and adapted technologies to meet their needs and improve their lives. The Inuit have survived in the Arctic for millennia by successfully adapting to changing conditions. Their culture in the 15th century was not the same as it had been 500 years earlier. When the Thule people, ancestors of today's Inuit, had first come to Canada's Arctic, the weather had been warmer, the ice less, and the big whales closer to shore. The weather turned colder, the migration patterns of the whales changed in response to the sea ice, new methods had to be developed to hunt on and under the ice and on land for new sources of nourishment. As they came into each new area, the people adapted their lives to the weather and food resources they found there. They adapted existing tools or invented the new technology they needed to survive in each environment.

The Inuit of Quebec have made great strides toward redefining education from the ground up and creating a school system which is based on Inuit values and the concerns and goals which they have for their children. Providing the variety and depth of training needed to prepare their young as Inuit and as members of the world community in the 21st century will be a daunting challenge. Building a regional economy that can provide employment opportunities for a rapidly increasing population will be equally difficult. The Inuit of Quebec bring to these challenges traditions of survival, co-operative sharing of resources, and innovative adaptation to changing environmental and social conditions. As they redefine education for their young, they will develop processes and institutions which work for them and may be of use to others concerned with reforming education in their own communities.

The Preamble to the 1989 Nunavik Constitution sets forth the tasks facing the Inuit of Quebec:

> WE, THE PEOPLE OF NUNAVIK, enjoying a special relationship to the land and wanting to govern ourselves on the principles of the supremacy of God, the rule of law and the equality of all peoples, hereby create and agree to live by this Constitution.
>
> AND:
>
> RECOGNIZING our right to maintain our freedom, our languages and our traditions;
>
> RECOGNIZING that an adequate land and resource base as well as a strong economic base are essential for the effective exercise of self-government in Nunavik;
>
> RECOGNIZING the need for us to clarify our status within Quebec and Canada and to create a new basis for our relationship with them;
>
> RECOGNIZING our desire to affirm, unify and protect our distinct cultural and linguistic ties;

RECOGNIZING the particular and special role of the communities and local administrations of Nunavik as central to the underlying strength and future of Nunavik;

RECOGNIZING that our participation in the development of renewable and non-renewable resources of Nunavik are essential to our present and future of Nunavik;

RECOGNIZING our desire and need to promote greater economic self-reliance for Nunavik;

AND WE FURTHER AFFIRM AND DECLARE:

THAT we alone are the ones responsible for our future and the survival and growth of our cultural identity;

AND we assume responsibility for the protection of our fragile environment; the development of our economies; and the education and welfare of our people;

AND

WE FURTHER COMMIT OURSELVES to determine in a spirit of co-operation the arrangements for practical achievement of these ends within the larger provincial and national legal and political framework of which we are part;

AND TO CARRY OUT these objects and aspirations and to promote and protect these many rights, for both present and future generations, in a fair, open, equitable and responsible manner, we hereby create through this Constitution a Charter of Rights and Freedoms and an elected Regional Assembly drawn from the people of Nunavik with a responsible Executive branch of government and an independent Judicial branch.

Appendices

A

Education Provisions of the James Bay and Northern Quebec Agreement

17.0.2 The Kativik School Board shall be governed by the provisions of the Education Act (1964, R.S.Q., c. 235, as amended) and all other applicable laws of general application in the Province, save where these laws are inconsistent with this Section, in which event the provisions of this Section shall prevail.

17.0.3 The School Board shall have jurisdiction and responsibility for pre-school, elementary, secondary and adult education.

The School Board shall also have, subject only to the annual approval of its budget by the Minister, the power to enter into agreements, concerning post-secondary education for persons in the jurisdiction.

17.0.59 The teaching languages shall be Inuttitut and with respect to the other languages, in accordance with the present practice of the territory. The Kativik School Board will pursue as an objective the use of French as a language of instruction so that pupils graduating from its schools will, in the future, be capable of continuing their studies in a French school, college or university elsewhere in Québec, if they so desire.

After consultation with the parents' committee, and having regard to the requirements of subsequent education, the commissioners shall determine the rate of introduction of French and English as teaching languages.

17.0.63 The Kativik School Board may establish a curriculum development center whose functions shall be:

1. to select courses, textbooks and materials appropriate for the Inuit population and arrange for their experimental use, evaluation and eventual approval;

2. to develop courses, textbooks and teaching materials in the Inuttitut language with a view to preserving and perpetuating the language and culture of the Inuit people;
3. to enter into agreements with persons, institutions, colleges or universities with a view to developing courses, textbooks and teaching materials corresponding to the programs and services it offers.

17.0.64 The Council may by ordinance provide for the establishment of programs, the teaching of subjects and the use of teaching materials in Inuttitut, English and French, based on Inuit culture and Inuttitut.

17.0.65 All ordinances shall be forthwith transmitted to the Minister of Education upon their passing. The Minister shall review such ordinances within forty (40) days and, except where the matters dealt with therein are based on Inuit culture and language, may disallow same in writing. Unless disallowed, all ordinances shall automatically come into force (40) days after the date of their passing or any earlier date indicated by the Minister.

17.0.66 It shall be the duty of the Kativik School Board to engage teachers duly qualified to teach in the schools under its control ... Section 203(1) of the Education Act shall not apply.

17.0.67 The Kativik School Board may establish by ordinance one or more school calendars, making use of existing rules but taking into consideration as well the special needs of its clientele. Such a calendar may consist of fewer than 180 school days provided that the time devoted to instruction remains the same.

17.0.68 The Kativik School Board shall, in consultation with the Minister of Education, negotiate the working conditions of its employees, except basic salary, basic marginal benefits and basic work load which are negotiated at the provincial level.

17.0.69 The Kativik School Board may establish by ordinance special training courses for teachers of Inuttitut, English and French, allowing the Inuit to be qualified as elementary and secondary school teachers and non-Inuit who are called upon to teach in schools of the school board to become familiar with the special needs of its clientele. Such courses may be given at schools of the school board or at any other place determined by the school board.

17.0.74 The Council may establish by ordinance qualifications and employment criteria for Native teachers involved in the teaching of Inuit culture and language. Such teachers shall not be subject to the provisions of the regulations in effect concerning teachers' qualifications.

17.0.80 Any child who maintains or helps to maintain his family may be declared exempt from compulsory school attendance by the Kativik School Board.

17.0.83 Subject to budgetary approval, provisions shall be made for maintaining the necessary levels of financial aid to students attending school outside the Territory when following courses not offered by the Kativik School Board.

17.0.84 Québec and Canada will jointly maintain, through the Kativik School Board, adequate funding for educational services and programs presently available to the population in the Territory.

17.0.85 Based on actual budgets providing for operating and capital costs approved by a joint committee named by Québec and Canada, each of the said Governments shall contribute to the approved budget of the Kativik School Board on the following basis:

Québec 75%
Canada 25%

This provision shall take effect two years after the execution of the Agreement.

Commencing in 1982 and every five (5) years thereafter, the percentage contribution of Québec and Canada shall be reviewed taking into account changes in the ratio of Native students to non-Native students under the jurisdiction of, and receiving services from, the Kativik School Board.

17.0.86 The Kativik School Board may make recommendations to the Lieutenant Governor in Council to declare inapplicable, in whole or in part, any regulation enacted under the Education Act which may affect it.

17.0.87 This Section shall come into force gradually over a minimum transition period of two (2) years to be jointly determined by the Kativik School Board and the Minister, beginning with the first complete school year following the execution of this Agreement...

17.0.88 The provision of this Section can only be amended with the consent of Québec and the interested Native party, save for the provisions of paragraphs 17.0.76, 17.0.77, 17.0.84 and 17.0.85 which in addition shall require the consent of Canada.

Legislation enacted to give effect to the provisions of this Section may be amended from time to time by the National Assembly of Québec.

B

November 1986 KSB Newsletter Anngutivik article on negotiations with the Quebec Ministry of Education

"Kativik School Board Meets With Minister of Education – A meeting took place on May 23rd between the Minister of Education Claude Ryan and the Kativik School Board Executive Committee and senior staff to discuss several unresolved issues. These included funding for program and material development, post-secondary activities, teacher training, building security and Adult Education. Discussion also centred on the Board's teacher allocation and overall budget conditions.

"The budget allocated to the School Board has been insufficient for the last six years due to the fact that the Board was placed under a fixed budget three years after it assumed the responsibility for education in Northern Quebec. Because the Board was only three years old, there was no way to identify all the needs in that short period. Thus, when the budget was frozen, needs such as student services, special education and post-secondary education had not yet been identified. Contrary to other school boards in the various regions, Kativik received very little in supplementary budgets for either special projects or specific needs.

"According to the James Bay and Northern Quebec Agreement, Kativik School Board has the mandate to develop a school curriculum to meet the specific needs of Inuit culture and language. Due to the School Board's frozen budget, limited funds have been given for this purpose, and while many needs have been identified and expenses incurred, the amount allocated has been merely indexed over the years. The School Board was encouraged by the Minister's recognition of the need for adequate funding.

"The School Board also has the mandate to train Inuit teachers. A request was made in 1982 to the Ministry of Education to increase the number of credits for the basic Teacher Training program from 30 to 45. It has taken almost four years for the

Ministry to finally approve the program extension. The budget for Teacher Training has been indexed, but it only covers the training of classroom teachers and certain language specialists enrolled in the 45-credit McGill University program. No extra funding has been received as yet for the training of culture and religion teachers. If Kativik School Board is to move into more specialized areas so that Inuit can be trained to teach in all subject areas and at all levels, the Ministry of Education has to increase training budgets and must respond to the Board's requests within reasonable time limits.

"The School Board is approaching a crisis situation concerning funding for post-secondary students studying in the South. The Minister stated that the students of Northern Quebec had the right to post-secondary education, and should never be refused that right ... While the James Bay and Northern Quebec Agreement doesn't specifically state that Kativik School Board has jurisdiction over post-secondary education, article 17.0.84 states that 'Quebec and Canada will jointly maintain, through the Kativik School Board, adequate funding for educational services and programs presently available to the population in the Territory.' Before Kativik School Board was created, the federal government had funds for post-secondary education. Therefore once the School Board took over the administration of education in the territory, it was entitled to receive these funds...

"The School Board has been very dissatisfied with the number of teachers allocated to it in the last three years. The number does not provide for specific needs such as special education and pre-kindergarten. The base number of teachers which the School Board has been allowed by the Ministry of Education is insufficient due to the following important factors: The limited experience of southern teachers – approximately 50% are on probation, while 80% have five years of experience or less. 80% of the Inuit teachers are still in training. 20% of the students have serious hearing losses, and there are students in several communities with other learning disabilities. Secondary teachers carry an immense load – they are expected to be generalists, unlike those in the South who specialize in one or two subjects. Children have very limited opportunities to express themselves in the second language outside of class. And finally, southern teachers must first adapt to the learning patterns of Inuit children, and all teachers must play a role in the development, experimentation and validation of programs, curriculum and materials.

"Certain groupings were recommended by the Ministry of Education in order to minimize the number of teachers required. These groupings cannot possibly work, because it would mean asking a teacher to teach six or seven subjects at three or four levels, or it would mean combining children in their first year of second language instruction with children in their second or third year. The School Board has devised a formula to determine the number of teachers needed to give the children of Northern Quebec the education to which they are entitled. The formula includes automatic allocation for pre-kindergarten classes, supplementary allocation for children with learning disabilities, special allocation for Inuttitut and culture teachers, and supplementary allocation for children to be taught at home (due to sickness). The School Board is presently waiting for the professionals within the Ministry of Education to study the request for additional teachers, and hopes to get a favourable reply very quickly.

"Since there are no housing provisions for adult education teachers who teach full-time in the North, the School Board requested additional funding for this purpose. The Ministry responded that no additional funds would be allocated, and that Adult Education housing could probably become an integral part of the School Board's regular sector construction needs. The School Board's five-year construction plan is full with the many other requests for regular sector facilities which also must be taken into consideration. The shortage of Adult Education staff housing means that many communities will have no or very seriously reduced Adult Education services available to them.

"Discussion took place concerning the request for a gymnasium in Salluit. At the time the Ikusiq School was built, the School Board had a contract with the municipality to use the Recreation Hall for physical education, and thus could not get funding for a gymnasium to be built in the new school...

"When Kativik School Board lost its third school to fire last year, additional funding was requested from the Ministry of Education for night security people. No response was ever received..."

C

Symposium '85 Workshop Recommendations

One of the strengths of Symposium '85 was the variety and scope of the workshops presented. In its report on the Symposium, the School Board summarized major recommendations made by conference attendees during the workshop sessions (numbers are the workshop number on the conference agenda).

1. The Inuttitut Reading and Writing Program

... Many of the workshop participants were impressed by how far Inuttitut materials development has come, though many felt that the School Board could use a lot of extra help from Inuit versed in Inuit traditions to work on producing more materials. The majority agreed that the teaching of Inuttitut was one of the most important responsibilities of the School Board.

Participants recommended that more time should be devoted to teaching Inuttitut at higher grade levels; Inuttitut words no longer in common usage should be taught; parents should also teach their children Inuttitut, and they should try to speak in pure Inuttitut (i.e., without English words) to reinforce what is taught at school; provisions should be made to continue teaching Inuttitut to post-secondary students, and to the children of Inuit who go South to work; Inuit teachers should get more assistance from counsellors; Education Committees should meet with Inuit teachers more often; and credits, recognized by the Ministry of Education, should be awarded to students upon completion of their Inuttitut studies.

2. Methods in Developing School Materials

Recommendations were that the Language Commission (located in the Avataq Cultural Institute) be involved in the development of school materials, and in reviewing the finished products; that a joint meeting be held twice a year between the Kativik School Board and the Language Commission; that an elder man be engaged to help develop more male-oriented school materials; that Inuit themes be used when writing stories, rather than using stories like "The Three Pigs" and "Goldilocks"; and that somebody be hired to co-ordinate the production of Inuttitut teaching materials between Avataq, the Kativik School Board Inuttitut Program Development Department, and the Northern Quebec Language Commission.

8. Creative Computing

... The animators stressed the necessity of creating educational computer programs which reflect Inuit ways of thinking and Inuit ways of building ideas. It was found that some people have fears regarding computers, and that participants in general have lots of questions.

The questions included whether children could become sick from working with computers too long; what happens to children emotionally and sociologically if they work with computers instead of interacting with other children; can computers change children's thinking patterns; and will only those people with computer training be able to find jobs in the future?

While some people felt that computers could too easily be misused, a lot of the workshop participants agreed that the computer provided a very positive way of learning, since students seem to be drawn to it naturally and are curious about it. There was also general agreement that computers will free people to do more interesting and worthwhile work.

Participants in this workshop recommended that the Kativik School Board provide training to secondary students and adults on how to use the computer as a job-related working tool; that the School Board does not use the computer with very young students until the research project being conducted at Laval University has been completed, and has shown the computer to be a safe and good educational tool for young students; and, that Inuit teachers be part of, and actively involved in, this research project.

11. Culture Programs

Participants felt that classroom sessions devoted to teaching culture should be longer than one hour; that womanhood should be taught at the secondary level, including sex education and pregnancy from an Inuit traditional perspective; that the archives collection belonging to the Federation of Co-ops should be circulated to all the schools; that culture teachers should construct a small tent in which to keep Inuit traditional materials, and in which to teach Inuit culture, values and life in general, and that Inuit culture programs should be developed at the university level.

12. Philosophy of Inuit Education

The different education systems which have operated in Northern Quebec were discussed with respect to course content, teaching methods, and advantages and disadvantages of each system. The difficulties encountered when Inuit try to learn through a Southern education system were described and the reasons why Inuit students should learn in Inuttitut first were explained.

Participants' comments were varied and included concerns that young people are being brought up by the ways of two different cultures and that Inuit should raise their children according to their own ways; that Elders should be respected for their knowledge; that the different organizations in the North should support education, so that the future of Inuit can be more certain – the more the Inuit are in unison, the stronger they are; that the teaching of culture should be accorded more hours; that the prevention of alcohol and drug abuse should be taught; that teachers and parents should communicate with each other to benefit the students; that religion should be taught at every grade level; that only certified teachers should teach; and that even though Inuit separate into communities, no community should see itself as better than any other.

13. Learning in a Second Language

Concerns expressed by participants included whether students will learn as well with the materials and programs presently being developed; whether teachers are taught how to teach the Kativik School Board second language programs; whether Southern teachers are sensitized to the Inuit culture and to the characteristics of Inuit children (before being sent to the communities); whether the second language counsellors are involved in the language development of the other programs (i.e., science, math, social studies); how the transition from Inuttitut to English or French affects the students; and whether the existing KSB programs will permit the students to pursue post-secondary studies in Southern institutions.

14. Adult Education and Regional Employment Strategies

Speaking on behalf of the Kativik School Board Adult Education students, Akenisie Qumaaluk: "There is a serious lack of facilities, teachers, courses and good boarding homes for Adult Education students. Insufficient housing is responsible for the lack of teachers and, subsequently, lack of courses in Adult Education. Typewriters, computers and textbooks are also needed. Many Adult Education students can't attend relevant courses given in other communities because of family and job responsibilities."

15. Towards the Holistic View of the Child

External factors which cause children to lose concentration were explained. Student counsellors participating in the workshops expressed concerns that all communities should have student counsellors; that student counsellors should work more closely with other organizations such as Social Services, hospitals and NNADAP (Northern Native Alcohol and Drug Abuse Program) so that students can get the help they need; and that more training should be provided for student counsellors. It was recommended that Education Committees in all communities formulate recommendations as to how the Kativik School Board can work towards meeting all the needs of the children. Participants also felt there should be more community effort and involvement in organizing activities at night for both adults and youths, including ongoing traditional activities. Efforts should also be made to bring more religion back to the communities.

Many of the recommendations concerned parental relationships including that the School Board should promote a policy that parents must play a larger role in terms of promoting the importance of education and in disciplining their children; that more support must be given by the parents to the teachers and counsellors; that discussion and information meetings should be held with parents concerning the total needs of the child; that parenting (child-rearing) programs should be made available in the communities; that parents should be good examples to their children. The comment was made that making people aware of the changes that have occurred in their lives as Inuit from the 1950's to the present may help people realize how these changes have affected their lives as Inuit and as parents and allow parents to gain more control of their own lives and to make the family unit a priority. Parents were encouraged to take a greater interest in education – to provide more input on education matters, and to see that their children not only attended school regularly, but that they also completed their education.

D

Makivik AGM Resolution Establishing NETF

WHEREAS   the Kativik School Board was requested by
Makivik Corporation to conduct a workshop of
Inuit education as part of the 1989 Makivik
Annual General Assembly;

WHEREAS   this request was based on the fact that Makivik
has, as one of its corporate objectives, "to promote
the welfare and the advancement of education of
the Inuit."

WHEREAS   Kativik School Board has jurisdiction and
responsibility for elementary, secondary and adult
education according to the James Bay and Northern
Quebec Agreement and the Education Act;

WHEREAS   in a discussion paper prepared by Makivik for
the educational workshop, the challenges faced
by the Kativik School Board in meeting its
responsibilities for developing the educational
services and programs needed to meet the current
and future needs of Inuit are recognized;

WHEREAS   on the basis of the points raised in this discussion
paper the workshop delegates reviewed the present
status and future development of education in
Nunavik;

WHEREAS   the Makivik Assembly recognized the importance
of education and the need to support the
continuing progress of Kativik School Board and
recommended that the work of the School Board
could be strengthened by the information that
would result from a review of the status of
education in Nunavik that would be carried out by
an independent task force;

On a motion moved by Minnie Grey, and seconded by Jobie
Epoo, it was unanimously resolved:

THAT An independent task force be created in order
to identify the educational successes as well as
the difficulties now encountered by Kativik School
Board;

THAT The task force would be chaired by
co-chairpersons, one of whom would be from
the outside with expertise in education and the
other would be from Nunavik. Additional members
would be determined by the co-chairpersons and
subject to acceptance by both the Kativik School
Board and the Makivik Corporation;

THAT The task force would follow a schedule and
procedure that would include a consultation
process that would be accessible to everyone within
the communities and institutions of Nunavik as
well as to other groups involved with, or having
expertise about, the development of education for
the Inuit of Nunavik;

THAT The task force would conduct their work through
public hearings and other meetings, written and
oral submissions and other appropriate means and
it would have the power to request special studies;

THAT The task force would report regularly to Makivik
Corporation and Kativik School Board. At the end
of its mandate, the task force will submit a final
report that summarizes their findings and states
specific recommendations to the Kativik School
Board and Makivik Corporation;

THAT The task force will be guided in its work
but not limited by the following points:
To consider the languages of education including
the importance of Inuttitut at all levels of education;
To examine both programs and school
curriculum in terms of their relevance to
educational objectives and standards as required
to meet the needs of the population;

To suggest ways in which parents, families and other institutions or organizations, can promote education in Nunavik including the development of extracurricular activities that will encourage good study habits and foster an interest in learning;

To examine educational development in relationship to a social and economic situation that now exists within the communities and which may serve to foster or retard the success of students at all educational levels;

To examine ways of encouraging and supporting students at the post-secondary level in academic, technical and vocational programs including the feasibility of offering post-secondary courses in the North, the establishment of "catch-up" programs, the creation of a CEGEP program that could respond more effectively to the special academic and social needs of Inuit students; and the possible role of private schools;

To recognize the critical importance of increasing the numbers and encouraging the further development of a core of Inuit teachers and to examine the ways in which non-Native teachers can become more effective in northern teaching.

E

Winter 1990 KSB Newsletter Anngutivik article on creation of the Nunavik Educational Task Force

"Independent Task Force to Study Education in Nunavik At the 1989 Annual General Meeting of Makivik Corporation, the Kativik School Board was asked to conduct a workshop on Inuit education. The purpose of this workshop was to review and evaluate the problems that must still be solved so that the Kativik School Board can deliver the best possible educational services to the residents of Nunavik. On the basis of the issues and concerns raised during this workshop, it was recommended that an independent Task Force be created to review educational policy and programs at all educational levels.

"A formal resolution creating the Nunavik Educational Task Force and describing its mandates was approved by the Makivik Annual General Meeting on March 21, 1989. The Kativik School Board gave its approval to the resolution and agreed to contribute one-half of its operating budget.

"Mandate of the Nunavik Educational Task Force: The Nunavik Educational Task Force will focus its attention on six major issues that affect the quality of education from primary through post-secondary levels including adult education. These issues are: 1) the languages of education including the importance of Inuttitut and the acquisition of second language fluency in English or French; 2) the content and quality of the school curriculum required for the academic or vocational needs of Inuit students; 3) the Inuit and non-Native teacher training programs required to develop a qualified core of professionally competent teachers; 4) the academic requirements needed for Inuit students to be successful in post-secondary education and advanced technical training; 5) the adult education programs that will best upgrade academic and vocational skills of Inuit; 6) the critical role of the family and community to support and encourage educational objectives.

"Organization: The Nunavik Educational Task Force is comprised of two primary units: an Educational Review Committee and Pedagogical Working Groups.

"The Educational Review Committee will be the primary body responsible for directing all of the activities needed to carry out the mandate of the Task Force and for writing a final report that will state the findings, recommend solutions and identify procedures for implementing these solutions. This Review Committee will select the members and supervise the activities of the Pedagogical Working Groups.

"The Review Committee is comprised of six Inuit who will be assisted by a Technical Advisor and Project Coordinator. The six members are: Johnny Adams, Minnie Grey, Josephie Padlayat, Mary Simon, Aani Tulugak and Jobie Epoo. The Co-ordinator is Wendy Ellis and the Technical Advisor is Bill Kemp.

"Five Pedagogical Working Groups will be established to carry out the specific work required to accomplish the mandate of the Task Force. Each Working Group will be comprised of at least three members, one of which must be a professional educator with expertise on the mandated topic.

"The Educational Review Committee and the Pedagogical Working Groups will require the active participation and co-operation of individuals and groups in all Nunavik communities. One of the first priorities of the Educational Review Committee is to develop a process that will enable individuals and community groups to state their concerns and opinions on issues identified in the mandate of the Task Force.

"Schedule of Activities: Members of the Educational Review Committee were selected by Makivik Corporation and Kativik School Board. Their first meeting was held in December 1989. Members of the Pedagogical Working Groups will be selected in early 1990.

"The Educational Review Committee and the Pedagogical Working Groups will carry out their work from January to December 1990. The Nunavik Educational Task Force will present its final report to all northern organizations and community delegates at the 1991 Makivik Annual General Meeting."

F

Interim Report of the NETF

The Language of Education: "... The primary role of the Task Force will be to carefully review all aspects of the language policy and program in relationship to curriculum material, teaching methods, and the values applied to Inuttitut and second language learning ... In addition, two other language related issues will have to be considered. The first issue involves the incredible demands currently placed on the educational system because it must now respond at an early stage of its development to providing quality materials and instruction in three languages. It is important for the Task Force to ask if these language demands may, in fact, overwhelm the educational system at this time. The second issue that will be reviewed by the Task Force is the policy of the School Board for evaluating the language ability and grade levels of students."

The School Curriculum: "Questions of curriculum development are linked very closely to those of language. It is certain that good language skills in Inuttitut and in English or French cannot be obtained unless language learning is supported by well-developed curriculum materials ... The Educational Task Force will review the policy as well as the specific objectives and content of the curriculum at all educational levels including adult education."

Encouraging Good Teaching: "The essential core of all educational programs is defined through the quality, commitment and dedication of teachers ... The creation of an Inuit teaching staff is a tremendously difficult undertaking, and many questions must still be addressed. The teacher training program that has been developed over the past years will be reviewed from the point of view of the School Board as well as from the perspective of the Inuit teachers. Are Inuit teachers satisfied with their training and what changes would they like to see in the program in order for them to further improve their knowledge of subject matter and teaching skills?

"The second major concern for the development of good teaching throughout Nunavik must address the quality and competence of non-Inuit teachers. The development of non-Inuit teachers involves questions of southern university training in relationship to the particular requirements of education in Nunavik. The Task Force will be asking the teachers themselves to comment on questions of qualifications, turnover and the difficulties in teaching in another cultural setting ... The Task Force will work with both Inuit and non-Inuit teachers in their review."

Education After High School: "... At the present time, all post-secondary schooling for either academic or professional purposes requires Inuit students to come to the South. Although this in itself can be an important educational experience, most students have found the change from a northern to a southern educational system very difficult. As a consequence, many students have returned home before finishing their course of study.

"The problems identified by students who have attended post-secondary schools almost always relate to some combination of difficult social adjustments to the South and a lack of academic preparation from their northern school ... The Educational Task Force will review the situation that now exists for post-secondary education. In particular, it will identify goals and objectives as defined by the students, teachers, pedagogical counselors and others in order to see where conflicts occur."

Family and Community Responsibilities: "The need to involve families and communities in the educational process at all academic levels is an essential part of educational development in Nunavik. The work of the Task Force will focus on four primary questions. The *first* question asks what can be done to create a better understanding by parents and family of the importance of education. The *second* question to be asked by the Task Force is how parents, family and community can participate in the day-to-day operation of the school. Parents and other community groups must be given a voice and the tools required to work with the school in a constructive manner. The *third* question asks how can the school facilities and its human resources be best utilized for extra-curricular activities and how can opportunities for out-of-school studying or other learning experiences be provided. This question is essential if the inter-relationships between the schools and the community are to work effectively. The *fourth* question relates to the role that the school can play to help alleviate social tensions and problems of drug and alcohol abuse that affect so many families and therefore students. The issues of substance abuse, suicide, violent behavior and disillusionment must be addressed at school, and through active intervention and leadership these issues must become a topic of active debate."

The Role Of Adult Education: "The final mandate of the Education Task Force will be to review the importance and role of adult education. It must be assumed that regardless of how effective the lower grade curriculum is or will become, there will always be a need for the continuing education of adults. Although there will always be the need for retraining in the rapidly changing work place of today, adult education should also provide an opportunity for people to improve their academic skills and to pursue their personal development."

G

NETF Report to the 1991 Makivik AGM

The written report began by acknowledging "the many years of hard work and selfless dedication given by the women and men who have built and established the Kativik School Board. Some of them will, no doubt, object to parts of this report that question particular structures and priorities. We hope that natural response will not prevent them from renewing their obvious commitment to education in Nunavik. It's time to move on...

"The study plan that had been developed for us by those initially engaged to establish the Task Force was narrowly focused and left no room to ask the kinds of questions we needed to ask in order to learn what quality education was and how to achieve it. All attempts to open up the inquiry or to bring in anyone critical of Kativik School Board's operations was met with stiff resistance from anyone connected to KSB. The message seemed to be that KSB already had all the answers, people who were critical were simply unobjective, and that if we just looked at what KSB was doing carefully enough we would understand all we needed to know...

"The significance of this connection between KSB and Ministère de l'Education du Quebec (MEQ) is very great ... for technical reasons that will be explained fully in the final report, the MEQ curriculum is set up in such a way that it cannot be easily adapted to community-based education, and in any case KSB did not have the expertise to do the job. So what happened is that the program that was supposed to be 'home grown' in Nunavik was actually imported from MEQ. Then, to add to the difficulty, KSB's adaptations seemed to be undermining the academic strength of the MEQ programs so that students were not getting a culturally appropriate education, but they also were not getting an education with enough quality to be successful in post-secondary studies.

"As we proceeded to uncover some of the difficulties and restricted vision in the present system, the resistance to our line of inquiry became more pronounced. There were concerns that people would be hurt if we were too critical. A lot of effort has gone into KSB. Many people have given much, even burned themselves out trying to make the system work. The fear seemed to be that by seeing its limitations clearly people might be discouraged. So there was more pressure to narrow our inquiry, be 'less adversarial' and to work hand in hand with KSB and keep whatever concerns we had between us and the Board authorities. It reached a turning point when one of our technical advisors resigned over the direction the inquiry was taking. Many people, but especially those at KSB, saw this as a sign that we did not know what we were doing.

"We knew what we were doing all right, and although we had anticipated some opposition, we did not realize to what extent it would come to and it took a lot of time, effort and energy to deal with it. However, the outcome resulted in us being able to set our own course and direction, and we decided it was time to hear the voices of the communities. This is something we had wanted to do from the start but for some reasons which were unclear to us it was advised as unnecessary.

"Furthermore, in each community, we wanted to have the views of a representative sample of interests and experience ... We have made records of all of this, many hundreds of pages and we have been drawing on this as our window on the realities of education in Nunavik. Except for those given in confidence these records are available for all to see. [There followed a list of specific problems.]

"If each of the problems the communities told us about had to be solved one by one it would take a long time. We have been analyzing these problems and have found that most of them are linked. In fact most of these problems cannot be successfully solved in isolation. To solve these problems you cannot just look at what you think is wrong, you also have to have a clear idea of what you think is right, you have to know where you are headed. It is only then that the significance of problems can be understood and you can get some idea of how to fix them. We will be saying much more about this in our final report...

"The voice of the communities was clear, but there was still a nagging doubt. KSB was saying that it was on the right track and that people would just have to be patient and everything would work itself out. It should be pointed out that KSB was very aware that things were not working very well, but this was seen as being caused by parents and students not understanding the value of education, difficulties in the communities, etc. In other words, in KSB's eyes, the problem was not KSB's it was the communities'.

"We do not pretend that our communities are without problems, and we had to check out the possibility that KSB might be right. Maybe they are doing the right things and we just have to be more patient. To check this out we sought out educators with proven track records, people who understood the problems and promises of education, people who know how to design and administer effective educational programs, people who understand second language instruction and who know North American standards of education...

"The communities are right to be impatient.

"There are serious structural and developmental problems with KSB. The education that KSB is delivering is well below North American standards. In fact the system has little or no quality control either for its own system of instruction or for student performance. Success in academic programs is achieved largely by lowering standards, a fact that becomes brutally apparent when our students enter schools in the south. The system has tried to explain this away as a difference in 'learning style' or problems of 'cultural adaptation'. We know from our research that these problems can be overcome, provided that people understand enough about how to design effective learning systems. Being patient, continuing on along the same path, would be not only futile, it would create more wasted years for more students, more burned out teachers, and slower social and economic development of Nunavik.

"We realize that this is not good news. But we do not blame anyone for this state of affairs, least of all the hardworking teachers in Nunavik who have tried to provide a good education for our children. They simply did not have the tools or support they needed to do the job effectively. We do not even blame the administration of the KSB. They thought they were doing the right thing when they 'protected' our culture by encouraging home-grown programs and fencing out all outside influences. Remember we went along with this for many years. We have had legal control of KSB since it was created. If we have been badly served by this organization in some ways, then we must also take some responsibility for it. *And we will!*

"In the final report we will offer a number of specific recommendations to deal with problems of education in Nunavik ... The ERC has been through a difficult process, yet we are very hopeful. Although we have seen and heard about many problems, we have also found that if you look for them there are also many solutions. Other people will not come and solve our problems for us, but there are tools, understanding and perspectives out there that can help us to solve our own. It is time to get on with it."

H

Silatunirmut/The Pathway to Wisdom:
Task Force Report and School Board Response

Establishment of a New Structure

#1: Create an integrated *Nunavik Education System (NES)* – directly accountable to the people of Nunavik – by restructuring and developing the existing education, training and cultural organizations and resources of Nunavik as part of the overall constitutional development plan. NES components are to be:

Nunavik Department of Education, Training and Employment (NDETE): Responsible for the overall development of education services. Directly accountable to the Nunavik Assembly. All other components of the NES will report to and receive their general policy direction from this authority.

Nunavik Futures Foundation (NFF): Responsible for developing and implementing a systematic fund-raising program to obtain funding from foundations, industry, governments, international and para-governmental organizations; also from Makivik and from a share of any compensation funds received as a result of negotiations with Hydro-Quebec and the Province of Quebec.

Nunavik School Board (NSB): Responsible for delivering high quality primary and secondary education.

Nunavik College (NC): Responsible for delivering high quality adult education, training and post-secondary services.

Nunavik Employment and Human Resource Planning Agency (NEHRPA): Responsible for manpower employment services and planning, including assisting individuals seeking employment and companies seeking employees.

Nunavik Educational Productions and Research Agency (NEPRA): Responsible for the design, development, production, and/or adaptation of high quality education, training, and heritage programs, curriculum, and materials.

Nunavik Heritage Institute and Land College (NHI/LC): Responsible for teaching, preserving, and researching Inuit heritage, language, culture, and spirit, and for developing archaeological and cultural collections.

KSB response: To be dealt with by Education Council and Council of Commissioners.

#2: Establish the Nunavik Education System Implementation and Planning Group to coordinate and control the creation and development of the NES...
KSB response: To be dealt with by Education Council and Council of Commissioners.

Catch-up Phase

#3: Develop and distribute to all residents a Charter of Educational Rights.
KSB response: At Kativik, we have a set of principles developed over the years since 1978, which consists of the Dual Mandate of the School Board and a set of objectives for education.

#4: Increase the base number of instructional days.
KSB response: Research shows that more school days do not make for more success in school ... KSB recognizes the value of family time that is essential for transmission of Inuit values and tradition ... Our efforts should be concentrated on making school time quality time...

#5: Establish after-school tutorials and learning programs in every school.
KSB response: In various communities there have been ... Kativik supports these types of programs. However, we recognize that individual communities and education committees have their own attitudes concerning "after-hours" school work.

#6: Implement individualized, competency-based, computer and multi-media assisted instructional programs to address urgent needs.
KSB proposal for action: KSB agrees that multi-media presentation is a valuable means of delivering educational material and we intend to continue our development in this area.

#7: Develop and implement summer training and education programs – on the land whenever possible.
KSB response: We support these types of recreation and development programs but believe that it is not the sole responsibility of KSB to administer these programs. The

initiative for these programs must come from the community level in consultation with the parents, the municipality and other local organizations.

#8: Establish a variety of innovative youth development programs.

KSB response: The Rediscovery Youth Program was used as a model to run a summer youth camp in Kuujjuaq and the extent of its success is questionable. The concept of Youth Development Programs is very interesting, however, these types of programs should be looked into in more depth to find the concepts or techniques which are applicable to our situation...

NES Component:
Nunavik Futures Foundation

#9: Launch fund-raising initiatives to obtain financial and other support from non-traditional sources.

KSB response: KSB already receives funding from other sources...

#10: Establish systematic co-operation among the world's Inuit and with other indigenous peoples.

KSB response: Professional staff of KSB have consistently been participating members of international and circumpolar organizations and conferences concerned with education ... Oftentimes, our professionals are among the presenters and organizers ... One problem of the School Board is that not enough organized communication and public relations, internally and externally, have been done on a regular basis...

NES Component:
Kativik School Board/Nunavik School Board Transition

#11: Restructure and rename KSB to make it more accountable as the NES component responsible for elementary and secondary education.

KSB response: To be dealt with by Education Council and Council of Commissioners.

NES Component:
Nunavik School Board (NSB) Purpose and Vision

#12: NSB policy should be based on a needs assessment of the people of Nunavik for basic education.

KSB response: KSB consults with the population through its Education Council and its Education Committees.

#13: NSB programs should be compatible with MEQ standards – but should be specifically designed for the needs of Nunavik, not bound by MEQ programs or regimes.

KSB response: KSB has adopted and pursues this policy in terms of students. However, in the matter of student ability to transfer to southern schools, it must be understood that a student who is in third grade is only in his first year of instruction in English or French ... It takes time for him to acquire equivalent skills in English or French. That does not mean that he is weak in concepts covered in the curriculum ... We must be aware that there are many other factors beside knowledge of course content which make transfer to Southern schools difficult for Nunavik students ... KSB recognizes the need to design curriculum and instruction so that the child will prosper in the bilingual environment of the School Board, and will be able to transfer his learning from language to language and even from North to South ... This recommendation seems to fight with itself and recommendation 12.

Clear Sense of Mission and High Operating Standards

#14: Set high standards – ones which exceed southern standards.

KSB response: This recommendation is contrary to basic pedagogical practice and theory ... we must be careful to create the possibility for all students to enjoy success, and not just make a school system which will have as its aim a set of standards equal to or exceeding an elitist "Southern" standard...

KSB proposal for action: ...The school system must present options for all students to make goals and work to obtain these goals...

#15: NSB curriculum and standards are to be authorized by, and controlled by, the Nunavik Government and until that is operational by Makivik.

KSB response: ... Such functions are presently within the scope of KSB. The Commissioners are quite capable of fulfilling those functions.

KSB proposal for action: KSB should review its policy on program development and implementation of new programs and materials. More information sessions such as the ones that have taken place in the past with the Commissioners would enhance the Commissioners' awareness ... Furthermore, there should be workshops with Education Services senior staff and Commissioners to deal with the issues of standards. Commissioners should also be actively involved in formal approval of programs, curriculum and material.

#16: A clear mission statement, system of objectives and methods, and statement of philosophy are to be developed for NSB operations and copies provided to each household.

KSB response: As part of the audit of curriculum which will be started by an external, objective educational team of experts in 1993, the goals of the School Board will be defined in such a way that they can be reviewed, revised as necessary and approved by all sectors of the School Board.

#17: The NSB Council of Commissioners is to set educational policies within guidelines established by the Implementation and Planning Group. Commissioners are to receive training in educational policy making, in institutional control, and in administration performance and evaluation techniques.

KSB response: The developing role of the Commissioners should be the subject of review...

#18: NSB administration will ensure that all staff and other stakeholders understand NSB's mission and commitment to high performance.

KSB response: The Board recognizes the need to strengthen in this area.

KSB proposal for action: The review committee will discuss this issue during community consultations and it will become part of our annual planning process. Greater use should be made of TV and radio...

Organization

#19: NSB will move its headquarters north in no more than 4 years.

KSB response: The Council of Commissioners has already taken action and made decisions on this matter ... In December 1991 the Commissioners made the decision to prioritize the provision of appropriate and complete school facilities in all communities before building administrative offices.

#20: NSB will establish clear leadership and administrative performance standards for all its administrators.

KSB response: ... KSB has offered professional development to all principals and centre directors.

KSB proposal for action: KSB, recognizing the need for quality education, should formalize the procedure by which administrators regularly review, evaluate and plan their work with their supervisor.

Administrative Personnel

#21: NSB should upgrade its headquarters-based instructional leadership and support services.

KSB response: Presently, the KSB provides a variety of means of support.

#22: All staff should receive specially designed pre-service and on-going training including intensive, individualized programs to train Inuit employees for administrative positions.

KSB response: ... The area of staff improvement and training is taken seriously and is continually being improved and increased.

KSB proposal for action: All training and development courses should continue. This area should be emphasized and expanded as much as possible particularly in the area of training Inuit staff to have more access to administrative positions.

Teaching Personnel

#23: Teacher Turnover must be reduced through improvements in recruitment of teachers, working conditions, and personal and professional rewards of working with NSB.

KSB response: Teacher turnover has decreased over the past five years in all language sectors. It is an oversimplification to suggest that just by putting more money into teacher recruitment or by improving working conditions we can reduce the turnover rate ... KSB has recruited teachers from major Universities across Canada ... All candidates are subjected to a pre-screening (for qualifications), an initial interview (for general suitability and aptitude) and a final interview (for specific attributes), before they are offered to a community selection team ... Kativik has since 1987-88 been offering courses to non-Inuit teachers on a voluntary basis.

KSB proposal for action: KSB must increase their recruitment campaign by aggressively advertising the opportunities, both personal and professional, that a career in Nunavik has to offer. In-Service cross/cultural orientation through a credit program must be provided for Second Language teachers. This type of course should be mandatory and be taught in the North...

Inuit Teachers

#24: NSB's professional teaching staff must reflect the indigenous population of Nunavik.

KSB response: To keep and attract Inuit teachers the Education Council recommended improving their working conditions by providing a training allowance.

KSB proposal for action: The Board must conduct a budget feasibility study and explore possible funding sources for providing training allowances. A formal training program for language, culture, religion and excursion teachers, that would lead to certification, must be developed...

#25: Peer and advanced-student teaching strategies should be used throughout the basic teacher-training program

KSB response: ... If conducted under proper guidelines these situations could be of benefit to all.

KSB proposal for action: Education Services will develop and provide guidelines to communities for student involvement in tutoring, peer helping and assistant teaching situations ... KSB's Co-operative Learning Program should be a mandatory course for all 1st and 2nd language teachers...

#26: A differentiated staffing strategy should be developed using classroom assistants from the community who will be encouraged to become qualified teachers.

KSB response: This has been initiated in one community and has proven to be successful.

KSB proposal for action: ...The communities may apply when there is an appropriate need...

#27: The teacher training plan must be clearly laid out in advance.

KSB response: This is already in place...

KSB proposal for action: It is very important to emphasize to the trainees the objectives and description of each course in the 45 credit program.

#28: The existing teacher training program must be redesigned.

KSB response: Consultation with teacher training counsellors and teachers indicated that they are satisfied with the teacher training program and there is ongoing improvement, therefore we don't feel there is a need to redesign the whole program. The McGill/Kativik program has acted as a model and an inspiration for other programs of aboriginal teacher education with which McGill has been involved...

KSB proposal for action: Close examination of the interactive media and distance education methods must be undertaken in order to evaluate them for suitability to our program and needs.

#29: Pre-service instruction should include the relationships between adaptive learning, empowerment and independence; education needs assessment; high order learning and teaching skills; the basics of instructional design; as well as global cultural access skills and perspectives.

KSB response: We do not feel such pre-service instruction is necessary. Kativik Teacher Training Program allows its teachers in training to gain all the skills indicated in this recommendation while working with children in actual classroom situations...

KSB proposal for action: Local courses should be developed with and for the teacher training counselors. Funding sources such as Adult Education and Manpower programs must be explored.

#30: The teacher instruction program should provide many possibilities for independent studies and the establishment of teaching schools on both coasts (Hudson and Ungava Bays).

KSB response: Independent studies are more appropriate for teachers pursuing their B.Ed. degree ... Instead of travelling staff we have local teacher training counsellors in each community. This exceeds the recommendation...

KSB proposal for action: A feasibility study is being conducted to investigate the possibility of securing funding that would allow all teacher training counsellors to work full time. A room for teacher training will be allocated to each school...

#31: The teacher training program and materials should be constantly evaluated, upgraded, and informed by ongoing professional research and evaluation.

KSB response: The Teacher Training Program has instituted an evaluation system that is ongoing for each course and we continually upgrade the program based on evaluations...

#32: Co-operative arrangements should be developed with a number of post-secondary institutions across North America.

KSB response: Through our involvement at the Circumpolar Conferences we have assessed the result of other Indigenous groups' experiences and have concluded that the KSB model best meets our needs at this time.

KSB proposal for action: Nevertheless, through our continued involvement with the various international indigenous groups, more particularly the Arctic College and Greenland Teacher Training Institutes, the experiences and practices of these groups will be monitored on an ongoing basis.

#33: Ongoing professional development of Inuit teachers should be improved by using interactive media and distance education technologies, improving instructional designs and materials for use by teachers, and establishing a teacher training coordinator at each school.

KSB response: This is put into practice through KSB's fall pedagogical days ... Making all teacher training counsellor positions full time would enable us to enhance the strong community centered training services that we already provide.

KSB proposal for action: A feasibility study will be done to secure funding for all teacher training counsellor positions to become full time.

Establishing a System of Community Schools

#34: Each school should be a true community school that makes parents a valued and welcomed part of the learning process and that helps people understand the potential and uses of education.

KSB response: ... One of the areas where the school board has had some weakness is in our support for community initiatives, or as the task force has put it, the development of community-based schools. While we have very often supported community projects on an ad hoc basis, we have not systematically built strong community structures, nor have we decentralized the necessary resources.

KSB proposal for action: A commitment has now been made to the principle of additional local autonomy, and the planning is now underway to build the capacity of the local education committees, as well as the local administrators, to take effective control over the schools in their communities. While board-wide quality and accreditation guidelines will still apply, the schools will be given greater autonomy in deciding the types of services they will offer, and the style of those services ... The board is identifying those budgets which can eventually be transferred to the communities so that they might control the resources they will need to effectively develop novel, locally based solutions to the educational problems they must face. A plan will be developed to carry out this transfer on a progressive basis, as the communities are ready to assume their new responsibilities. More workshops will be provided to parents at the local level on the philosophy of education...

#35: Communities must have the control to create programs which use local human resources and facilities to meet locally defined needs.

KSB response: First, KSB has the responsibility to work with all communities to determine a base of knowledge and skills to be acquired by all children. Then, within the broadly defined goals of education, curriculum should be developed that allows villages locally to adapt curriculum to meet locally defined needs. Some of the recommendations of the Task Force actually work counter to this recommendation. For example, in Recommendation 11...

#36: Retaining experienced, effective teachers must be a top priority which communities should assist in.

KSB response: See response under recommendation 23.

#37: School education committees are the critical link between school and community and they should receive training.

KSB response: The training for locally elected people is an ongoing problem for all organizations and has only recently become a priority throughout Nunavik. Lack of time and resources have been a problem. It should be noted that many of the education committees are very effective in fulfilling their role even without formal training.

KSB proposal for action: As part of our plan to decentralize more powers and resources to the communities a special training plan for local administrators and education committees will be developed.

#38: A review process to resolve conflicts between school education committees and the NSB must be established.

KSB response: KSB and the Education Committees are part of the same organization. Conflicts are resolved the same way they are between any two parts of an organization. Through discussion, consultation, and mutual understanding.

KSB proposal for action: Roles and responsibilities should be clearly defined to help avoid misunderstandings.

#39: Parents, administrators, teachers and students must agree on basic rules of conduct for each school.

KSB response: There is a board-level discipline policy as well as a policy for transfer students which are applied by the individual schools.

KSB proposal for action: A larger discussion and consultation should be carried out with the parents and communities about the very nature of discipline and the concepts of correction and punishment so that a policy can be developed that can be understood and supported by everyone.

#40: Instruction must be organized to promote high levels of learning time. Homework is essential, as is tracking student progress.

KSB response: See response to recommendation 4. The matter of homework and tracking of student progress involves strengthening our partnership with parents so they can fully understand the need...

#41: Schools should strive to develop humane, high quality education by being publicly committed to certain operating principles.

KSB response: These are the operating principles of all good school boards including KSB.

#42: Roles and qualifications of Principals and Centre Directors should be clarified.

KSB response: ... In the evolution of KSB more and more Inuit have become trained for school administration, and the potential for the role of the Centre Director has likewise changed. It is time to consider making this role of the Centre Director more pedagogical, so that total administration of the school can be shared.

KSB proposal for action: As the human resources become available for supervision of school administrators, and as their respective roles are defined and redefined, there must be consistent supervision of administrators and in-service support of their pedagogical activities.

#43: Pre-service and in-service training programs in community-based education should be designed and implemented.

KSB response: See response to recommendations 22 and 44.

#44: Administrators should be selected and trained in techniques of management and support of community-oriented teachers and teaching practices.

KSB response: KSB is committed to providing training for their school administrators ... It is the aim of the School Board to move toward having Inuit administrators who are properly trained to carry both the physical and pedagogical administration of the school.

KSB proposal for action: Training for school administrators will be continued...

A comprehensive training program should be developed to encourage Inuit to take on more administrative roles. A process of evaluation is presently being set up, through Education Services, to allow board-wide performance review.

School Organization and Calendar

#45: The school calendar must be modified to meet the needs of culture-related activities and catch-up programs.

KSB response: ... Communities who want to alter their calendars have always had the right to do so since the signing of the JBNQA.

#46: Schools should be able to deploy and organize staff in flexible ways according to local needs and community circumstances.

KSB response: Community school administrators and Education Committees have always had latitude in the organization of their schools ... KSB supports, through its organization principles and professional development for principals, the process of consultation and co-operative action in school projects.

KSB proposal for action: Decentralization of budgets will allow for even greater flexibility in school organization.

Student Affairs

#47: Students should become respected and responsible partners in maintaining an active community for learning.

KSB response: KSB has always encouraged athletic and recreational activities for our students through extra-curricular programs and sports tournaments. Student initiative programs are encouraged by community administration and teaching staff, and this type of program can be offered through extra-curricular activities.

KSB proposal for action: Inter-community sports activities and student workshops will continue with the securing of adequate funding.

#48: A system-wide student discipline policy should be developed in co-operation with parents, students and educators.

KSB response: Such a policy has existed in KSB since Dec. 1991. Parents, students and educators were consulted on the drafting of this policy beginning in 1989.

Teaching Strategies and Methods

#49: NSB should be in the forefront in the use of new educational technologies and delivery systems.

KSB response: In 1984, Inuit teachers were able to work on IBM computers at KSB, thanks to the development of a special chip by consultants of the Board which allowed use of syllabics on the computer. Since that time, the Board has used a combination of the IBM and Apple formats to introduce computer use to students, teachers and administrators ... KSB was one of the early experimenters in the use of Autoskill: computer-assisted remediation combining specific testing and evaluation of student needs with the appropriate elements of the programme, under the supervision of a trained teacher. We are now testing new programmes by the Autoskill company for mathematics, and again are the leaders in Canada in this piloting...

KSB proposal for action: Kativik will continue its innovation in the use of technology.

#50: NSB should have a coherently organized curriculum with teaching and testing components carefully integrated and coordinated.

KSB response: Kativik Staff agree that this is a good direction to take in program development. In fact is is already being done...

#51: NSB should develop and maintain a variety of program delivery systems permitting flexible scheduling, continuous progress, and individualized mastery-based learning.

KSB response: This is a recommendation with merit, which should be investigated carefully and implemented as possible.

#52: Teachers should be trained to use a variety of instructional strategies and methods and be able to adapt and develop curriculum.

KSB response: KSB recognizes that it must take the initiative to present a variety of strategies for student support so that the Education Committees, in harmony with administrators and teachers and students, can create their own school projects to give additional support which they feel is necessary. The community must be in agreement with these local initiatives, and they cannot be imposed by the Board. The Board's role is to provide research and practical ways and means for implementation.

#53: NSB should make sure students have adequate "hands-on" learning opportunities including manipulative materials as well as laboratory and field experiences in science.

KSB response: ... Many teachers who taught in our schools and then moved south are totally surprised as to how well our schools are equipped as compared to southern schools ... It is also policy and an integral part of our curriculum that hands on learning in all areas is recommended ... Schools are all provided with science rooms, but a resourceful teacher can make the regular classroom a living lab.

KSB proposal for action: What is recommended is just sound pedagogy... The Board intends continuing to pursue this path.

#54: NSB should promote whole language approaches to reading including libraries in every elementary classroom.

KSB response: The whole language approach is one that is integrated in our curriculum in English and is becoming more so in French and Inuttitut ... Learning style of the child, however, is most important, so that a variety of approaches may be necessary in any one school and even in any one classroom.... Classroom libraries are very desirable. Whether libraries are centralized or not is a local decision, but classroom hoarding limits access to books. Moreover, it would be quite difficult to find 200 books in Inuttitut appropriate...

#55: Fine arts and a wide range of practical communications and media projects should be emphasized throughout the curriculum.

KSB response: Perhaps this is an area where recommendation 35 could be used to pass on traditional music, dance, sculpture ... by using local artists and travelling specialists, all teachers could be trained to work in these areas while their students are learning.

KSB proposal for action: KSB should look for these skills when interviewing new teachers. KSB should encourage local artists to come into the classroom and teach. We should consider the possibility of travelling specialists...

#56: School programs should use community resource people.

KSB response: KSB is in full agreement with this recommendation.

KSB proposal for action: KSB should provide training for local resource people so they can be more effective and comfortable in the formal learning situation. Sensitization about the North must be provided to visiting "experts"...

Standards, Quality Control and Shareholder Reporting

#57: System-wide achievement standards should be developed. Student advancement should be based on mastery, with clear indications that achievement standards have been met.

KSB response: This is a recommendation with merit which should be investigated carefully and implemented as possible.

#58: A set of evaluation instruments, benchmark studies and a student progress tracking system should be established for years 4-8-12.

KSB response: The suggestion of Board-wide standardized testing is interesting as a method of comparing, administratively, the extent of learning in the various communities. This would be a tool valuable to programme developers to see to what extent curricula and/or materials and/or teaching strategies were successful. However, if this were to lead to comparison of achievement either between individual students or communities, this provides a far too simplistic view of the success of our students or our schools ... School Board examinations which indicate the degree of growth towards a standard which they hope to achieve is more important for the purpose of evaluation of student progress.

#59: Every school should be given an accreditation review within 3 years (and thereafter every 5 years) with results of these reviews made public.

KSB response: This is a recommendation with merit, which should be investigated carefully and implemented as possible.

Language Learning and Instruction

#60: NSB should establish guidelines for language learning and instruction. It should be up to each community to decide how to structure their programs within those guidelines.

KSB response: See response to Recommendation 35 ... Identifying qualified programme developers is no easy task ...Therefore, finding people locally to develop programs in all communities would seem to be an impossible task ... The Task Force has proposed the creation of NEPRA to do a variety of things – the creation of an external agency to do the work of programme development is unnecessary. It is a special concern that an independent organization would only be a means of controlling development, and would not be responsive to needs ... In principle, we do not believe that one organization should be solely responsible for its own evaluation ... The evolution of the process of curriculum and programme development in KSB has been steady, and now there is a more formalized department which deals with programme development (for the new social studies programme). It is necessary for educators with classroom experience to be involved...

KSB proposal of action: We cannot over-emphasize the need for coordination in development, and the need for consultation among all parties involved in creating and teaching programs.

#61: The instructional program must be truly bilingual.

KSB response: ... We realize that there is not a progression in difficulty in the Secondary program, and that a challenge is necessary for students to have a sense of accomplishment. Therefore, the themes in Secondary will be reorganized ... This work will, by its very nature, progress slowly, since it involves the development of human resources in Nunavik ... In principle, KSB believes that as much quality teaching as possible should happen in the mother tongue, especially at the primary level. This is a model we adopted through the democratic process of leadership by consultation. When consultation was done in the communities, most were found to be in support of Kativik's language policy.

KSB proposal of action: As programs, material and teachers become available, Inuttitut instruction time should increase.

#62: English or French first language students should be encouraged to take Inuttitut courses, as should second language teachers.

KSB response: In meeting with members of the Task Force, the Review Committee was told that this recommendation refers to Inuit children whose first language was English or French. The Board believes, and our research supports, that all Inuit children should have a firm foundation in Inuttitut as mother-tongue ... There is some question as to the value of a second language teacher who is not an Inuk using Inuttitut in his second-language teaching. We know that it is necessary for those teachers to be aware of culturally appropriate techniques in questioning and classroom management...

#63: NSB should develop and apply an advanced, whole language learning philosophy and strategy including use of appropriate curriculum materials.

KSB response: As in other cases where single specific strategies are suggested, we hesitate to use only one strategy in our development and teaching activities.

#64: NSB should not waste energy and resources developing routine second language materials which are available from other places.

KSB response: This recommendation ignores the reality of our second-language goals. The MEQ and other programs are meant for people to learn a second language for conversational purposes, in order to co-habit with other language speakers and to survive in other cultures. One of our greatest needs for second language learning is to permit student access to vocational and post-secondary institutions ... A strictly second language programme is clearly unacceptable for the needs of our students...

#65: Workshops should be organized at the community level to explain and demonstrate language teaching philosophies and programs.

KSB response: This is a recommendation with merit, which should be investigated carefully and implemented as possible.

#66: NEPRA should undertake a system-wide independent study on the status of first and second language proficiency with the results made public.

KSB response: ... The making public of testing is of questionable value. The result of testing should only be used to improve instruction...

#67: Programs should be implemented to send students outside their territory for language immersion courses.

KSB response: The majority of schools in KSB have participated and continue to participate in cultural exchange trips between our schools and schools in southern Canada....

#68: Start second language instruction as early as possible, but maintain most of the early teaching in Inuttitut.

KSB response: That is what KSB does ... Many people in Nunavik do not subscribe to this philosophy. They look to the experience of the Federal school as one that was very powerful, and people realize that Inuttitut suffered through this time as the language deteriorated and was devalued. The process of rebuilding the value of the language is a long one, and will require much consultation and public information on the subject.

#69: NSB needs a more effective French program including the training of all French second language teachers in the communicative language approach.

KSB response: Material for the Kativik French Program (FRANNORD) has been developed over a long period of time (from 1976 to 1992) ... Some of that material is no longer appropriate, and should be revised...

KSB proposal for action: A change has occurred in the method of course development. In the past, most of the initiative has come from outside developers responding to needs as expressed by teachers. Development will now be guided by the Pedagogical Counsellor, with outside consultants working on specific development to fall within an overall plan developed in the School Board...

#70: Ways must be found to keep French teachers longer.

KSB response: ...We do not feel it is warranted to treat any particular linguistic group differently...

Programs and Operations

#71: The school's role should include emphasizing, and training students to deal with, the process of change taking place within northern society.

KSB response: Programs should include instruction in critical thinking, especially in terms of appreciating cultural differences...

KSB proposal for action: Teacher Training courses should include elements of critical pedagogy. Program development should consider the pedagogy of transcultural processes...

#72: Qualified authors and journalists should be commissioned by NSB and NEPRA to rewrite the NSB social and history curriculum programs.

KSB response: ... It appears that the Task Force was not aware of what was happening in program development in the School Board, even though a presentation was made....good curriculum materials are created by good teachers...

KSB proposal for action: KSB should continue to develop programs as it is at the moment, using elders and other experts for consultation in subject matters and cultural matters.

#73: Health education and prevention programs should be developed in co-operation with local health organizations and NEPRA.

KSB response: KSB has always co-operated with health organizations in health and prevention programs...

KSB proposal for action: KSB will continue to operate as it has been in this area.

#74: Career counseling programs should be started in Secondary I as part of an expanded community service and economic skills acquisition program.

KSB response: ... Counseling for career and life planning must take into consideration the economic reality of the community in which students live. This means that greater co-operation in terms of economic development and long-term job creation programs must occur between all the government agencies. Any counseling must be done in consultation with agencies which have the power to create and sustain employment opportunities in the communities ... See proposal for Recommendation 71...

KSB proposal for action: KSB should continue to work in co-operation with other agencies....

#75: Curriculum program development needs and priorities should be established on a systematic, long-term basis.

KSB response: In the early years of the Board, program development tended to be done as part of the teacher training process. There was a tendency to create programs to meet needs, rather than work from a long-term plan with dedicated resources and a common goal ... In addition, it was not until the school year 1988-89 that adequate funding was even available for program and curriculum development. Before this time, funding was squeezed from other operational budgets.

KSB proposal for action: ... Over the past fourteen years, in responding to the needs of our students, we have developed informal patterns and styles of development that meet the needs of our population. These should be formalized and put into such a form that development can occur where the resources (human and financial) and the need exists ... Program development planning should coordinate the curricula to promote the principles of transference of learning and addictive bilingualism.

#76: Early childhood programs should be set up for parents and for children.

KSB response: Before-school help has been tried in individual cases of disabled children in Nunavik ... This was carried out in the home, with the assistance of a shadow teacher ... There is some doubt about the successes or the viability of the Head Start program in the United States ... We believe ... that unstructured play is necessary in the early years, outside with their own friends ... culture is transmitted through natural activities, especially before children start school. That notwithstanding, the School Board should look to outside models...

KSB proposal for action: Liaison with Social Services is essential to provide early intervention for children with special needs ... Family literacy programs should be encouraged...

#77: Effective assessment procedures, programs and followup are required for special needs students.

KSB response: Effective assessment tests have been developed in Inuttitut ... Individual Education Programs are being prepared for every special needs student ... Since 1989/90 funding has been negotiated for, and thus the provisions for the assessment of students and the implementation of our special education services have been greatly increased.

Extracurricular and Enrichment Activities

#78: A full range of extracurricular activities should be developed.

KSB response: Extracurricular activities are encouraged ... The participation of other organizations at the community level should be encouraged.

KSB proposal for action: KSB will continue to foster involvement in a full range of extracurricular activities at both the community and board-wide levels.

NES Component:
Nunavik Human Development Agency

#79: Strategic planning programs for leaders and management, including management skills, analytical skills, and political skills, should be developed and implemented as a priority.

KSB response: Management training programs have been offered through Adult Education Services during the past ten years. A previous attempt to set up a comprehensive management training program was not supported by the regional organizations, and recent courses given to the staff of various organizations have been ad hoc and less effective than they might have been...

KSB proposal for action: Manpower Services and Adult Education should give a higher priority to management training....

#80: Regularly scheduled training programs for School Commissioners and education committees should be developed and implemented.

KSB response: ... the newly elected council receives basic orientation regarding the KSB mandate under the JBNQA education act. The education committees receive basic role and responsibility booklets...

KSB proposal for action: We recognize further training must be developed to expand this area.

Community and Adult Education Services

#81: Youth Environmental Service (YES) projects should be established.

KSB response: While we agree with the ideas presented in this recommendation, KSB cannot be the only organization dealing with these types of programs. Rather, a partnership must be and in fact is being built to offer these programs...

#82: Nunavik Youth Initiative Projects (YIPS) should be developed, tested and implemented at the community level, in which young people themselves are primarily responsible for the project planning, organization, and operations.

KSB response: KSB is now taking advantage of the STAY IN SCHOOL program which is funded by the federal government. These programs are designed to encourage at risk students to continue their education in a more unique setting which is suited to their individual needs and abilities.

KSB proposal for action: KSB will continue to expand the use of these and other such programs.

NES Component:
Nunavik College

#83: A junior college should be created that will provide, among other services, an optional two-year post-secondary preparation program for students prior to further post-secondary education outside of Nunavik.

KSB response: The optional post-secondary program could be acceptable as long as accredited courses are offered. However, the idea of one college in one location needs further assessment...

#84: Adult Education courses, including mathematics courses in Inuttitut, should be taught as a priority.

KSB response: Adult Education courses have been in existence for many years ... It would be a valuable exercise for teachers who are trying new approaches to document their successes so that innovative ideas could be given trial on a larger scale...

#85: Nunavik College should make a firm commitment to train local Adult Education teachers.

KSB response: In the past Adult Education Teachers have attended Teacher Training courses, to some extent, when it was appropriate to their teaching duties. This practice should be continued and even increased...

KSB proposal for action: Adult Education in consultation with Teacher Training will determine guidelines for the training required by Adult Education teachers.

#86: Vocational training should be coordinated with employment opportunities.

KSB response: This has been done for a number of years through the Kativik Regional Employment and Training Committee. This approach has been further consolidated by the transfer of all manpower responsibilities to KRG.

KSB proposal for action: Economic development plans should be well defined to allow for the closest link to training.

#87: Empowering community programs and seminars should be implemented on personal and social development issues.

KSB response: ... We have consistently invested a great deal of human and financial resources in these programs, both for the general population and for the school population.

KSB proposal for action: Resources should especially be given to local initiatives, since they will have the greatest chance for success...

#88: An information clearinghouse should be created for referring national and international post-secondary education and training opportunities to students and to trainees. This service should establish close ties with others already in existence such as the Roger Lang Clearinghouse for Circumpolar Education.

KSB response: The idea of creating a new clearinghouse service would be duplication of the services of other agencies...

KSB proposal for action: ... A comparison study will be made by Kativik, through the Department of Northern Affairs Library, to determine which of these services would best serve our needs.

NES Component:
Nunavik Education Productions and Research Agency

#89: A regular sample survey of youth and adult students concerning education, career and social matters should be undertaken.

KSB response: Two major surveys in this area have been carried out by the Kativik Regional Government (1987 & 1991). The school board participated actively in both of these surveys and both were widely publicized.

KSB proposal for action: KRG should be encouraged to continue this on a regular basis.

#90: Curriculum and other materials on Nunavik Inuit should be developed and marketed or exchanged with southern school boards and other organizations.

KSB response: This is a recommendation with merit which should be investigated carefully and implemented as possible.

#91: Co-operative arrangements with Quebec, Canadian, and international post-secondary institutions should be developed for the research and production of curriculum programs and materials.

KSB response: ...The position of the School Board is that development of program is essentially part of development of human resources (teachers) and the total school programme (goals of education). These cannot be implanted on the school system; neither can programmes be taken from other institutions without a serious consideration as to their adaptability within the context of a commonly agreed set of goals of education. Working from the base of our goals of education, we will make use of whatever expertise is applicable...

#92: A major effort should be placed on the creation of materials required for subject matter courses in Inuttitut.

KSB response: We are firmly convinced that development of Inuttitut language and culture curricula cannot happen outside of the School Board. There is a strong relationship between the teaching process, teacher training activities and the development of program and learning materials and the piloting of these programs. Some work has been done with Avataq concerning the development of materials, and this should continue and grow ... We will need the co-operation of people both within and from outside the School Board to assist in the planning and creation of vibrant, interesting and practical Inuttitut-language content courses...

#93: Programs should be implemented that are intended to develop and assist the development of Inuttitut media.

KSB response: As a starting point in this direction ... the development of the new grade three to seven program in Inuttitut will be a language-arts based development. This will include the use of language in various media: print, radio, television...

#94: A strategy should be developed for identifying and engaging the human resources required for advancing Inuttitut language instruction.

KSB response: ... As part of a Board-wide audit of curriculum, the Inuttitut program will be investigated in order to develop culturally-appropriate measures that will set a high standard for program development and evaluation.

#95: Creative, educational, and recreational programs should be developed that will stimulate and challenge youth, and that will enhance physical and mental conditioning.

KSB response: We encourage inter-community physical and intellectual competitions. As stated in recommendations 78 and 82 programs and activities that are already done should be continued.

#96: Programs should be designed to train teachers to work within a wide curriculum accommodation range. The program should ensure that teachers, and the teaching environment, can handle multi-grade teaching.

KSB response: All newly hired teachers receive an information session in August prior to their placement in the North. Support is also given by a travelling pedagogical counsellor.

KSB proposal for action: Programs should be developed to train teachers in areas such as multi-level teaching techniques and second language learning approaches. This would be in addition to what is proposed for recommendation 24.

#97: Programs should be designed that use simulations to teach students about the justice system and the courts, politics, and Inuit organizational management.

KSB response: The fact that the court has often been held in community schools has made it possible for students to know something about the justice system. However, there are cultural questions whether children should be exposed to certain proceedings or discussions of the court or elders. It is the responsibility of organizations and the local populations to find ways to assure that everyone is aware of the political process...

KSB proposal for action: KSB should continue its Social Studies development and its in-service support of a variety of teaching techniques...

#98: The instructional design team must be able to integrate the critical MEQ standards and elements in all NSB curriculum materials to ensure easy integration with MEQ programs, while at the same time addressing Nunavik's unique needs.

KSB response: This is already done. The current development in Social Studies is following the elements and standards of the MEQ programmes, but the consultation with elders, Education Committees, and development through committees involving many resources persons is intended to make the programmes pertinent to the needs of our students.

#99: NES should learn, use and adapt where necessary, excellent curriculum and teaching materials and programs that have been developed elsewhere. There is a pressing need to identify excellent Inuit instructional designers.

KSB response: ... Representatives from Baffin came to KSB in December 1992 and met with us to look at our program and curriculum. They are impressed with the progress we have made, and want the benefit of sharing our experience. This will be a two-way sharing process.

#100: Special efforts and innovative support programs should be designed to seek out, encourage, and challenge the brightest students.

KSB response: School standards for all of our students have to be measured in terms of their needs and their abilities. KSB must serve all students of Nunavik within its schools, including the handicapped and the gifted ... KSB's policy is that students are promoted within their age group and not isolated from their peers. Therefore we encourage horizontal enrichment for gifted students.

NES Component:
Nunavik Heritage Institute/Land College

#101: The teaching of Inuit language and culture must be integrated with the real lives of hunters and fishers. Programs must be developed that apply strong, effective culture programs that genuinely encompass the Inuit spirit, and that encourage youth to get involved in cultural and linguistic preservation activities.

KSB response: The excursion program has already created situations in the communities where teaching of Inuit culture can be integrated with the real lives of hunters and fishers. Guidelines for the running of excursions have been reworked to ensure that the activities of the excursion come back into the classroom to be made part of the formal learning process ... Generally speaking, elders are involved in the development of all learning materials.

National Curriculum Audit Center Report

NCAC ANALYSIS OF NETF RECOMMENDATIONS

Major Theme	Corresponding Recommendations
1. Redesign organizational structures	1, 2, 10, 11, 15, 17, 19, 21, 34, 35, 37, 38, 42, 83, 92, 93 (16 total)
2. Revise certain KSB policies, beliefs	12, 41, 48, 60 (4 total)
3. Recruit and train teachers and administrators	23, 24, 26, 44 (4 total)
4. Redesign staff evaluation procedures	42, 70, 80 (3 total)
5. Establish a collaborative curriculum design plan	57, 73, 75, 90, 91, 94, 99 (7 total)
6. Develop and communicate student outcomes, standards, and specific programs	7, 8, 13, 14, 16, 18, 39, 55, 64, 69, 71, 72, 74, 87, 97, 98 (16 total)
7. Design program and student assessment procedures	58, 59, 66, 79, 89 (5 total)
8. Provide training for various constituents	17, 21, 22, 27, 28, 29, 30, 31, 32, 33, 37, 43, 52, 65, 79, 80 (16 total)
9. Change certain delivery systems	4, 25, 26, 40, 45, 46, 51, 53, 54, 56, 68, 84 (12 total)
10. Establish specific programs through which to deliver instruction	2, 6, 47, 54, 61, 62, 63, 67, 76, 78, 81, 82, 86, 88, 95, 97, 100, 101 (18 total)
11. Provide equitable learning opportunities	3, 5 (2 total)
12. To establish fiscal efficiency and adequacy of support base	9 (1 total)

NCAC ANALYSIS OF KSB RESPONSE
TO NETF RECOMMENDATIONS

Recommendations Accepted by the Board:

1 Integrated services of education and training agencies and eventual self-government
2 Transition oversight
6 Individualized technology for special populations
11 Restructure the Kativik School Board
16 Mission and objectives development by NES
18 Communicate mission and standards to all stakeholders
19 Relocate NSB to Nunavik
22 Staff and administrative training for Inuit
23 Teacher recruitment and retention
24 Inuit teacher recruitment, training and retention
25 Students teaching students
26 Community classroom assistants
27 Clear Inuit teacher training program
36 Teacher retention
37 School Committee training
46 Flexible staffing
50 Curriculum integration and coordination
51 Variety of program delivery systems
53 Adequate instructional resources
55 Fine arts curriculum emphasis
56 Use of community resource people
59 Individual school accreditation
61 Bilingual program
65 Community training on language programs
71 Transcultural programs
78 Full range of extracurricular activities
79 Leader and management strategic planning training etc.
82 Youth initiative projects
87 Personal and social development
89 Youth and adult student survey
90 Market or exchange of Nunavik curriculum
94 Inuttitut language instruction/staff readiness
95 Creative, educational and recreational programs
97 Teaching about justice, politics and Inuit organizations
99 Identify exemplary Inuit designers and materials

Recommendations NOT Accepted by the Board:

4 More school days and year-round school

14 Set high student achievement standards

15 Control of curriculum and standards by Nunavik
Department of Education

17 Commissioners' control: policy control, performance
evaluation

29 Pre-service instructional components

32 Post-secondary co-operative arrangements

35 Community latitude to create local programs

40 Learning time

48 Collaborative system-wide student discipline policy

63 Co-operative development of whole language learning

64 Development of second language materials

70 French teacher retention

88 Referral clearinghouse for education and training

91 Co-operative curriculum development

92 NEPRA responsibility for quality Inuttitut materials

**Recommendations Where the Board's Response
Is Not Clear And More Clarification/Dialogue Needed:**

3 Educational rights for all children to effective learning
program

5 After-school tutorials/learning programs at each school

7 At-risk summer program

8 Youth development programs

9 Financial support review and expansion

10 Create co-operative structure to adapt to change

12 Policy reflect needs of community

13 Responsiveness to MEQ standards and local needs

20 Establish administrative performance standards

21 Upgrade leadership and support services through training and technology

28 Teacher training program redesign

30 Access to teacher instruction program

31 Continual improvement of teacher training materials.
Advanced programs in second language

33 Improvement of professional development

34 Community schools

---

38 Review process for Committee/Board conflicts
39 School academic and social behavior goals
41 Operating principles
42 Principals and Center Directors role/qualifications
43 Community-based education systems training
44 Administrative support of community-oriented teachers
45 Modified school calendars
47 Student-initiated programs
49 Use of technology
52 Instructional strategies training
54 Whole language approaches
Classroom Libraries
57 Co-operative curriculum development
58 Evaluation instruments, benchmark studies, tracking system
60 Preserving the Inuttitut language
62 Teaching Inuttitut to students and teachers whose first language is another
66 Study of first and second language proficiency
67 Travel and exchange programs for language development
68 Maintain early teaching in Inuttitut
69 More effective French program
72 Nunavik social and history curriculum
73 Co-operative health education development
74 Secondary career counselling program
Community service and economic skills acquisition
76 Early childhood programs
77 Special needs student assessment
80 Regular training for commissioners and committees
81 Youth environmental service projects
83 Junior college creation in Nunavik
84 Adult education courses taught in Inuttitut
85 Local adult education teachers at Nunavik College
86 Collaborative vocational training
93 Development of Inuttitut media
96 Multi-grade teaching capability
97 Simulations to teach about justice, politics, and Inuit organizations
98 Integrate MEQ standards in NSB materials
100 Challenging programs for brightest students
101 Integrate teaching of Inuit language and culture with real lives of hunters and fishers

J

Settlement Descriptions

Akulivik
Meaning: Central prong of a kakivak (spear)

Akulivik takes its name from the surrounding geography. A peninsula jutting into Hudson Bay between two small bodies of water, the area evokes the shape of a kakivak, a traditional, trident-shaped spear used for fishing. To the south is the mouth of the Illukotat River, and to the north is a deep bay which forms a natural port and the village against strong winds. Ice around the peninsula tends to break up particularly early in the spring, making the area good for hunting. The soil around Akulivik carries vestiges of the last ice age: its white, sandy texture is the crumbly remains of fossilized seashells.

The area around Akulivik teems with game. The many lakes of the region abound in fish. The Youville Mountains, or "Qimiit" in Inuktitut, are the natural habitat of ptarmigan, Arctic hare, and foxes. Numerous islands near the village are the summer refuge of various species of birds. The steady currents of Hudson Bay make the area a favorable habitat for marine wildlife and flora. In winter, Akulivimmiut practice a unique method of harvesting mussels in nearby shallow waters. After piercing holes through the ice, they use a hooped net fixed to one end of a long pole to scoop mussels from the sea floor.

Akulivik was incorporated as a community in 1976. However, the history of the area goes back thousands of years. More recently, in 1610, the explorer Henry Hudson passed by Qikirtajuaq. Later, in 1750, the island was given the name Smith Island in honor of Sir Thomas Smith, merchant, first Governor of the Company of Adventurers and discoverer of the Northwest Passage.

In 1922, the Hudson's Bay Company (HBC) established a post on the site of today's settlement. The outpost was moved to a more strategic and accessible point on Qikirtajuaq in 1926. Inuit at that time were still living all the coast. However, over time, some groups began to congregate around the trading post. Between 1922 and 1955, the area where Akulivik is located today was the summer camp of these groups. By 1933, according to HBC records, there were about 140 Inuit living on Qikirtajuaq. In 1952, the post was closed, forcing the now somewhat sedentary groups to move to Puvirnituq, the next closest trading post.

The displaced people, however, never forgot the land where they had grown up. In 1973, one family moved back to the area. The following year, many others followed and, together, they built the village of Akulivik.

Aupaluk
Meaning: Where the earth is red

Aupaluk, the smallest Nunavik community, is located on the southern shore of Hopes Advance Bay, an inlet on the western shore of Ungava Bay. It is about 150 kilometers north of Kuujjuaq and eighty kilometers south of Kangirsuk. The village is built on the lowest of a series of natural terraces about forty-five meters above sea level. The village offers a superb view of Ungava Bay. Aupaluk owes its meaning to the reddish color of its ferruginous soil. This soil constitutes the northern reaches of the Labrador Trough, which is rich in iron deposits. There was mining activity in the region in the late 1950s.

Unlike the majority of Nunavik communities, Aupaluk did not develop around a trading or mission post. With its abundance of caribou, fish, and marine mammals, it was a traditional camp. In 1975, Inuit from Kangirsuk and some other villages relocated to this area where several generations of hunters before them, their ancestors, had sojourned and built temporary camps. For the first time in the Canadian Arctic, Inuit themselves planned and conceived the site of their village. Aupaluk was incorporated as a Northern Village in 1981 and opened its co-operative store in the early 1980s. The life of Aupalummiut remains essentially centered on traditional activities.

Inukjuak
Meaning: The giant

Inukjuak is located on the north bank of the Innuksuak River, known for its turquoise water and turbulent rapids. The many archaeological sites scattered along the meandering river evidence thousands of years of inhabitation. The land around Inukjuak is marked by gently rolling hills and open spaces, which give the landscape a "silent beauty," in the words of local Inuit. In spring, ice between the Hopewell Islands and the mainland is moved by the action of tides and currents to create a spectacular field of immense, upraised blocks of ice.

At the beginning of the twentieth century, the area was given the name "Port Harrison" and the French fur-trading company Révillon Frères established a post here. The Hudson's Bay Company (HBC) opened its in 1920. Competition between these companies ended in 1936 when the HBC bought out Révillon Frères.

The subsequent HBC fur trade monopoly continued until 1958. The St. Thomas Anglican mission was founded in 1927, and, in the years following, the federal government began delivering basic community services in Inukjuak: a post office and a Royal Canadian Mounted Police detachment were opened in 1935, a nursing station in 1947 and a school in 1951. In 1962, the co-operative store opened, and, in 1980, Inukjuak was legally established as a municipality. Throughout this period, most Inuit continued to prefer their traditional lifestyle on the land and only began settling in the village in the 1950s.

A much more painful period in the history of Inukjuamiut involves Resolute Bay and Grise Fjord, communities created two thousand kilometers away in the High Arctic. In 1953, Inuit from Inukjuak were involuntarily relocated north by the Government of Canada. History should remember these people for their important role in establishing Canada's presence in the High Arctic.

Ivujivik
Meaning: Place where ice accumulates because of strong currents

Roughly two thousand kilometers north of Montreal, Ivujivik is Quebec's northernmost village. Nestled in a small, sandy cove, the village is surrounded by imposing cliffs that plunge into the waters of Digges Sound. This is the place where the strong currents of Hudson Bay and Hudson Strait clash. On the Ungava Plateau which crowns the cliffs around Ivujivik, the only plants that cling to the rocky tundra are lichen.

Located thirty kilometers northeast of Ivujivik is Cape Wolstenholme. Its cliffs are the nesting place of one of the world's largest colonies of thick-billed murre. To the northwest of Ivujivik are Nottingham and Salisbury Islands with their impressive walrus populations.

Different peoples, including most recently the nomadic ancestors of the Inuit, have inhabited the coast and islands of this area for about four thousand years, with seal, walrus, and beluga forming their staple food source. Marine animals tend to be abundant as these waters are a migratory pass between Hudson Bay and Hudson Strait. Strong currents prevent the sea from freezing and allow hunting to be carried out year-round. In addition, the myriad of islands offer shelter for waterfowl in summer.

The first recorded encounter between Europeans and Inuit of Nunavik took place in 1610 on nearby Digges Island during Henry Hudson's last and fatal expedition to the Arctic in search of a polar route leading to Asia. Later, in 1697, Captain Pierre LeMoyne D'Iberville and his crew, in search of commercial opportunities in Hudson Bay, met Inuit at Cape Wolstenholme. In 1909, the Hudson's Bay Company established a trading post on the site of today's settlement. In 1938, a Catholic mission was also founded, but it was only after 1947 that Inuit gradually began to settle close to these two establishments. When the mission closed in the 1960s, the federal government took over delivery of services in the emerging Inuit village. In 1967, the Inuit of Ivujivik founded a co-operative store.

Kangiqsualujjuaq
Meaning: Very large bay

Kangiqsualujjuaq is the easternmost village of Nunavik, located about 160 kilometers to the northeast of Kuujjuaq. It is situated twenty-five kilometers from Ungava Bay on the George River, nestled at the end of a cove called Akilasakalluq. Tidal movements reach as far upstream as the village so that, at low tide, water recedes almost entirely from the cove. Kangiqsualujjuamiut's summer life is therefore closely linked to the rhythm of the tides. The village itself stands in the shadow of an imposing granite rock outcropping which rises to the north of the bay.

The calving grounds of the George River herd, the largest ungulate population in the world, estimated at several hundreds of thousands of head, is nearby. The George River, as well as other rivers in the area, teem with fish, particularly Arctic char, Atlantic salmon, and a variety of trout. About a hundred kilometers to the east of Kangiqsualujjuaq are the Torngat Mountains. This range stretches for three hundred kilometers along the Quebec–Labrador border, between Ungava Bay and the Labrador Sea.

Known also as simply George River, Kangiqsualujjuaq did not really develop as a village before the early 1960s. The Hudson's Bay Company operated a post south of today's village during the periods of 1838–42, 1876–1915, and 1923–32. However, Inuit of the area never settled around the post, preferring to live along the coast in summer and setting their camps about fifty kilometers inland in winter. In 1959, local Inuit established, on their own initiative, the first co-operative in Northern Quebec for the purpose of marketing Arctic char. The construction of the village began in 1962 and, a few years later, all inhabitants of George River lived in prefabricated houses. A school was built in 1963 as well as a co-operative store and government buildings. In 1980, Kangiqsualujjuaq was legally established as a municipality.

Kangiqsujuaq
Meaning: The large bay

Kangiqsujuaq occupies an exceptional site, ten kilometers from the Hudson Strait, on the southeastern shore of Wakeham Bay. The village is snuggled in the hollow of a valley surrounded by mountains. Fifteen kilometers southeast of the village are petroglyph masks dating back to the late Dorset period, about twelve hundred years ago, and remnants of semi-subterranean houses built by Inuit of the Thule period, eight hundred years ago.

Of particular note is the method employed by local Inuit to harvest mussels in winter. As the tide ebbs in shallow areas, they pierce holes in the sea ice. When the water recedes, they lower themselves through these holes and are able to crawl under the ice to collect this succulent seafood delicacy.

In 1884, members of the Canadian Hudson's Bay Expedition, aboard the steamship *Neptune*, arrived in the area to establish a commercial route to Europe through Hudson Strait. An ice observation and a meteorological station were built at Stupart Bay, called "Aniuvarjuaq" by the Inuit. Inuit began to trade frequently with observers posted at the station: sealskin mitts and boots for tobacco and gun powder.

Wakeham Bay takes its name from Captain William Wakeham who, in 1897, led an expedition to determine whether Hudson Strait was safe for navigation. In 1961, the provincial government renamed the settlement "Sainte-Anne-de-Maricourt," until, with the establishment of a municipality, it officially readopted its Inuttitut name: "Kangiqsujuaq."

In 1910, the French company Révillon Frères established a post at Kangiqsujuaq. Four years later, the Hudson's Bay Company (HBC) followed suit. In 1928, the HBC established an experimental fox farm, which it operated for twelve years. In 1936, the Révillon Frères trading post was closed, but a Catholic mission was established. Many Oblate priests have lived at the mission, among them, Father Dion since 1964. In 1960, the first school was opened, followed the next year by a nursing station. An Anglican church was established in 1963. Kangiqsujuammiut established their co-operative store in 1970.

Kangiqsujuaq is located north of the Cape Smith belt, an area rich in mineralization. Since the 1950s, mining has been carried out irregularly. Through the 1970s and 1980s, asbestos was mined at Purtuniq. Today, a copper and nickel mine is operated by the Société minière Raglan du Québec in the area. Roughly fifteen percent of this mine's workforce is drawn from Nunavik communities.

Kangirsuk
Meaning: The bay

Kangirsuk, meaning "the bay" in Inuktitut, is located on the north shore of the Payne River, thirteen kilometers inland from Ungava Bay. The village lies between a rocky cliff to the north and a large, rocky hill to the west. It is situated 118 kilometers south of Quaqtaq and 230 kilometers north of Kuujjuaq. Not far from the village on Pamiok Island is the stone foundation of a long-house, which some archaeologists believe to be vestiges of Vikings, presumed to have sojourned in the area in the eleventh century.

The numerous lakes and rivers of the area are well known for their Arctic char and lake trout. The strong tides that occur on the Payne River make it an extraordinary place for mussel harvesting. On the islands of Kyak Bay and Virgin Lake, located to the east and north-east of Kangirsuk, respectively, important colonies of eider ducks nest every year. Inuit women collect the down of those birds to make the warm parkas which protect Kangirsumiut from the biting, winter cold.

Kangirsuk, like many Inuit villages of Northern Quebec, developed around trading posts. The French fur company Révillon Frères built a trading post in 1921 and, four years later, the Hudson's Bay Company followed. Both trading posts were managed at times by Inuit. The federal day school was inaugurated in 1959. Thereafter, Inuit from the region started to settle permanently in the village.

In 1961, the federal government introduced health, housing, and social services to Kangirsuk, and throughout the 1960s the community developed intensively. In 1965, an Anglican mission opened a church in Kangirsuk, and the following year the local co-operative store was established. In 1981, Kangirsuk was incorporated as a municipality.

Kuujjuaq
Meaning: Great river

Kuujjuaq, Nunavik's largest community, is located on the west shore of the Koksoak River, about fifty kilometers upstream from Ungava Bay. Daily life in this community is closely tied to the river. The ebb and flow of its tides are continually altering the landscape, and they impose their rhythm on the practice of traditional summer activities.

The boreal forest is near Kuujjuaq, where patches of black spruce and larch stand in marshy valleys. Kuujjuaq also witnesses annual migrations of the George River caribou herd throughout August and September.

Kuujjuaq was known before by the name of Fort Chimo. "Chimo" is a mispronunciation of the phrase "saimuk," "Let's shake hands!" Early fur traders were often welcomed with this phrase, which they eventually adopted as the name of the trading post.

The first Europeans to have contact with local Inuit were Moravian missionaries. Around 1830, the Hudson's Bay Company (HBC) started the fur trade business in Nunavik by establishing their first post on the east shore of the Koksoak River, about five kilometers downstream from the present-day settlement. The post closed in 1842, then reopened in 1866. At that time, Inuit, Montagnais, and Naskapi came to trade at the post.

The construction of a U.S. Air Force base (Crystal 1) in 1942 on the west shore of the Koksoak River, the site of today's settlement, and the occupation of the site by the American army between 1941 and 1945 sped up the development of the community. After the end of World War II, the United States turned the base over to the Canadian government. In 1948, a Catholic mission was established, followed by a nursing station, a school, and a weather station. When the HBC moved upstream closer to the airstrips in 1958, the remaining families that still lived across the river at Old Fort Chimo followed. In 1961, a co-operative was created.

With its two airstrips, Kuujjuaq is the transportation hub of the entire region. The village has a number of hotels, restaurants, stores, arts and crafts shops, and a bank.

Kuujjuarapik
Meaning: Little great river

Kuujjuarapik is nestled in golden sand dunes at the mouth of the Great Whale River. Beyond the village, the land is rather flat; a carpet of moss and rock unfold as far as the eye can see. From the crest of the dunes, there is a good view of Hudson Bay and the Manitounuk Islands which are just a little to the north along the coast.

These islands are representative of the Hudsonian cuestas that rise along the eastern shore of Hudson Bay. They are characterized by rocky beaches on the side facing the open sea and by cliffs on the coastal side. The Manitounuk Islands provide ideal shelter for birds, seal, whale, and beluga.

Kuujjuarapik, Nunavik's southernmost village, is a bicultural community of Inuit and Cree. The Cree community is called Whapmagootsui ("where there are whales," in the Cree language). This village is also officially designated Poste-de-la-Baleine, making it one of the few places in Canada with three official names.

Ancestors of the Inuit, as well as Cree, have occupied the area for roughly 2,800 years. In the eighteenth century, hunters travelled throughout the region setting up camps on Richmond Gulf, Little Whale River, and Great Whale River. The Hudson's Bay Company opened a trading post called Great Whale River in 1820 on the site of today's Kuujjuarapik. The main activities at the post were processing whale products from the commercial hunt and trading furs. An Anglican mission was established in 1882 and a Catholic mission in 1890. Although the federal government set up a weather station in Great Whale River in 1895, it only started providing some medical assistance and policing services through the Royal Canadian Mounted Police in the first half of the twentieth century.

The village itself started to develop in the late 1930s. During World War II, the United States built a military base and airport in Kuujjuarapik, which they turned over to the Canadian government in 1948. This base was also the control station of the Mid-Canada Line, a line of military radar stations constructed in 1955 from the Atlantic Ocean to Hudson Bay along the fifty-fifth parallel. The population of Kuujjuarapik decreased significantly in 1985 when many families, fearing the negative impacts of the Great Whale River hydro-electric project, decided to relocate to Umiujaq, another Inuit community about 160 kilometers north of Kuujjuarapik.

Puvirnituq
Meaning: Place where there is a smell of rotten meat

Located four kilometers from Povungnituk Bay, on the north shore of the major river by the same name, this village is surrounded by an expansive plateau with a mixture of lakes and rivers, abundant wildlife, and arctic plants and flowers. For several days every fall, thousands of caribou from the Leaf River herd arrive and plunge across the Povungnituk River in a spectacular display.

Two explanations are commonly given for the peculiar name of this village. The first recounts that, years ago, when migrating caribou attempted to cross the river, many were swept downstream and drowned. Their carcasses were washed up on shore where they began to rot, producing a putrid odor. The other explanation of the site's name tells how everyone living in the area were once the victims of a deadly epidemic. In the end, there was no one left to bury the dead bodies. When the corpses began to decompose, the air was filled with an awful stench.

The whole area, however, is also known by a more pleasant name. "Amaamatisivik" means the place where women breast-feed their babies. According to legend, women in this area would continually breast-feed their babies to keep them from crying and disturbing the herds of migrating caribou.

In 1921, the Hudson's Bay Company (HBC) established an outpost at Puvirnituq. Inuit who came to trade their furs in these early years occupied various camps scattered throughout the region. In 1951, the HBC opened a general store in Puvirnituq and closed its posts at Qikirtajuaq (Cape Smith near Akulivik) and Kangirsuruaq. Inuit living in those areas had no other choice but to relocate in the following years to Puvirnituq.

In 1956, a Catholic mission was founded in Puvirnituq. Two years later, Father André Steinman inspired residents to form the Carvers Association of Povungnituk, which became the Co-operative Association of Povungnituk. Today, a symbol of the community's solidarity and independence, it is one of the most dynamic co-operatives that make up the Federation of Co-operatives of Northern Quebec.

At the beginning of the twenty-first century, Puvirnituq is the hub of the Hudson coast and gateway to more remote communities. Puvirnituq and Kuujjuaq, Nunavik's administrative centers, are connected directly by plane two times a week.

Quaqtaq
Meaning: Tapeworm

The village of Quaqtaq is located on the eastern shore of Diana Bay (called "Tuvaaluk" – "the large ice field" in Inuttitut) on a peninsula which protrudes into Hudson Strait where it meets Ungava Bay. Mountains stand on the peninsula to the north, and to the southeast are short, rocky hills. The region around Diana Bay is rich with land and sea mammals, as well as fish, mussels, scallops, and clams.

Evidence found nearby shows that different people have occupied the area for about 3,500 years. People of the Thule culture, the ancestors of today's Inuit, arrived around AD 1400 or 1500. Up until the early 1930s, the peninsula was known as "Nuvukutaaq" ("the long point"). However, according to stories still told, a man who once came to the area to hunt beluga acquired parasites. His hunting companions began to call the place "Quaqtaq" ("tapeworm"), and the use of this new name spread rapidly.

An independent trader built the first trading post in 1927 at Iggiajaaq, a few kilometers southwest of Quaqtaq. It operated for eleven years. At that time, the site of present-day Quaqtaq was one of the Tuvaaluk Inuit's winter campsites. It was near the limit of land-fast ice, and sea mammals were abundant at this place during the cold season. In 1931, the French fur trading company Révillon Frères opened a second store at Iggiajaaq, which the Hudson's Bay Company (HBC) assumed control of in 1936. A Baffin Trading Company (BTC) post was established in 1939 in the same area, and the following year the HBC closed its post at Iggiajaaq. The BTC post closed ten years later, and the Inuit who normally wintered at Iggiajaaq moved to Quaqtaq. In 1947, a Catholic mission was established at Quaqtaq.

Because Quaqtaq was considered too small, public services were not delivered in the area as early as in other communities. Only after a measles epidemic tore through the area in 1952, killing eleven adults – ten percent of Quaqtaq's population, did the federal government begin delivering some basic care. In the 1960s, the Quebec government opened a store and a post office equipped with a radio-telephone. A nursing station was built in 1963. In 1974, the store became a co-operative and, in 1978, Quaqtaq was legally established as a Northern village.

Akpatok Island, which rises like a fortress out of the waters of Ungava Bay to the east of Quaqtaq, has long been known as the finest area in the region for walrus and polar bear hunting. The rocky cliffs that guard the island are the nesting areas of a large summer colony of thick-billed murre.

Salluit
Meaning: The thin ones

Salluit stands at the far end of the narrow Sugluk Inlet, ten kilometers inland from Hudson Strait, hidden between high, rugged mountains rising close to five hundred meters. Salluit, being the middle point between Nunavik's fourteen communities, is a strategic location for meetings attended by people from the Hudson and Ungava coasts.

Though the village's name suggests that it has not always been the case, the area is rich in wildlife and arctic plants. The coastal seabed teems with mussels and clams. Sallumiut enjoy a variety of dishes, which include arctic char, caribou, bannock, berries, roots, and herbs. The very harsh climate endured by the Sallumiut is indelibly engraved in their way of life, endowing them with an incredible sense of survival. An explanation for the name of this village recounts that, long ago, some Inuit were told the region abounded in wildlife. Yet, when they arrived, they found almost nothing to eat and, as a result, suffered near starvation.

In 1958, archaeological work was carried out on Qikirtaq Island, at the entrance of Sugluk Inlet. The evidence collected showed that people of the Dorset period occupied the area from approximately 800 BC to AD 1000. The three sites excavated were named Keataina, Tyara, and Toonoo. The Sugluk Masquette, a minuscule mask two centimeters in size carved out of ivory, was excavated from the Tyara site and dates back to about 400 BC.

In 1925, an independent trader opened a trading post on the site of present-day Salluit. Competition was fierce, and the Hudson Bay Company (HBC) quickly established its own post on the far shore of Sugluk Inlet. The following year, the HBC moved to Deception Bay, but, in 1930, it built a combined store and dwelling at present-day Salluit. In 1932, it closed its post at Deception Bay. The golden years of fur trading came to an end around 1936 when the price of pelts plummeted. Although a Catholic mission was established in 1930, it operated for only some twenty years. In 1955, an Anglican mission was established, and, two years later, a federal day school was opened. As more public services were being delivered, Inuit settled around the small village, and the first residential houses were built in 1959. Sallumiut joined together in 1968 to open a co-operative store. Salluit legally became a municipality in 1979.

Tasiujaq
Meaning: Which resembles a lake

Tasiujaq was built on the shores of Leaf Lake at the head of Deep Harbour on the Finger River. It lies a few kilometers north of the tree line where the shrub tundra finally gives way to the arctic tundra. "Tasiujaq," which means "resembling a lake," actually refers to the whole of Leaf Basin: Leaf Lake, Leaf Passage, and Leaf Bay. Leaf Basin is renowned for its high tides, which regularly exceed fifteen meters.

The region is very rich in marine mammals (seal and beluga), fish (Arctic char, Atlantic salmon, trout), ducks (particularly eider) and many seabirds. As well, close to a thousand musk-ox roam the surrounding area. Gyrfalcons and peregrine falcons are commonly found nesting on the islands of Leaf Basin and surrounding cliffs.

The French fur company Révillon Frères and the Hudson's Bay Company each opened trading posts in 1905 and 1907, respectively, on a site located east of today's settlement. This settlement was along a traditional dogsled route used by Inuit to travel between Kuujjuaq and Kangirsuk. However, both posts closed by 1935 without any village ever having developed around them.

In the 1950s, when the federal government opened a school in Kuujjuaq and started delivering social services, many Inuit congregated around that emerging village. The wildlife resources of Kuujjuaq, however, were scarce, and many Inuit were forced to rely on government allowances. In 1963, the Northern Quebec directorate of the provincial government, hoping to partially remedy this problem, decided to create a new village on the south shore of Leaf Lake where wildlife resources were more plentiful.

In 1966, with the project about to start, Inuit families were divided as to where their future village should be built. A choice had to be made between a site known as Qaamanialuk Paanga and the site of the old trading posts. Qaamanialuk Paanga was finally selected because it was easily accessible by boats used for summer hunting and fishing; nearby Finger

River provided necessary drinking water; and there was room to construct a landing strip. Subsequently, the new village was given the name "Tasiujaq." The old trading post site was not selected as the site because its foreshore (tide land) was dotted with large boulders, and access by boat in summer would have been difficult. In 1971, once the community was organized, a co-operative store was established independently by residents. It continues to be the only Nunavik co-operative not associated with the Federation of Co-operatives of Northern Quebec.

Umiujaq
Meaning: Which resembles a boat

Umiujaq was established at the foot of a hill resembling an overturned umiaq (traditional Inuit walrus-skin boat). Richmond Gulf (Tasiujaq), located fifteen kilometers east of the village, is an immense inland bay. It is joined with Hudson Bay by a rocky, glacier-polished canyon called the "Goulet." Due to the strong current, the passage does not freeze even in winter. The western shores of the Gulf are bordered by beaches and remarkable cliffs. The many rivers flowing into the Gulf make its water a healthy habitat for brook trout and whitefish, seal and beluga. This sheltered maritime environment also nurtures scattered black spruce and larch, defying the surrounding tundra. On the south shore, there can still be seen the remnants of an abandoned Hudson's Bay Company trading post.

From the cliffs of Richmond Gulf, there is a spectacular view to the west of Hudson Bay and the nearby Nastapoka Islands. Many species of birds, such as common loons, eider ducks, and peregrine falcons, find summer shelter and nest here. Like the Manitounuk Islands near Kuujjuarapik, the Nastapoka are, in geographical terms, cuestas. The abrupt, rocky cliffs plunge into Nastapoka Sound, where the water can reach 110 meters deep.

Located about 160 kilometers north of Kuujjuarapik, Umiujaq was established in 1986. In light of the La Grande hydroelectric project and the proposed Great Whale hydro-electric project, Inuit negotiated a clause into the 1975 James Bay and Northern Quebec Agreement that provided for the relocation of Inuit from Kuujjuarapik to Richmond Gulf. In 1982, through referendum, they opted to create a new community where they could preserve their traditional lifestyle in an area where fish and game were not threatened. After numerous archaeological, ecological, and land planning studies, construction of the little village of Umiujaq began in the summer of 1985 and ended in December 1986. During the construction period, Inuit from Kuujjuarapik, who had decided to relocate to Umiujaq, lived in tents in the area of their future community.

Bibliography

Arnold, Robert D. (1976) *Alaska Native Land Claims.* Anchorage: Alaska Native Foundation.

Barman, Jean, Yvonne Hébert and Don McCaskill, Editors. (1986) *Indian Education in Canada – Volume 1: The Legacy.* Vancouver: University of British Columbia Press.

Barman, Jean, Yvonne Hébert and Don McCaskill, Editors. (1987) *Indian Education in Canada – Volume 2: The Challenge.* Vancouver: University of British Columbia Press.

Bothwell, Robert. (1995) *Canada and Quebec: One Country, Two Histories.* Vancouver: UBC Press.

Brody, Hugh. (1975, 1991) *The People's Land: Inuit, Whites and the Eastern Arctic.* Vancouver: Douglas & McIntyre.

Canada. (February 1982) *James Bay and Northern Quebec Agreement Implementation Review.* Ottawa: Indian and Northern Affairs Canada.

Canada. (July 6-8, 1993) *National Round Table on Education: Discussion Papers.* Ottawa: Royal Commission on Aboriginal Peoples.

Canada. (1996) *Royal Commission on Aboriginal Peoples – Final Report.* Ottawa: Royal Commission on Aboriginal Peoples.

Canada. (December 1990) *"You Took My Talk": Aboriginal Literacy and Empowerment – Fourth Report of the House of Commons Standing Committee on Aboriginal Affairs.* Ottawa: Queen's Printer for Canada.

Cram, Jack. (1987) "Some Notes on Teacher Training in the Circumpolar Region." *Education, Research, Information Systems and the North"*, 114-15. Ottawa: Association of Canadian Universities for Northern Studies (ACUNS).

Cram, Jack. (1987) "Northern Teachers for Northern Schools: An Inuit Teacher Training Program." *Education, Research, Information Systems and the North*, 116-23. Ottawa: Association of Canadian Universities for Northern Studies (ACUNS).

Dickason, Olive Patricia. (1992) *Canada's First Nations: A History of Founding Peoples from Earliest Times.* Toronto: McClelland & Stewart.

Dorris, Michael. (1994) *Paper Trail: Essays by Michael Dorris.* New York: Harper Collins.

Fullan, Michael G. with Suzanne Stiegelbauer. (1991) *The New Meaning of Educational Change.* New York: Teachers College Press.

Fullan, Michael G. (1993) *Change Forces: Probing the Depths of Educational Reform.* London, England and Bristol, Pennsylvania: The Falmer Press.

Fullan, Michael G. (1997) *What's Worth Fighting for in the Principalship.* New York: Teachers College Press.

Gordon, Mark R. (March 1987) "The Struggle for Self Determination" – Presentation at Seminar on Self Determination and Indigenous Peoples, November 2-3, 1984. Copenhagen: *International Work Group for Indigenous Affairs/IWGIA Document 58*, 121-30.

Graburn, Nelson H.H. (1969) *Eskimos Without Igloos: Social and Economic Development in Sugluk.* Boston: The Little, Brown Series in Anthropology.

———. (1976) *Ethnic and Tourist Arts: Cultural Expressions from the Fourth World.* Berkeley: University of California Press.

Grand Council of the Crees. (October 1995.) *Sovereign Injustice: Forcible Inclusion of the James Bay Crees and Cree Territory Into a Sovereign Québec.* Nemaska, Eeyou Astchee.

Grant, Shelagh D. (1988) *Sovereignty or Security? Government Policy in the Canadian North 1936-1950.* Vancouver, University of British Columbia Press.

Grenier, Annie, Sarah Bennett and Elaine Armstrong. (Summer 1997.) "*Satuigiarniq*: Reclaiming Responsibility for Education." *Journal of Staff Development* 18 # 3.

Harper, Kenn. (September 1983) "Writing in Inuktitut: An Historical Perspective" *Inuktitut Magazine* 53, 3-35.

Henchey, Norman and Donald Burgess. (1987) *Between Past and Future: Quebec Education in Transition.* Calgary: Detselig Enterprises.

Iglauer, Edith. (2000) *Inuit Journey: The Co-operative Adventure in Canada's North.* Madeira Park, British Columbia: Harbour Publishing.

Inuit Cultural Institute. (1979) *Inuit Education Concept.* Arviat.

Irwin, Colin. (1988) *Lords of the Arctic: Wards of the State – The Growing Inuit Population, Arctic Resettlement and Their Effects on Social and Economic Change.* Report prepared for Health and Welfare Canada.

Jenness, Diamond. (May 1964) *Eskimo Administration: II. Canada.* Montreal: Arctic Institute of North America – Technical Paper No. 14.

———. (May 1965) *Eskimo Administration: III. Labrador.* Montreal: Arctic Institute of North America – Technical Paper No. 16.

———. (March 1968) *Eskimo Administration: V. Analysis and Reflections.* Montreal: Arctic Institute of North America – Technical Paper No. 21.

Kleinfeld, Judith S., G. Williamson McDiarmid and David Hagstrom. (1985) *Alaska's Small Rural High Schools – Are They Working?* Anchorage: Institute of Social and Economic Research and Center for Cross-Cultural Studies, University of Alaska.

Lamont, Lansing. (1994) *Breakup: The Coming End of Canada and the Stakes for America.* New York and London: W.W. Norton & Co.

Lauritzen, Philip. (1989) *Highlights of an arctic revolution: The first 120 months of Greenlandic Home Rule.* Nuuk: Atuakkiorfik.

Macpherson, Norman John. Edited by Roderick Duncan Macpherson. (1991) *Dreams & Visions: Education in the Northwest Territories From Early Days to 1984.* Department of Education, Government of the Northwest Territories.

Madsen, Andrew. (Fall 1995) "The First School in Inukjuaq." *Tumivut 7,* 31-34. Avataq Cultural Institute.

Man in the North Project: Education Task Force. (March 1973) *Report Three: Southern Teachers for the North.* Montreal: Arctic Institute of North America.

McPhee, John. (1976, 1977) *Coming Into The Country.* New York: Farrar, Straus & Giroux.

Morgan, Robert (1994) "Educational Reform: Top-Down or Bottom-Up?" in Reigeluth, Charles M. and Robert J. Garfinkle, Editors. (1994) *Systemic Change in Education.* Englewood Cliffs, New Jersey: Educational Technology Publications.

Pauktuutit – Inuit Women's Association of Canada. (No publication date given.) *The Inuit Way: A Guide to Inuit Culture.* Ottawa.

Quebec. (1976) *The James Bay and Northern Quebec Agreement (Éditeur officiel du Québec).* Quebec City.

Reigeluth, Charles M. and Robert J. Garfinkle, Editors. (1994) *Systemic Change in Education.* Englewood Cliffs, New Jersey: Educational Technology Publications.

Rich, Bruce. (1994) *Mortgaging The Earth: The World Bank, Environmental Impoverishment, and the Crisis of Development.* Boston: Beacon Press.

Richardson, Boyce. (1991) *Strangers Devour The Land.* Post Mills, Vermont: Chelsea Green Publishing.

Saladin d'Anglure, Bernard. (1984) "Inuit of Quebec" *Handbook of North American Indians: Volume 5, Arctic.* Washington: Smithsonian Institution.

Sarason, Seymour B. (1990) *The Predictable Failure of Educational Reform.* San Francisco: Jossey-Bass Publishers.

Swisher, Karen Gayton and John W. Tippeconnic III, Editors. (1999) *Next Steps: Research and Practice to Advance Indian Education.* Charleston, West Virginia: ERIC Clearinghouse on Rural Education and Small Schools.

Tester, Frank James and Peter Kulchyski. (1994) *Tammarniit: Inuit Relocation in the Eastern Arctic 1939-63.* Vancouver: University of British Columbia Press.

Wall, Steve and Harvey Arden. (1990) *Wisdomkeepers: Meetings with Native American Spiritual Elders.* Hillsboro, Oregon: Beyond Worlds Publishing.

Wiles, Jon W. (1993) *Promoting Change in Schools: Ground Level Practices That Work.* New York: Scholastic Leadership Policy Research.

Wilson, Kenneth G. and Bennett Daviss. (1994) *Redesigning Education.* New York: Henry Holt & Co.

Index

www.ingramcontent.com/pod-product-compliance
Lightning Source LLC
Chambersburg PA
CBHW070758300326

41914CB00053B/726